Lincoln and the Indians

Lincoln and the Indians

Civil War Policy and Politics

David A. Nichols

 Minnesota Historical
Society Press

CLEAN
WATER
LAND &
LEGACY
AMENDMENT

www.mhspress.org

The Minnesota Historical Society Press is a member of the Association of American University Presses.

Manufactured in the United States of America

10 9 8 7 6 5 4 3 2

∞ The paper used in this publication meets the minimum requirements of the American National Standard for Information Sciences—Permanence for Printed Library Materials, ANSI Z39.48-1984.

International Standard Book Number
ISBN: 978-0-87351-875-8 (paper)
ISBN: 978-0-87351-876-5 (e-book)

Library of Congress Cataloging-in-Publication Data
Nichols, David A. (David Allen), 1939–
    Lincoln and the indians : civil war policy and politics / David A. Nichols.
        p. cm.
    Originally published : Columbia, MO : University of Missouri Press, 1978.
    Includes bibliographical references and index.
    ISBN 978-0-87351-875-8 (pbk. : alk. paper) — ISBN 978-0-87351-876-5 (ebook)
    1. Lincoln, Abraham, 1809–1865—Relations with Indians of North America.
    2. Indians of North America—Government relations. 3. United States—
    History—Civil War, 1861–1865. I. Title.
    E457.2.N6N53 2012
    973.7092—dc23

                                                              2012010382

*To the Native Americans who suffered so much
on the American frontier and, in particular,
to the Dakota people who have been enthusiastic
advocates for the republication of this book.*

Abbreviations in Footnotes

AGO   Adjutant General's Office
AR   Annual Report
CIA   Commissioner of Indian Affairs
ID   Indian Division
JCCW   *Report of the Joint Committee on the Conduct of the War*
LAM, with appropriate year—Lincoln's Annual Message
LC   Library of Congress
LR   Letters Received
LS   Letters Sent
M   Microcopy
NA   National Archives
OIA   Office of Indian Affairs
OR   *The War of the Rebellion: A Compilation of the Official Records of the Union and Confederate Armies* (with series, volume, and page numbers listed respectively)
OSI   Office of the Secretary of the Interior
RG   Record Group
SF   Special File
SI   Secretary of the Interior
SW   Secretary of War

Contents

Preface

"SURELY, LINCOLN DID NOT HAVE TIME for Indians." That provocative statement is as true today as it was in the 1860s and in 1978, when this book was first published. And now, *Lincoln and the Indians* is born again—thanks to the 150th anniversary of the U.S.–Dakota War of 1862 in Minnesota, the passionate interest of Dakota leaders whose ancestors fought in that war, and the generous response of the Minnesota Historical Society Press. I am honored that my Native friends in Minnesota have discovered, in this chronicle, information that enhances their understanding of their own past.

So, let us ask once again: "Why did Lincoln, in the midst of a bloody civil conflict, take time to deal with Indian affairs?"

First, he took time because of the Civil War itself. In the Indian Territory (now Oklahoma), the so-called "five civilized tribes" allied themselves with the Confederacy. Lincoln first abandoned the Indian Territory, but a flood of Indian refugees from the Territory into Kansas resulted in intense political pressure on the president to retake it. He eventually approved an expedition that included Native fighters, only to have that expedition torpedoed by Union troops who mutinied against their commander. In the aftermath, Kansas was the scene of a tragedy all too common on the frontier—the presence of starving, suffering, ruthlessly exploited Natives whose situation was made worse by the government's mismanagement.

Lincoln expended even more time and energy in dealing with the Dakota War. When fighting broke out, Minnesotans could not fulfill their commitment to provide soldiers for the war with the South. Lincoln, desperate for manpower, ordered, "Attend to the Indians," and dispatched General Alexander Pope to put down the uprising.

But, when the fighting ceased, Lincoln was presented with an even more time-consuming, morally wrenching problem—Pope's plan to execute 303 Dakota men.

What contemporaries called "the Indian System" was the catalyst for the situations in Kansas and Minnesota. It demanded Lincoln's attention because it was a system of political patronage, not a system designed to serve the needs of Indians.

Complex and corrupt to the core, the Indian System was administered by the Office of Indian Affairs and provided financially lucrative jobs to superintendents, Indian agents, and other officials. These officials, in turn, disbursed government largesse to traders, contractors, and claimants. The president's political allies routinely lined up for these jobs, usually recommended by their state's congressional leaders.

The system's operations were both ingenious and cynical. Following warfare, Indian tribes were often removed from land that white men wanted. Removal was formalized by means of sham negotiations with the leaders of allegedly independent tribal nations. A treaty was then signed which, in return for the confiscated land, provided for annuity funds held in trust in Washington. These funds, ostensibly committed to meeting tribal needs, were doled out each year through the Indian Office and, on the local scene, by the Indian agent.

The Indian System revolved around the efforts of rapacious white men to commandeer these monies. Again and again, tribes were moved to barren country where they could not sustain themselves, either by hunting or farming. That opened the monetary floodgates, creating a demand for contractors and traders to provide provisions, with payment overseen by the Indian agent. The system featured every conceivable kind of financial corruption—kickbacks, inflated prices, false claims, and payments for goods and services never actually delivered.

Most of this money never trickled down to the Natives. Starving Indians became commonplace in the West; such starvation was precisely what touched off the Indian war in Minnesota in 1862.

This story reminds us that the issue of money in American politics is not just a modern phenomenon. In Lincoln's time, the Indian System provided a pathway to power, whereby ambitious men could get rich and go into politics. It is no accident that the first two governors of Minnesota, Henry Sibley and Alexander Ramsey, were products of this money machine. The enduring contribution of *Lincoln and the Indians* is its description of this system of institutionalized corruption.

The Indian System cried out for reform, and a handful of brave reformers campaigned for the removal of politics from the system. Minnesota's Episcopal Bishop, Henry Benjamin Whipple, was the most persistent. Whipple lobbied relentlessly for justice for the Indians of his state, personally traveling to Washington to confront Lincoln. Whipple's vivid account of tribal suffering so moved the president that Lincoln pledged he would seek reform of the system "if we get through this war, and I live."

We will never know if Lincoln, who faithfully played his political role in the Indian System, would have kept that promise. Even before Lincoln's death, Whipple gave up on the president and supported his opponent in the 1864 election. But Whipple captured the evils of the system in one powerful sentence: "It commences in discontent and ends in blood."

That is what happened in Minnesota in 1862. As a result, Abraham Lincoln was forced to confront the legacy of the Indian System there, described by one investigator as "a system of wholesale robberies." Lincoln was not a man who shrank from bloodshed in his determination to preserve the Union. In prosecuting the war against the South, he discarded generals right and left until he found a man, Ulysses S. Grant, who would shed enough blood to get the job done. But even Lincoln, that hard-nosed commander in chief, could not quite stomach General Pope's plan to hang 303 Dakota men. In effect, Lincoln ordered: "Halt!" After his lawyers reviewed the skimpy trial transcripts, Lincoln recognized the consequences of his original orders to the Minnesotans, invoking the stark declaration: "Necessity knows no law."

Lincoln reduced the execution list from 303 to 38. He still sanctioned the largest official mass execution in American history and tacitly approved the imprisonment and removal of others, resulting in more deaths. When I read those trial transcripts, I cringed at how thin most of the justifications for executions were. I confronted the fact that my political hero, Abraham Lincoln, had determined that he had no choice but to authorize a blood sacrifice to appease the Minnesotans. Otherwise, that state's angry citizens might have taken the law into their own hands and executed all the condemned men.

The descendants of those men, especially Sheldon Wolfchild, have instigated the revival of this book. One day, reflecting on this story, I remarked to Sheldon that I have now concluded that there was, in a sense, an American "holocaust."

Yes, Lincoln was no Hitler. There are stark differences between Nazi Germany and America in the 1860s. But for the descendants of those executed in Minnesota, this ugly story feels like it happened yesterday, and—at least spiritually—to them. In the collections of the Minnesota Historical Society, a noose from the hangings furnishes a vivid reminder that we Americans, for all our founding ideals, are capable of cruel and indefensible behavior.

Someone will say, "But we did not have concentration camps like the Nazis." No, but it's hard to argue that the internment camp at Fort Snelling, where hundreds of women and children were held in the winter of 1862–63, was anything else. And we established *reservations.* In reading *Lincoln and the Indians,* you will discover that "concentration"—that was the term the government used—*concentration* of the Indians on reservations became the settled policy of the U.S. government.

We have made no attempt to rewrite the book. It reads as it did in 1978, including the use of the tribal names employed by government officials at the time. The modern nomenclature is an interesting mixture of old and new. "Indian" is still with us because Christopher Columbus did not know where he had landed. The Santee Sioux, Chippewa, and Winnebago tribes are now more accurately known as the Dakota, Ojibwe, and Ho-Chunk tribes. Four of the five tribes in the Indian Territory—Creeks, Cherokees, Chickasaw, and Choctaw—are now known as the Muscogee, Tsa-la-gi (or A-ni-yv-wi-ya), Chikasha, and Chahta, although the old names are still around. The Seminoles, whose name was a corruption of *cimarrón*, a Spanish term for "runaway" or "wild one," has stuck, even though the tribe's origins were closely associated with the Muscogees.

Much of the content in *Lincoln and the Indians* has stood the test of time. The book is still definitive on aspects of the Indian System and the politics of Indian affairs in the Lincoln era. But it is time for an updated study, hopefully written by a Native scholar.

This started out in 1978 as a book about Lincoln. In 2012, the descendants of those who died on the gallows in 1862 have inspired us to understand that this book, in some respects, is truly about them and their Dakota forbears. I dedicate this new edition to them and to the Dakota people. They have survived in spite of everything.

David A. Nichols

Lincoln and the Indians

I. Introduction

SURELY, LINCOLN DID NOT HAVE TIME for Indians. That assumption has ruled the historiography of Abraham Lincoln's presidency. Much has been said about the tendency of historians to burden the past with the conflicts of their own time. The neglected corollary is the inclination to read back an absence of conflict that was quite real in an earlier era. The conquest of the American Indian seems painfully inevitable to modern scholars who study the American past. It was not so readily predictable, at least in certain situations, for those who inhabited nineteenth-century America. So it is with Lincoln and the Indians. Scholars have assumed that Indian affairs had little impact on mainstream events and decisions, especially during the Lincoln years. In fact, Indian history became (and still is, despite its recent popularity) an antiquarian study, segregated from the major developments of American history.

This has led to a neglect of the Lincoln years in Indian affairs until very recently. Historians have continued to disdain interest in Indian peoples and Indian policy during the Civil War or they have compartmentalized Indian history in a fashion that distorts the proper place of Indian affairs in mainstream Civil War history. Indian historiography has been plagued by a lack of integration.[1]

The premise in this book is that no such compartmentalization existed. It is the invention of modern, specialized scholars who have assumed that Indian history is the story of a defeated, primitive people who have been marginal to American development. There

1. Annie H. Abel, *The Slaveholding Indians,* is a classic example of the compartmentalized approach.

is no desire here to make the opposite error of overemphasizing their importance, but Indians were not always marginal for Lincoln. For him Indian affairs were inextricably enmeshed in a labyrinth of financial, political, social, and military problems. Significant linkage existed between matters historians have traditionally segregated—Indian wars and the Civil War, the use of Indian and black troops, abolitionism and Indian policy reform, colonization and Indian removal, political patronage and the Indian System, and Lincoln's program for western development and the ultimate decimation of the western Indian tribes. Furthermore, white Americans of the Lincoln era defined themselves and their destiny in terms of Indian stereotypes and related conceptions of savagery and civilization. They knew better than we, in our specialized world, that our past is one fabric in which relationships among parts are as significant as the parts themselves.

The focus of *Lincoln and the Indians* is on Lincoln and his subordinates rather than the Indians themselves, on Washington and its political intrigues rather than the frontier scenes of Indianwhite confrontation. Therefore this study does not pretend to cover all the territories under the jurisdiction of the Indian Office. It is a white man's perspective on the main themes of the politics of Indian affairs, for which no apology is offered. Politics in America is never a narrow subject. In the Lincoln era, it embraced basic ideology and attitudes, social and economic concerns, military affairs, the growth of fundamental American institutions and the central values of American culture. The logic of this perspective eventually leads to some examination of the impact of the politics of Indian affairs on Native peoples. A major theme is the need for reform of the Indian System, the ultimate failure of the reform movement, and that System's impact on government policy and Indian peoples. It is not derogatory to the central role of the tribes, in concern for the dynamics of the situation, to concentrate on the question: "Why did white men act as they did?"

Important among those white men was Abraham Lincoln. There is little record of Lincoln's early relationships with Indians or concerning his attitudes toward them. That is probably because his contact was minimal. His grandfather was killed by Indians in 1784, orphaning Lincoln's father at the age of six and contributing to hardship in young Abraham's household. Lincoln volunteered for the Black Hawk War in 1832 (fought largely in Wisconsin and Illinois), but he saw no combat. Years later, Lincoln joked about his achievement as a "military hero" when he "bent a musket pretty badly on one occasion" and "had a good many bloody struggles with the musquetoes [sic]."[2]

Lincoln learned how to use Indian affairs for political advantage and understood the potency of the Indian-fighter image in the age of Andrew Jackson. When the Black Hawk War ended, he attempted to capitalize on his new military record and ran unsuccessfully for the Illinois state legislature. Years later, as a presidential candidate, Lincoln caused his campaign biographies to highlight his election as a captain in that war, calling it "a success which gave me more pleasure than any I have had since."[3] When Zachary Taylor died in 1850, Lincoln eulogized Taylor's military exploits against Indians. In 1852, he campaigned for Winfield Scott, calling him a "noble hearted man and Christian gentleman who as the agent of a democratic administration, removed the Cherokee Indians from their homes to the west of the Mississippi in such manner as to gain the applause of the great and good of the land."[4]

Lincoln, in the years before he became president, apparently never challenged the American consensus on the necessity for Indian removal to make way for white progress. There was, however, a more human side to his pattern that distinguishes him from a great majority of his contemporaries. It emerged only when he was confronted personally. The story (perhaps a legend) is told

2. Abraham Lincoln to Solomon Lincoln (a distant relative), 6 March 1848, in Roy P. Basler, ed., *The Collected Works of Abraham Lincoln*, 1:455–56, 509–10.

3. Ibid., 1:5; Lincoln to Jesse W. Fell, 20 December 1859, Basler, ed., *Collected Works*, 3:512; a similar statement is found in Basler, ed., *Collected Works*, 4:64; Anthony F. C. Wallace, "Prelude to Disaster: The Course of Indian-White Relations Which Led to the Black Hawk War of 1832," in *The Black Hawk War, 1831–32*, ed. Ellen M. Whitney.

4. Basler, ed., *Collected Works*, 2:83–84, 159; Don E. Fehrenbacher, *Prelude to Greatness: Lincoln in the 1850s*, pp. 27–28.

that during the Black Hawk War, an old Indian wandered into Lincoln's camp. His men immediately prepared to exterminate the old man, but Lincoln defended him. The men grumbled and accused their captain of cowardice. Lincoln reportedly said, "If any man thinks I am a coward, let him test it." The soldiers backed way from the confrontation.[5]

The Black Hawk War symbolized Lincoln's relationship with Indians. He found them politically useful following the war. His noncombatant status foreshadowed the detachment that would characterize his presidential actions. Although the incident with the old man is illustrative of Lincoln's humanity when confronted personally by Indians and Indian problems, his public attitude characteristically returned to one of detachment and political preoccupation. That set the pattern for Lincoln and the Indians.

5. Carl Sandburg, *Abraham Lincoln: The Prairie Years*, pp. 90–91.

II. The Indian System
"A Sink of Iniquity"

ON 20 MARCH 1861, Abraham Lincoln penned a note to his secretary of the interior, Caleb B. Smith, "Please make out and send blank appointments for all Indian places, to service in Wisconsin, in favor of the persons united [*sic*] recommended by the Wisconsin Congressional Delegation." The new president did the same concerning Minnesota. By these actions, Lincoln set in motion what contemporaries called, "The Indian System." That System, more than anything else, shaped the policies of the Lincoln administration toward Native Americans.[1]

Lincoln and the Indian Patronage

Lincoln was performing the normal presidential ritual by rewarding his political friends with the "spoils" of office. This was not unusual for him. The year previous, Lincoln's convention managers had traded the positions of secretary of interior and commissioner of Indian affairs for Indiana's twenty-six votes at the Republican presidential convention. Caleb Smith of Indiana, who had seconded Lincoln's nomination, was appointed as secretary of the interior. Lincoln reserved the commissioner's job for an Illinoisan, William P. Dole. Both men were lifelong politicians and neither had any particular expertise in Indian affairs.[2]

1. Roy P. Basler, ed., *The Collected Works of Abraham Lincoln*, 4:297–98.
2. Harry J. Carman and Reinhard H. Luthin, *Lincoln and the Patronage*, p. 76; Harry Kelsey, "William P. Dole and Mr. Lincoln's Indian Policy," p. 484; James H. Lane to Abraham Lincoln, 21 February 1861, Roll 17, Abraham Lincoln Papers, LC (for "Abbreviations in Footnotes," see p. vi).

Qualifications for the Indian service were not generally considered in making other appointments either. Commissioner Dole made a typical recommendation just following the inauguration, "Dr. Stephenson was one of our efficient speakers in Eastern Ill during your contest with Judge Douglass in 1858 as well as in the canvass of 1860 and I trust he may receive the reward he merits."[3]

This political approach disappointed people who had expected "Honest Abe" to take a higher road. His new superintendent in Washington Territory managed to offend a number of churchmen. One complained, "I had looked forward to the Administration of Mr. Lincoln with high hopes and expectations of future good to the Indians." Instead, Lincoln's new political appointee was committing "outrages" that were being tolerated in Washington. However, finding an honest man for the job had not been easy. Lincoln had already withdrawn the appointment of one nominee in Washington, Anson Dart, following disclosure that Dart had offered a one-thousand-dollar bribe to an Oregon senator to obtain the superintendency there. Dart, a shrewd operator, managed to get a bill through Congress in 1864 for "the relief of Anson Dart," indemnifying him for the loss of his position and forcing the Lincoln administration to pay the claim.[4]

Nevertheless, by normal political standards, Lincoln did his work well. In September 1861, Orville Hickman Browning told his old friend in the White House not to worry about Illinois and patronage jobs, "I am not conscious of any restlessness for new positions."[5]

Institutionalized Corruption

The Indian service to which Lincoln was making appointments already had quite a reputation. Almost everyone agreed with Bishop Henry Whipple of Minnesota "that the Indian Department

3. William P. Dole to Lincoln, 16 March 1861, Roll 18, Lincoln Papers, LC.

4. Anson G. Henry to Dole, 28 October 1861, Roll 28, Lincoln to Dole, June 1861, Roll 23, ibid.; Edward Bates to Lincoln, 8 October 1864, Roll 1, M825, LR, ID, OSI, RG48, NA.

5. Orville Hickman Browning to Lincoln, 30 September 1861, Orville Hickman Browning Papers.

was the most corrupt in our government." It was, Whipple said, "characterized by inefficiency and fraud."

Whipple articulated the evils of the System better than anyone. It was based on a "falsehood," he said, the idea of treating Indians as independent nations with whom treaties could be made. It destroyed tribal government so that chiefs "became the pliant tools of traders and agents powerful for mischief, but powerless for good." Law and order were nonexistent around reservations. Annuities were plundered by fraudulent claims. This System, said Whipple, did nothing to civilize the Indians. Instead, it threw "the weight of official influence on the side of savage life."[6]

Whipple was not alone in this indictment. Another Minnesotan told Lincoln that the Indian System was held together by "the cohesive power of public plunder." He maintained that the cause of Indian wars lay "in the thievish and dishonest conduct of Government Agents, Officers, Traders, and the vile confederates that procured their appointment and share their plunder and then gloss over and hide their iniquity."[7]

Sen. James Nesmith of Oregon summarized:

> If there is any one department of our Government worse managed than another it is that which relates to our Indian affairs. Mismanagement, bad faith, fraud, speculation and downright robbery have been its great distinguishing features.[8]

What discouraged the critics was the extent to which the corruption was integral to the System. It was so structured as to attract an almost endless stream of job seekers and entrepreneurs. Once the political jobs were filled, the System revolved around attempts to tap the federal money that flowed through its machinery. Competition for these funds took the form of an uninhibited

6. Henry Benjamin Whipple to Henry Halleck, 4 December 1862, Box 40, Letterbook 3, Henry Benjamin Whipple Papers; "The Duty of the Citizens Concerning the Indian Massacre," Box 39, Letterbook 3, Whipple Papers.

7. Lewis H. Morgan to Lincoln, 3 December 1862, Roll 20, M825, LR, ID, OSI, RG48, NA; George A. S. Crooker to William H. Seward, 8 October 1862, enclosed in a letter to Lincoln, 7 October 1862, Roll 42, Lincoln Papers, LC; also found in Lincoln Papers, Minnesota Historical Society.

8. U.S., Congress, Senate, *Congressional Globe*, Debate on the Indian Appropriation Bill, 37th Cong., 2d sess., 13 May 1862, pt. 3:2095.

capitalism, operating virtually without rules. It attracted to reservations a breed of men whose only aim was the accumulation of wealth and power. Any means to those ends were tolerated, even if they exploited the suffering of Indian men, women, and children. The System permitted and encouraged this aggrandizement openly and without fear. It was, in short, a system of institutionalized corruption.

No president, including Lincoln, could escape the demands of his victorious followers for their share of the rewards. Consequently, Lincoln's first contacts with the Indian System focused on the stampede for jobs and money rather than on the welfare of the Indians.

The Origins and Structure of the System

The Indian System originated in the treaty process initiated by the British in colonial America. Treaties became an orderly way to facilitate the westward movement of European populations. After the Revolution, the new nation continued this practice of making treaties. The use of treaties allowed white Americans to imply a recognition of Indian sovereignty while nearly always obtaining additional Indian land, in the process establishing trust funds and regulating trade and other Indian-white relations.

The diplomatic contacts became so numerous and complex that the government eventually employed agents to oversee them. The first Office of Indian Affairs was established by the secretary of war in 1824. In 1832 the president was authorized to appoint a commissioner of Indian affairs who reported to the secretary of war. Two years later Congress approved legislation providing for agents and superintendents in a fully organized Indian service. The Office of Indian Affairs was moved to the Interior Department in 1849. When Lincoln assumed office in 1861, it was the focal point for a powerful bureaucracy. The Indian System had acquired both political and economic significance.[9]

9. Edmund Danziger, *Indians and Bureaucrats: Administering the Reservation Policy during the Civil War*, pp. 3–4.

One contemporary called the system that Lincoln inherited in 1861 a "political machine."[10] The president stood at the pinnacle of the formal political structure. He had the power to appoint officials at all levels. A change in administration usually dictated a change in all positions in the Office of Indian Affairs. However, the power of appointment did not give the president absolute authority over the operation of the System. Others, especially congressmen, shared that political power.

The secretary of the interior reported to the president, and the commissioner of Indian affairs was responsible to the secretary. The commissioner headed regional superintendents who supervised a varying number of Indian agents attached to particular tribes or reservations. During the Lincoln years, thirteen large superintendencies and nearly three dozen additional agencies completed the formal bureaucracy for the System.

Other agencies were closely allied to the Indian System. The General Land Office was often involved in the disposition of Indian lands acquired by treaty. The functions of the Interior Department related to railroad and mineral development were frequently linked to the operation of the Indian System. Although the War Department no longer supervised Indian affairs directly, the army was frequently called on to intervene in violent conflicts between Indians and whites. The army sometimes supervised Indians on reservations or during the process of removal. The territorial governments, especially the governors, participated in the System. Territorial governors often served as superintendents of Indian affairs. Once a territory became a state, congressmen assumed primary responsibility for representing their state's interests in the System.

Congress was central to the System. Senators approved the treaties that provided the money and the jobs that made the System work. They recommended appointments to Indian patronage jobs at all levels, and the president was expected to heed the desires of his party's congressmen, especially concerning superintendent

10. William H. Rector to Dole, 23 January 1863, Roll 21, M825, LR, ID, OSI, RG48, NA.

9

and agent positions. Congressmen acted as channels for claims, special interests, and job seekers.

Congressional committees in each house exercised much influence over Indian affairs. The Indian Affairs committees were normally dominated by congressmen from western states that had Indian populations. These men had a vested interest in legislation affecting Indians, Indian lands, and the operation of the Indian Office. Sen. Henry M. Rice, a Democrat, testified to the power of the Minnesota congressmen who served on these committees, "The Secretary of the Interior and the Comr of Indian affairs give much *attention* to their suggestions."[11]

The formal structure, then, was made up of the president, his appointees, and Congress. It was essentially a political structure.

The Money Machine

In addition to being an official political machine, the Indian System unofficially was a vehicle for economic gain. A large and complex informal structure had developed, based on the availability of the large sums of money that were channeled through the political machine. That flow of funds had originated in the treaty system. Treaties always led to Indian removal. By the 1860s, this normally meant that Indians were removed to poor lands where they became dependent on the government for survival. In return for ceded lands, tribes were granted annuities to be held in trust and doled out each year by the local Indian agent. The practice varied widely but most of these payments were in cash. Much of the money was spent for services and supplies required by the Indians. By the 1860s, the Indian System had become a sophisticated arrangement for the disbursement of federal funds.

The ceded lands themselves were an obvious source of wealth for opportunists who sought to exploit the System. The land speculators have been discussed in depth by historians, and the subject needs little elaboration here. Land could be farmed,

---

11. Henry M. Rice to Whipple, 22 April 1862, Box 3, Whipple Papers.

developed for mineral wealth, and exploited indirectly through speculation and fraud in government bonds derived from the sale of Indian lands.[12]

Less is known about the network of persons who sought to tap the annuity funds set aside by the government for the tribes. The first group was made up of claimants—men who filed claims with the government alleging Indian destruction of property or other losses. Many such claims were undoubtedly legitimate, but there was pervasive fraud. Claims were numerous and investigation was inconsistent. A white man's claim against Indians was generally assumed to be valid. It could be paid as long as there were annuity funds available. Thus, most claims were allowed. The converse was not true—Indians normally had no machinery for processing claims for depredations by whites against Indians. A typical message recommending the payment of two claims against Indians was sent Lincoln in 1862 by Caleb B. Smith, "The law requires such payments to be made upon the order of the President."[13] As long as the local Indian agent cooperated, almost any claim could be approved. Moreover, because Indians did not vote, a prudent president would find it advantageous to approve white claims.

The commissioner of Indian affairs was continually inundated with claims for substantial amounts. In October 1862, nine persons were awarded $72,517.04 from Winnebago trust funds. Only slightly more than $12,000 was disallowed and $29,000 was still under consideration, with the chances excellent for approval.[14]

The flow of claim money increased when congressmen got into the act. Congressmen were able to push minor claim bills through the legislative process without debate or question—simply as a courtesy from colleagues. Many claims were channeled to the

12. An example is furnished by Lincoln's report to the Senate on the "Russell Fraud" in 1864. This concerned theft and fraud in securities based on Indian trust lands in Kansas. Lincoln to the Senate, 14 March 1864, Basler, ed., *Collected Works*, 7:246. An example of a land sale is found in William Lamb to Dole, 20 August 1863, Roll 936, M234, LR, Winnebago Agency, OIA, RG75, NA.

13. Caleb B. Smith to Lincoln, 13 February 1862, Roll 32, Lincoln Papers, LC.

14. Smith to Dole, 4 October 1862, Roll 4, M606, LS, ID, OSI, RG48, NA.

Indian Office by congressmen; Commissioner Dole would customarily respond that he would recommend "that it be allowed and charged appropriation fulfilling Treaty . . . annuities."[15]

The corruption in the claim process existed, but it was hard to prove. It was legal corruption as long as the appropriate officials approved the claims. Hence, public scandal rarely resulted from its operation.

That was not the case with the contractors, the second major group in the informal structure of the Indian System. Contracting was big business and its impact in some locales was very great. A number of contractors transcended state and regional lines. Major superintendencies spent hundreds of thousands of dollars per year for contracted goods and services, and their records are filled with advertisements and bids to meet the needs of the tribes.[16]

Here, the corruption was plainly evident. On taking office, Commissioner Dole informed Lincoln he was going to have to repudiate contracts approved by his predecessor "at *fraudulently* high prices & with the concurrence of the Sec of the Interior."[17] Dole was a shrewd politician. It probably occurred to him that it would be helpful to replace these Democratic contracts and contractors with Republicans. However, changing parties certainly did not end the fraud. One highly publicized incident concerned R. S. Stevens, who was given contracts by the Lincoln administration to build buildings for two Indian agencies in Kansas at a cost of $179,000. Sen. James H. Lane told Lincoln: "The contract as originally made is a gross fraud. The buildings themselves are a fraud. Stevens is a fraud."[18]

15. U.S., Congress, Senate, *Congressional Globe*, 37th Cong., 2d sess., 12 July 1862, pt. 4:3289; Dole to Cyrus B. Aldrich, 18 April 1862, Roll 68, M21, LS, OIA, RG75, NA.

16. An example is found in Clark W. Thompson to Dole, 14 May 1861, Roll 599, M234, LR, Northern Superintendency, OIA, RG75, NA; Branch to Dole, 11 July and 1 November 1861; Advertisement for Supplies, 17 April 1862, Roll 57, M234, LR, Northern Superintendency, OIA, RG75, NA.

17. Dole to Lincoln, 1 April 1861, Roll 19, Lincoln Papers, LC.

18. R. S. Stevens to Charles E. Mix, 19 August 1861, Roll 57, M234, LR, Central Superintendency, OIA, RG75, NA; this is the first of a series of letters regarding this scandal. More on the Stevens case can be found in M606, LS, ID,

Congressmen were vital to the contracting process. They kept themselves informed concerning the funds available. Armed with such information, they could frame legislation or encourage friends to make applications designed to tap those monies. A key figure in this process was the regional superintendent, who estimated the costs of goods and services, solicited bids, and had considerable discretion in exercising his authority.[19]

The records of every superintendency are filled with contracts of every type and description. Missionaries received contracts to vaccinate against smallpox. There were contracts for food, supplies, buildings, printing, removal, and transportation. Legal contracts did not exhaust the potential for profit. Contractors and bandits stole goods in transit. When the Sioux were removed from Minnesota in 1862, a missionary wrote Bishop Whipple that only fifty out of a promised one hundred tons of freight ever arrived in Dakota Territory.[20]

Critics of the System expressed harsh judgments concerning a third group in the informal structure, the traders. Traders were quasi-official in that they were licensed by the government. Licensing was originally intended to control unscrupulous commerce, but the licensing process gave some traders monopolies on reservations. This practice provided an opportunity for corrupt bookkeeping and the charging of unreasonable prices. Traders had a close relationship with agents because they were normally licensed on the recommendation of agents, other Indian officials, or congressmen.

Bishop Whipple called the trading system "ruinous to honest traders and pernicious to the Indians." Gen. John Pope agreed, "As long as our present policy prevails, the money and goods

---

OSI, RG48, NA, an example of which is Smith to Mix, 22 August 1862, Roll 4, M606, Lane to Lincoln, 25 July 1862, both in Roll 20, M825, LR, ID, OSI, RG48, NA.

19. Dole to Aldrich, 14 February 1863, Roll 13, M348, Report Books, OIA, RG75, NA.

20. S. M. Irvin to Mix, 8 May 1862, Roll 57, M234, LR, Central Superintendency, OIA, RG75, NA; S. D. Hinman to Whipple, 6 January 1864, Box 3, Whipple Papers.

furnished to the Indians will be a constant and sufficient temptation to the unscrupulous white man."[21] The secretary of the interior, Caleb B. Smith, made a scathing attack on the traders in his 1861 report. He found that money paid to Indians went immediately to the traders. The payments never quite covered the debts already accumulated by the Indians. Because of this dishonest accounting, tribesmen were kept in perpetual debt. Traders could accomplish the same thing by charging inflated prices. They often concluded their dealings by going to Washington and demanding that the government pay the debts the Indians were unable to pay. Smith told how this worked, "Witnesses are produced, who establish the debts by evidence, which cannot be contradicted by any available proof, sufficient to absorb most of the proceeds of their [the Indians'] lands." The secretary estimated that licensed traders enjoyed a profit margin ranging anywhere "from one to three or four hundred per cent."[22]

Reformers called the monetary annuities "the *great* curse of the present system." Traders included not only businessmen who attempted to maintain the appearance of respectability but also "gamblers, whiskey-traffickers, fugitives from civilized justice and desperate men of every known vice." One observer explained, "Where the carcass is there will the vultures go." Whiskey smoothed the way for much fraud. One technique was to employ an Indian as a clerk to sell the liquor on the reservation.[23] A special agent informed Gov. John Evans of Colorado that liquor was central to the cheating of the Indians by the traders.

Liquor was not the only nefarious traffic going on in Colorado. The agent reported a lively trade in Indian prostitutes around military posts. He accused one commanding officer of making "prostitutes of their women" and he found, "Licentiousness and

21. "The Duty of Citizens," Box 39, Letterbook 3, Whipple Papers; John Pope to Edwin M. Stanton, 6 February 1864, U.S., Congress, *Report of the Committee on the Conduct of the War*, 2:193.

22. AR, SI, 1861, p. 12.

23. B. B. Meeker to Bates, 2 November 1862, Thompson to Dole, 3 July 1861, Roll 599, M234, LR, Northern Superintendency, OIA, RG75, NA.

venereal diseases prevail in and around all the military posts that [I] have visited to an astonishing extent."[24]

Claimants, contractors, and traders all took advantage of the opportunities available through the Indian System. Their activities partook of the enterprising spirit of the time and the intense drive for western development. Many of them saw themselves as legitimate aspirants to wealth that the Indians could not and would not utilize. They represented entrenched interests, resistant to change and unlikely to be moved by the cries of a handful of reformers.

The Indian Agent and Corruption

Reformers reserved their harshest language for the Indian agents. Since agents were ordinarily responsible for approving trading licenses, they were seen as the root of much corruption. A Minnesotan reported: "It is believed that the trader is, in all cases, a partner of the Agent. He is usually a near relative."[25] In such arrangements, the potential for kickback schemes was virtually unlimited.

Superintendents and agents stood at the center of the system of institutionalized corruption. Their salaries were insufficient to draw hordes of job seekers—normally superintendents received two thousand dollars and agents, fifteen hundred dollars. In 1863 a special agent told Lincoln that so many people wanted these jobs because shrewd superintendents and agents could "in *four* years lay up a fortune more than your Excellency's salary—this is not known to the world." Another correspondent told Lincoln how farming appropriations were exploited by agents, "They are now chiefly used by the agents to plunder both the Indians and the government."[26]

Commissioner Dole knew his agents were corrupt. He was

24. H. T. Ketcham to John Evans, 4 April 1864, Ketcham to Evans, 1 July 1864, Roll 197, M234, LR, Colorado Superintendency, OIA, RG75, NA.

25. John J. Porter to Alexander Ramsey, 3 October 1862, Roll 20, M825, LR, ID, OSI, RG48, NA.

26. Branch to Dole, 1 November 1861, Roll 57, M234, LR, Central Superintendency, OIA, RG75, NA; George E. H. Day to Lincoln, 24 April 1863, Roll 599, M234, Morgan to Lincoln, 3 December 1862, Roll 20, M825, LR, Northern Superintendency, ID, OSI, RG48, NA.

informed early in his term, "There is no doubt in the world that the impolitic system of Indian agents is the cause and the whole cause of the imbecility and depreciation of the Indian tribes." Dole pleaded for "honest and capable Superintendents and Agents who will be satisfied with their salaries for their services instead of wishing to double them by speculations off the Indians they are employed to protect." Dole's personal obsession was the corruption in the California Superintendency, where he found agents defrauding the government at every turn. Little of the food shipped by his office from New England ever reached the Indians. He called the California Indian schools "mere nuisances, mere traps set to filch the money from the Indians."[27]

Wherever Dole looked, he found incredible examples of agent fraud. In Colorado, Simeon Whitely declined to live with his tribe and instead used government money to live in a fine house in Denver. Whitely had a clerk to do his accounts and managed once to have his quarterly salary paid twice. Another agent built buildings, including a large house for himself, at "wholly unauthorized expense" and brought financial ruin to his Indian charges. Dole pronounced agent A. D. Barrett guilty of a "swindle" and told him, "You have sacrificed the public to your private interest."[28]

Sometimes a shrewd trader moved up the ladder to become an agent. Fielding Johnson, agent to the Delawares, managed this feat. The Indians charged him with fraud in 1862. The Delawares wrote Lincoln that Johnson had, as a trader, cheated them and corrupted the agent. Now, as a new agent, he had become partner in a new store and "the Agent is giving orders to all of our people desirous of purchasing goods at the store, and promising to retain it out of the next payment."[29]

27. J. B. Chapman to Dole, 22 July 1861, Roll 57, M234, LR, ID, Central Superintendency, OSI, RG48, NA; Dole to John Beeson, 3 May 1861, Roll 65, M21, LS, OIA, RG75, NA; Dole to Elijah White, 9 June 1862, Roll 59, M574, SF201, OIA, RG75, NA.
28. Dole to Evans, 14 July 1864, Roll 74, Dole to H. W. Farnsworth, 3 January 1862, Roll 67, Dole to A. D. Barrett, 8 November 1864, Roll 75, all in M21, LS, OIA, RG75, NA.
29. Chiefs of the Delawares to Lincoln, enclosed in Smith to Dole, 20 December 1864, Roll 276, M234, LR, Delaware Agency, OIA, RG75, NA.

Oregon furnished some of the most extraordinary corruption stories. An 1859 audit revealed that liabilities of over $265,000 had been incurred in violation of Indian Office regulations. That report also revealed that one agent had retired after two years, on a $1,000 per year salary, with a $17,000 fortune. Another accumulated $41,000 in three years. No wonder Supt. William H. Rector concluded that his department "has been heretofore and is liable to be used again by designing men for base and selfish purposes."[30]

The agents were not totally responsible; Congress condoned these actions through treaties that they were responsible for approving, which set the process in motion. Sen. William Pitt Fessenden of Maine complained to his colleagues: "I have been told on very good authority that very little of the large appropriations we generally make to negotiate a treaty goes to the Indians. It goes to a lot of people who get together and have a good time and divide the spoils and make a treaty."

In May 1862, the Indian Committee of the Senate requested $15,000 to negotiate a new treaty with the Chippewa of Minnesota. Fessenden opposed the appropriation and informed the Senate that he knew a man who had been offered a bribe to promote this bill. The committee opposed Fessenden, insisting the treaty and the funds were necessary. Sen. Morton Wilkinson of Minnesota was especially outspoken in defense of the treaty that was to be negotiated in his home state. Suddenly, Sen. John Sherman of Ohio inquired whether "there was not an appropriation for this very object last year?"

> Mr. Wilkinson: There was.
> Mr. Sherman: What became of it?
> Mr. Wilkinson: A wicked and corrupt Administration appointed an incompetent man, Goddard Bailey, and he squandered the whole of it.

Asked what had become of Bailey, Wilkinson replied that the agent had been arrested for stealing $870,000 in bonds out of a safe in the Interior Department. Wilkinson quickly assured his colleagues that such corruption ended with the election of Abraham

30. Rector to Dole, 23 January 1863, Roll 21, M825, LR, ID, OSI, RG48, NA.

Lincoln and that the new administration appointed only "honest men." Thus reassured, the senators passed the appropriation.[31]

A Pathway to Wealth and Power

By the 1860s, the Indian System had become more than a source of corruption. It had become a vehicle for social mobility. It translated uninhibited capitalism into political power and wealth for ambitious men.

One example was Sen. Samuel C. Pomeroy of Kansas. Pomeroy went to Kansas from Massachusetts, first serving as a financial agent for the New England Emigrant Aid Society. Pomeroy obtained ninety thousand acres of Pottawatomie land after helping negotiate a treaty with those Indians. He received fifty thousand acres of Kickapoo land in a similar fashion. He speculated in other lands and in railroad bonds. Pomeroy became wealthy, entered politics, and became a senator.[32]

Pomeroy carried out his most notorious scheme in 1862, and it was not discovered until years later. On 22 July 1862, he wrote a letter to W. W. Ross explaining a plan to obtain Indian funds. J. K. Tappan of New York had obtained an exclusive government license to sell goods to the Pottawatomies. Orders were to be charged against annuities. "This proceeding is recognized here at the [Interior] Department," Pomeroy told Ross, "and is all right." Pomeroy and Ross were to each receive one quarter of the profits. "We have nothing to do, only to take our share of profits at each payment." Pomeroy gave Ross a prewritten letter to channel through the superintendent and the commissioner of Indian affairs. Presumably, Commissioner Dole would then check the matter with Senator Pomeroy who would urge approval. The boondoggle was on its way.[33]

31. U.S., Congress, Senate, *Congressional Globe*, Debate on the Indian Appropriation Bill, 37th Cong., 2d sess., 13 May 1862, pt. 3:2091–92.

32. Martha B. Caldwell, "Pomeroy's 'Ross Letter': Genuine or Forgery," p. 463.

33. S. C. Pomeroy to W. W. Ross, 22 July 1862, Kansas City *Star*, 2 September 1945; also found in the Samuel C. Pomeroy Papers; Caldwell, "Pomeroy's 'Ross Letter,'" p. 472.

Henry Hastings Sibley of Minnesota provides an even clearer example of how the System could be a "pathway to power" for a clever man. Sibley was born in Michigan. At the age of twenty-three, he became a manager for the American Fur Company in the Minnesota region. Sibley entered politics in 1848 and in 1849 was elected a territorial delegate to Congress. He continued in the fur trade and represented the traders at the Sioux treaty negotiations of 1851. That treaty promised the Santee Sioux $475,000 in exchange for land. Henry Sibley succeeded in claiming $145,000 of that amount as money due him for overpayments to the Sioux for furs! The Sioux objected to this obvious fraud, but the claim was approved by agent Alexander Ramsey. Henry Sibley became a rich man and in 1856 was commissioned a major general in the militia. He became the first governor of the state of Minnesota in 1858. His successor as governor was, not surprisingly, Alexander Ramsey. Sibley was later commissioned as a brigadier general for his service in the Indian war of 1862. The Indian System served Sibley well, as it did many other ambitious men.[34]

The Lincoln Administration and Corruption

The evidence was abundant that the Indian System to which Lincoln made appointments was corrupt. The new administration's attempts to deal with that corruption were fitful and ineffective. Sometimes the exposers of fraud found themselves in more difficulty than the perpetrators. For example, Supt. William H. Rector of Oregon made charges in 1862 that read like a catalog of all the corrupt practices ever conceived by the Indian agents—kickbacks from contracts, false reports on expenses and services, sale of food intended for the Indians, use of government funds to speculate in land, failure to harvest the potato crop, and "gross carelessness and wilful neglect of duty."[35]

Rector's honesty did not pay. By early 1863, a number of people

34. Dee Brown, *Bury My Heart at Wounded Knee*, p. 49; Henry Hastings Sibley Papers.
35. Rector to Dole, 7 June 1862, Roll 613, M234, LR, Oregon Superintendency, OIA, RG75, NA.

in Oregon wanted to get rid of him. A congressional delegation pressured Secretary of the Interior John P. Usher who, in turn, urged Lincoln to fire Rector. One Oregonian told Lincoln that Rector's "official conduct will bring more reproach on your administration than you can remove." Lincoln evidently refused to buckle to these demands, but he was distinctly warned, "You will have cause to remember with regret your official action toward the actual and hard working Republicans of this state." Lincoln faced "a day of reckoning."[36]

There were continual intimations that there was corruption among higher officials in the Lincoln administration. In September 1862, Walter A. Burleigh was accused of fraud at his Yankton Agency in Dakota Territory. Burleigh's alleged crimes involved high government officials. They included using government funds to pay the cost of transporting his own goods, hiring his daughter to teach at a nonexistent school, buying farm implements that no one could locate, and hiring men to work at half the price he reported to the government. On hearing these charges, Lincoln told Dole, "I think you should suspend his official functions until these charges be heard, and that the charges be brought to a hearing as soon as possible."[37] Dole objected because this would leave the Indians without an agent, and he argued that Burleigh should continue to serve while being investigated. A year later, Burleigh was still in office. In 1864, Dole scolded Burleigh for his contracting and spending actions. The Burleigh scandal became so notorious that the House of Representatives ordered an investigation in 1866. One investigator later testified that he saw an 1864 payroll that had penciled-in payments of twenty-five thousand dollars to Burleigh, ten thousand dollars to the secretary of the interior, and five thousand dollars to the commissioner of Indian affairs. These charges were never fully substantiated, but Burleigh's subsequent career is

36. John P. Usher to Lincoln, 8 January 1863, Roll 4, M606, LS, ID, OSI, RG48, NA; Amory Holbrook to Lincoln, 29 January 1863, Roll 21, M825, LR, ID, OSI, RG48, NA.

37. Usher to Dole, 1 September 1862, Roll 957, M234, LS, ID, Yankton Agency, OSI, RG48, NA; this is the letter ordering the investigation and only one of a whole set of papers concerning Walter A. Burleigh; George H. Phillips, "The Indian Ring in Dakota Territory, 1870–1890," 2:350.

revealing as to the public's feeling toward morality with regard to Indians in frontier regions like Dakota Territory. A few years later, he was elected territorial delegate to the Congress.[38]

Other charges of corruption were leveled at men high in the administration. Joseph Cody, a Kansas agent, claimed that Commissioner Dole was guilty of fraud: "If I chose I could do something more than implicate. I could convict him of enough to dam him up forever." Dole appointed a cousin and a brother-in-law to choice positions in the Indian System, and he was rumored to be speculating in Indian lands. Eventually, Dole's conduct became a great public scandal following the Sand Creek Massacre in 1864. The charges against Dole were especially significant because no other person was so influential with Lincoln concerning Indian affairs.[39]

The allegations did not stop with Dole. There were intimations of conflicts of interest throughout John P. Usher's tenure as assistant secretary and then secretary of the Interior Department. His private papers furnish evidence of speculation in railroad bonds and other financial matters revolving around the exploitation of Indian lands.[40]

The pervasive, institutionalized corruption of the Indian System was symbolized by the sale of Sac and Fox trust lands in Kansas in 1864. Tracts of land were purchased by Commissioner Dole, Secretary of Interior Usher, Comptroller of the Currency Hugh McCulloch, and John G. Nicolay, who was Lincoln's personal secretary.[41]

The Impact of the System on the Indians

The public claim for the Indian System was that it was designed to serve and protect Indians. In fact, it rarely fulfilled those

38. Dole to Lincoln, 5 January 1862, Roll 67, Dole to Burleigh, 1 May 1863, Roll 70, Dole to Burleigh, 10 May 1864, Roll 74, all in M21, LS, OIA, RG75, NA; Phillips, "Indian Ring," pp. 350–52.

39. Joseph Cody to Elvira Cody, 20 July 1863, Cable-Cody Collection; Harry Kelsey, "The Background to Sand Creek," p. 298.

40. John P. Usher Papers.

41. Kelsey, "Sand Creek," p. 298.

purposes. By the 1860s, Indian peoples, in region after region, agency after agency, were destitute and miserable. Observers reported that the "dreadful havoc" of smallpox had decimated many tribal groups.[42] Starvation and exposure killed many more.

In 1861, Lincoln's Indian officials sent out special agents to inspect the tribes of the Central Superintendency, primarily to ascertain their loyalty in the impending conflict with the South. T. C. Slaughter called the Kansas Indians "the most destitute" and described their life as "squalid and miserable." Augustus Wattles found similar conditions in that region. Wattles described a "rude and destitute" people at the Sac and Fox agency, and he reported that the Indians were being cheated by the traders. The traders threatened Wattles and said they would spend thousands of dollars "to send agents to Washington to buy influence, etc." One trader allegedly made out orders for Indians in the precise amount of annuity payments and then told each Native that he had already received his goods. The Indians protested to the agent, who checked the records and pronounced the trader guiltless. This trader even owned the wholesale outlet in Minnesota that had furnished the goods in the first place. This same trading company was regularly recording false figures on dividends to the Indians and thereby obtaining thousands of dollars extra in annuity funds.[43]

Meanwhile, the Indians starved. Wattles observed: "Nearly every family is out of provisions, living scantily on one meal a day. Women and children look particularly thin & hunger [*sic*] now." Most of them were virtually naked. Among the Kansas Indians Wattles found truly desperate conditions—no houses, oxen, cows, implements, food, or clothing. "I have never seen so poor and so miserable a community of people before," the shaken agent reported.[44]

42. Irvin to Dole, 24 February 1862, Roll 57, M234, LS, Central Superintendency, OIA, RG75, NA.

43. Dole to T. C. Slaughter, 6 April 1861, Roll 65, M21, LS, OIA, RG75, NA; Slaughter to Dole, 21 June 1861, Roll 57, M234, LR, Central Superintendency, OIA, RG75, NA; Augustus Wattles to Dole, 1 June 1861, Roll 59, M574, SF201, RG75, NA.

44. Wattles to Dole, 26 May 1861, Wattles to Dole, 15 June 1861, Roll 57, M574, SF201, RG75, NA.

These reports could be duplicated all across the nation. Bishop Whipple best summarized what the System did to the Indian: "It gathers about him a whole load of harpies to prey on him & rob him and goad him to madness. It makes promises to the ear and breaks them in life. It commences in discontent and ends in blood."[45]

A System to Serve White Men

There were fundamental reasons why the Indian System failed to meet its stated goals of serving native peoples. It was not really designed to protect Indians. It had its roots in the growth of a white population and a dynamic, aggressive culture bent on the acquisition of material wealth.

The United States Senate recognized this truth. One day in 1862, the senators debated the need for a treaty in Oregon. They confronted an accomplished fact—gold hunters were moving by the thousands onto Indian land. Sen. James Harlan of Iowa described these migrants accurately, "They are the class of men who will not permit the Indians to remain in their way." Therefore, he concluded, "The Indians will be driven off whether we agree to it or not." Another senator foresaw a war if they did not act. The whites were there illegally, but the Indians had to be removed, partly for their own protection.

The senators demonstrated the institutionalized power of the Indian System by what was left unsaid in that debate. It hardly occurred to them that the army could be used to *enforce* the law. It would be unthinkable to use force against whites on behalf of Indians. Removal was the only course open. Removal, of course, meant beginning again the cycle that nourished the Indian System, providing money and jobs for ambitious men of the Lincoln era.[46]

The Indian System mirrored the basic drives of American society—social mobility, the acquisition of wealth, unrestricted capi-

45. Wattles to Dole, 18 June 1861, Roll 57, M574, SF201, RG75, NA; Whipple to [Dole], 2 November 1863, Box 40, Letterbook 4, Whipple Papers.
46. U.S., Congress, *Congressional Globe*, Debate on Indian Appropriation Bill, 37th Cong., 2d sess., 14 May 1862, pt. 3:2121.

talism, and political activism. It was a pathway to power and wealth for the ambitious, closely allied to the struggles for power and influence in newly formed territories and states. It was also more important to the government in Washington than historians have generally realized because those regions were on the cutting edge of economic development and population migration. It served some groups extremely well—politicians, claimants, traders, contractors, and agents. Indian removal and its attendant activities had always been initiated to serve the needs of European Americans, not the needs of Native Americans. It produced a system of, by, and for white men.

As he wrote his appointment orders to Secretary Smith, Abraham Lincoln, like presidents before him, was the servant of this System. Nevertheless, Augustus Wattles found one remarkable emotion among the destitute Indians he visited, "Their veneration for the President is very profound, and their awe, when speaking of his power, is like that which children feel when listening to ghost stories." These people believed "that if the ear of the Great Father can be reached, all will be well with them."[47] Some native leaders were not so naive. Clear Sky, an aged Chippewa chief, succinctly characterized what the Indian System had done to his people:

> Dam rascal plenty here. He steal him horse. He steal him timber. He steal him every thing. He make him good business. Many agents come here. Sometimes good. Sometimes bad. Most bad. The agent say, you must not do so. The next one come, he say you do very foolish. The Government not want you to do so. Agent much dam rascal. Indian much dam fool.[48]

47. Wattles to Dole, 15 June 1861, Roll 59, M574, SF201, RG75, NA.
48. Wattles to Dole, 26 June 1861, Roll 59, M574, SF201, RG75, NA.

III. Lincoln and the Southern Tribes "Our Great Father at Washington Has Turned Against Us"

LINCOLN WAS UNDERSTANDABLY unconcerned about corruption in the Indian System in early 1861. His administration confronted a military showdown in South Carolina. The new Republican leaders barely considered even the potential military role of Indian tribes in any civil conflict.

A few unorthodox Northerners included Indians in their military schemes for defeating the South in a Civil War. These focused their attention on the "Five Civilized Tribes" in the Indian Territory (later Oklahoma). The Cherokees, Creeks, Choctaws, Chickasaws, and Seminoles were numerous. Their geographic location was strategically important. The Indian Territory, controlled by the North, could provide a base for attacks on Arkansas and Texas. Controlled by the Confederacy, it could be used to attack Kansas. The disorganization of the new administration, however, prevented any serious action from being taken on these considerations. Federal policy toward the tribes was consequently weak and contradictory.[1]

Lincoln Abandons Indian Country

Southern leaders were not so indecisive. They recognized the Indian Territory's strategic importance and sought immediately to control it. On 29 January 1861, Gov. Henry Rector of Arkansas appealed directly to Principal Chief John Ross of the Cherokees.

1. Sammy David Buice, "The Civil War and the Five Civilized Tribes" (Ph.D. diss.), p. 15.

Rector searched for common ground with the Indians and found it in the institution of slavery. The Cherokees, he wrote Ross, were "allied to the common brotherhood of the slaveholding states." Rector envisioned a great development of slave labor in the Indian Territory if Ross joined forces with white Southerners. If he did not do so, Rector predicted Lincoln's people would find Indian country "ripe for the harvest of abolitionism, freesoilers, and Northern mountebanks."[2]

A similar message went to other tribes. Confederates reaped early success with the Choctaws, who announced their determination to join the South. Their justifications included slavery and "the natural affections, education, institutions, and interests of our people, which indissolubly bind us in every way to the destiny of our neighbors and brethren of the Southern states."[3]

Northern leaders were not ignorant of Confederate activity in Indian country. The Office of Indian Affairs learned of Rector's contact with the Cherokees in mid-February 1861. The commissioner under the outgoing Buchanan administration was advised that troops would be necessary to counter these Southern influences, but the federal government failed to act. Following Lincoln's inauguration, the new secretary of the interior discovered that the Indian agent for the Cherokees was working actively for the Southern cause.[4]

These Confederate attempts to win over the Indians might have had less success had it not been for some serious grievances the tribesmen held against the federal government. Their loyalty to it was diluted by recollections of the government's forcibly removing them from the southeast a generation earlier. That government had failed to fulfill treaty obligations. The Indians also feared they

2. Henry M. Rector to John Ross, 29 January 1861, OR, 1:1, pp. 683–84 (for "Abbreviations in Footnotes," see p. vi).

3. Resolution of General Council of the Choctaw Nation, 7 February 1861, OR, 1:1, p. 682.

4. R. T. Corvant to H. B. Greenwood, 13 February 1861, John B. Ogden to the Secretary of the Interior, 4 March 1861, both Roll 99, M234, LR, Cherokee Agency, OIA, RG75, NA.

would lose their slaves and tended to believe Southern arguments that Northerners eventually intended to invade their land. The Lincoln administration did not inspire confidence in Indian country. Some Republican leaders, it was rumored, were openly advocating driving the Natives out of the Indian Territory.[5]

The Lincoln administration made feeble attempts to counter Confederate influences. Commissioner William P. Dole wrote the tribes that "the government would under no circumstances permit the smallest interference with their tribal or domestic institutions." He said that Southern agents were spreading an "erroneous impression" about government policy on slavery. This comforting message was not delivered to the tribes because of the pro-Southern activities of the Indian agents.[6] Instead, the slaveholding Indians heard the same words from Lincoln that so disturbed white Southerners, "One section of our country believes slavery is *right,* and ought to be extended, while the other believes it is *wrong,* and ought not to be extended."

Lincoln's other public declarations were not conciliatory. His theory of the Union did not allow secession and *"resolves and ordinances* to that effect are legally void, and that acts of violence, within any State or States, against the authority of the United States, are insurrectionary or revolutionary." Lincoln meant to "hold, occupy, and possess" federal properties. What did such words mean for Indian country? They sounded threatening. White Southerners were saying that Northerners would use war as an excuse to overrun the Indian Territory. That reasoning apparently made sense to the tribal leaders.[7]

The Lincoln government took only minimal actions in Indian country. In April, Lincoln appointed a new superintendent to the Southern Superintendency to replace an official who had declared his allegiance to the Confederacy. On 12 April, the day the Con-

---

5. Buice, "Civilized Tribes," p. 25; Annie H. Abel, *The Slaveholding Indians,* 1:58–59.

6. William P. Dole to Ross et al., 11 May 1861, AR, CIA, 1861, pp. 650–51.

7. Roy P. Basler, ed., *The Collected Works of Abraham Lincoln,* 4:253–58.

federates fired on Fort Sumter, Sen. J. C. Pomeroy of Kansas urged Commissioner Dole to find some way to fulfill financial obligations due the Indians by treaty. Agent John Crawford pleaded with Dole for action: "The excitement here is at an alarming pitch. . . . I wish to God those in power would do something."[8]

Those in power did nothing. In fact, the Lincoln government was preparing to withdraw from Indian country. Military posts were abandoned by the federals by 18 May. This left the tribes with no alternative but to join the South. The Chickasaws did just that on 25 May 1861, proclaiming their concern for "our social and domestic institutions" and predicting that Lincolnian rule would surpass the horrors of the French Revolution. The Choctaws took formal action on 14 June.[9]

Lincoln obviously placed a low priority on holding the Indian Territory at that moment. He was more concerned with the border states and protecting Washington. Commissioner Dole dissented from that policy. He pressed Secretary of Interior Caleb Smith on the "necessity of sending a military force in the Indian country west of Arkansas." Dole maintained that, although most of the tribes were loyal, they could be lured into war by Southern attentions. Dole wanted two or three thousand men to stabilize the situation. Smith endorsed the request and sent it to the War Department, but nothing was done.[10] The only concession was the authorization of the use of Indian spies in the Southwest where there was some concern over Confederate instigation of "Indian depredations."[11]

8. Caleb B. Smith to Dole, 5 April 1861, Roll 835, M234, LR, Southern Superintendency, OIA, RG75, NA; J. C. Pomeroy to Dole, 12 April 1861, Roll 58, M234, LR, Central Superintendency, OIA, RG75, NA; John Crawford to Dole, 21 April 1861, Roll 99, M234, LR, Cherokee Agency, OIA, RG75, NA.

9. S. T. Benning to L. Pope Walker, 14 May 1861, OR, 1:1, p. 653; Resolutions of the Chickasaw Legislature, 25 May 1861, OR, 1:3, p. 585; Proclamation of the Principal Chief of the Choctaw Nation, 14 June 1861, OR, 1:3, p. 593.

10. Dole to Smith, 30 May 1861, AR, CIA, p. 651; Smith to Simon Cameron, 30 May 1861, Roll 3, M606, LS, ID, OSI, RG48, NA.

11. A. L. Anderson to William Chapman, 19 June 1861, pp. 40–41, E. R. S. Canby to the Governor of Colorado, 6 July 1861, pp. 52–54, Canby to the Assistant Adjutant General, 29 July 1861, p. 61, all in OR, 1:4.

In July, Commissioner Dole and Secretary Smith requested an armed force for Arizona and New Mexico "as will insure to the loyal citizens of the territory and the officers of this Department therein located, that protection to which they are entitled from the Government of the U. States."[12]

Concern also surfaced in the Congress. On 22 July, the House of Representatives demanded that the secretary of war tell congressmen "whether the Southern Confederacy . . . has in their service any Indians; and if so, what number and what tribes." Simon Cameron reported that he had "no information" on the subject—an inexplicable falsehood. Union officials knew that their own agents had defected and that the Confederacy was negotiating treaties. It is highly probable that they knew that Indian troops were being organized. On 1 August, Confederate President Jefferson Davis was informed that a regiment of "mounted rifles" had been organized among the Choctaws and Chickasaws and was ready for battle.[13]

Abraham Lincoln had abandoned Indian country. Opothleyaholo, a Creek leader, was bitter over the Union betrayal. He wrote Lincoln a long letter recounting the broken promises of many years. The "Great Father" (meaning Lincoln's predecessors) had promised that "in our new homes, we should be defended from all interference from any people, and that no white people in the whole world should ever molest us unless they came from the sky." Now, the old chief found that the heavens were producing white men who urged them to fight with the South. He demanded that the president tell him what to do. "We do not hear from you," he complained. Southern agents told the Creeks that "the Government represented by our Great Father at Washington has turned against us."[14]

12. Smith to Cameron, 19 July 1861, Roll 3, M606, LS, ID, OSI, RG48, NA.
13. Resolution of the House of Representatives, 22 July 1861, OR, 3:1, p. 340; Cameron to Galusha A. Grow, 25 July 1861, OR, 3:1, p. 348; Albert Pike to Jefferson Davis, 1 August 1861, OR, 1:3, p. 625.
14. Opothleyaholo to Abraham Lincoln, 15 August 1861, White Chief et al. to Lincoln, 18 September 1861, both in Roll 59, M574, SF201, OIA, RG75, NA.

The Confederacy Gains Some Allies

The Confederate government had moved quickly to secure the loyalty of the tribes. On the day of Lincoln's inauguration (4 March), the Confederate Congress sent a special agent to the tribes west of Arkansas. On 15 March, a Bureau of Indian Affairs was established. By May, Albert Pike was commissioned to negotiate treaties with the Indians.[15]

Although the Confederates were interested in controlling the Indian Territory to expand their geographical domain, they also wanted manpower. One recommendation called for enlisting two thousand Cherokees and "send[ing] them that they may go and fall suddenly upon the unpeopled prairies and unannounced upon the Northwestern Territories and States."[16] On 13 May, the Confederate secretary of war ordered the occupation of the Territory and the raising of two regiments of Indian troops. On 17 May, the Confederacy annexed the Indian Territory. That same month, Stand Watie of the Cherokees offered to organize troops and was made a colonel in the Confederate Army.[17]

Albert Pike's efforts in the Indian Territory were soon rewarded with all the tribes except the Cherokees. Among the Cherokees, the former New Englander and longtime friend of Indians attempted to exploit a split between mixed-blood slaveowners and antislavery fullbloods. The superintendent of the Southern Superintendency was informed, "The influence of Capt Pike the Rebel Commissioner is second to no man's among the Southern Indians & I fear that he may succeed in his intrigues with the other tribes."[18]

The man who resisted Pike's entreaties the longest was John Ross. Ross rebuffed Pike's first overtures and many Cherokees were loyal to the old leader, now more than seventy years of age. He had led his people a generation before along the "trail of tears" from

15. Buice, "Civilized Tribes," pp. 10, 26.
16. Felix W. Robertson to Davis, 3 May 1861, OR, 1:53, p. 676.
17. Walker to Benjamin McCulloch, 13 May 1861, OR, 1:3, p. 575; Buice, "Civilized Tribes," p. 28; J. Frederick Neet, "Stand Watie, Confederate General in the Cherokee Nation," p. 38.
18. Buice, "Civilized Tribes," pp. 43–46; E. H. Carruth to W. G. Coffin, 11 July 1861, Roll 835, M234, LR, OIA, RG75, NA.

Georgia to the Indian Territory.[19] Now another crisis threatened his people.

The inaction of the Lincoln government left Ross with few alternatives. He chose the only policy that could possibly spare people bloodshed—neutrality. Ross's neutrality was early established. He answered Henry Rector's letter of 29 January with non-committal assurances. He announced his neutrality policy publicly in May 1861 and refused to approve the organization of troops for the Confederacy. He told a Northern commander, "We do not wish our soil to become the battle ground between the States and our homes to be rendered desolate and miserable by the horrors of civil war."[20]

Commissioner Dole made attempts to reach Ross in his May 1861 messages that went undelivered. These notes assured the Cherokee leader on slavery, accused "bad and unscrupulous men" of misrepresenting the president on that issue, and said Dole had requested troops and weapons for the Indian Territory. Caleb Smith's accompanying message said, "I have assured the President that he need have no apprehension of trouble with your people."[21] Ross never read those words. In any event, federal withdrawal demonstrated what the policy behind the words really was.

Ross continued to hold out. Confederate Gen. Benjamin McCulloch warned his superiors that "John Ross . . . is only waiting for some favorable opportunity to put himself with the North."[22] Confederate Commissioner of Indian Affairs David Hubbard pressured Ross in June, warning him that Northerners would take Cherokee slaves, land, and default on Cherokee money invested in bonds issued by Southern states if the Union won the war. Actually,

19. The best account of the removal is still Grant Foreman, *Indian Removal: The Emigration of the Five Civilized Tribes of Indians*.

20. Ross to Elias Rector, 22 February 1861, OR, 1:13, pp. 491–92; Ross to J. R. Kannady, 17 May 1861, OR, 1:13, p. 493; Gary E. Moulton, "Chief John Ross During the Civil War," p. 315.

21. Dole to Ross, 11 May 1861, Roll 65, M21, LS, OIA, RG75, NA. Also found in AR, CIA, 1861, pp. 650–51; Smith to Ross et al., 11 May 1861, Roll 59, M574, SF201, OIA, RG75, NA; AR, CIA, 1861, p. 627.

22. David Hubbard to Ross, 12 June 1861, Ross to Hubbard, 17 June 1861, OR, 1:13, pp. 497–99; McCulloch to Walker, 22 June 1861, OR, 1:3, p. 595.

McCulloch had Ross militarily surrounded. The Choctaw and Chickasaw regiment was organized to the south, Arkansas was on the east, and McCulloch had forces on the Cherokees' western border. John Ross had no alternative but to join the Confederacy.

Ross soon realized how untenable his position was. On 21 August, the Cherokees agreed to seek an alliance with the Confederacy. On 31 August, McCulloch reported, "The Cherokees have joined the South, and offered me a regiment." The alliance was consummated on 9 October and the Cherokees sought to convince Southerners of their sincerity in language denouncing the Lincoln government as a "military despotism" guilty of crimes against the constitution and humanity.[23]

The Cherokees had some reason for hopeful results from the new relationship. Albert Pike had promised them a degree of equal treatment they had never enjoyed with the federal government. Indian troops were to select their own field officers. They were promised representation in the Confederate Congress. The Congress, however, diluted this pledge by disallowing voting rights and permitting only one delegate per tribe.[24] Nevertheless, these concessions were more satisfactory than any proposal ever offered by the national government.

Lincoln Changes His Mind

The Lincoln government learned in late August that the Cherokees had joined the Southern cause. By September, the military was getting worried. Gen. John C. Frémont warned that the Confederates were organizing Indians and "that the frontier is utterly unprotected and that the inhabitants have applied in vain for aid to the State Authorities." The Indian Territory was in complete

23. Resolution of the Cherokee Council, 21 August 1861, OR, 1:13, pp. 499–500; Ross to McCulloch, 24 August 1861, OR, 1:13, p. 673; McCulloch to Walker, OR, 1:13, p. 689; McCulloch to Ross, 1 September 1861, OR, 1:13, p. 690; Message of John Ross to the Cherokee Council, 9 October 1861, Declaration by the Cherokee National Committee, 28 October 1861, OR, 1:13, pp. 500–505; Moulton, "Chief John Ross," pp. 318–19.

24. Walker to Pike, 24 August 1861, OR, 1:13, p. 671; Resolution by the Confederate Congress, July 1861, OR, 4:1, p. 443; OR, 4:1, pp. 1190–91; Abel, *Slaveholding Indians*, 1:159.

control of the Confederacy. C. H. Carruth told James H. Lane that John Ross had joined the Confederacy and "all there is left to do, is to kindle civil war over his head."[25]

What worried some Unionists was the apparent intention of the Confederates to do more than merely hold their position in Indian country. General McCulloch ordered Col. Stand Watie "to move into neutral land and Kansas, and destroy everything that might be of service to the enemy."[26] This destruction, especially in the pockets of Indian resistance to the Confederate control, resulted in a flood of refugees into Kansas.

Union leaders could no longer ignore the strategic threat in the Indian Territory. One report warned that the Indian alliances gave Southerners a potential army of sixty-four thousand men in the region covering the Indian Territory westward. These troops, a New Mexican officer informed a superior, would form "an efficient army for operations upon these territories, familiar with this country, and allied to the Georgians, who sympathize with secession, and form a large proportion of our mining population."[27]

On 22 November 1861, the Confederacy organized the Indian Territory into a separate military department and designated Albert Pike as commander.[28] On 3 December, Abraham Lincoln reported to the Congress, "The Indian country south of Kansas is in possession of insurgents." He also noted press reports that the Confederates were organizing Indian troops.

Lincoln was forced to change his mind. He had ignored the Indian Territory, withdrawn Union forces, and given leaders like John Ross no place to go but the Confederacy. That was beginning to look like a military blunder. Lincoln told the Congress, "It is believed that upon repossession of the country by the federal forces the Indians will readily cease all hostile demonstrations, and resume their former relations to the government."[29]

25. John R. Howard to Charles Robinson, 18 September 1861, Correspondence of the Kansas Governors, 1861–1865; Carruth to James H. Lane, 9 October 1861, Roll 57, M234, LR, Central Superintendency, OIA, RG75, NA.

26. McCulloch to Sterling Price, 22 October 1861, OR, 1:3, p. 721.

27. William Gilpin to Canby, 26 October 1861, OR, 1:4, p. 73.

28. Abel, *Slaveholding Indians*, 1:253.

29. Basler, ed., *Collected Works*, 5:46.

This meant that the president had decided to retake the Indian Territory. Now, the cost would be far greater than it would have been had it been initiated when Commissioner Dole first urged action in May 1861. The greatest price was being paid by the Indians who, due to the Confederate scorched-earth policy in neutral areas, were being driven into Kansas by the thousands.[30]

Lincoln, Jim Lane, and Indian Troops

Lincoln's decision to retake Indian Territory had unexpected ramifications. Because of the shortage of soldiers for the theaters of conflict farther east, it was inevitable that Indian troops would have to be used in Indian Territory. Public opinion was generally opposed to the use of Indian manpower in the army, although the army had utilized Indian scouts and spies. For this reason, Lincoln had already rejected the idea of Indian soldiers. In May 1861, Hole-in-the-Day, a Minnesota Chippewa leader, offered a hundred men to the government. The secretary of war replied, "The President as well as this Department is much pleased," but turned down the offer. Simon Cameron's language mirrored the fears of whites, "The nature of our present national troubles, forbids the use of savages."[31]

William P. Dole had pressed for a military force in Indian country in May, although he did not specify Indian troops. An agent on the scene was more precise, "Let me beg of you that you will lay the matter before the President, and see if possible that some measures are taken to rescue the southern Indians from the rebels." He specifically suggested "the formation of a brigade of *friendly* Indians" to combat the Cherokees armed by the Confederates. This agent claimed that all the other agents favored such a plan. He then revealed the probable author of the scheme: "Gen'l Lane is also heartily in favor of it."[32]

30. Abel, *Slaveholding Indians*, 1:259.

31. D. Cooper to Cameron, 1 May 1861, OR, 3:1, p. 140; Cameron to Cooper, 9 May 1861, OR, 3:1, p. 184.

32. Dole to Smith, 30 May 1861, AR, CIA, 1861, p. 651; George Cutler to Dole, 21 October 1861, Roll 28, Abraham Lincoln Papers, LC.

More than anyone else, James H. ("Bloody Jim") Lane was responsible for persuading Abraham Lincoln to use Indian troops. Lane was unscrupulous and unpredictable. He had gone to Kansas from Indiana in 1855, where his political career had been ruined by his escapades. Lane found Kansas the perfect environment for his style of activity. He changed parties (Democrat to Republican) and began the career that made him a folk hero and elevated him to the United States Senate in 1861. Lane's brigade, composed of drifters, blacks, and Indians, became notorious for missions that frequently plundered Unionist civilians as readily as the Confederates.[33]

Lane became a powerful man in Washington, and his influence on Lincoln was remarkable. Military patronage in Kansas was controlled by Lane, not by the governor, as was the normal practice. Lincoln even humiliated Gov. Charles Robinson over this. In August 1862, Secretary of War Edwin Stanton told Lane to report the names of officers selected. Governor Robinson would be asked to commission them. If he refused, Stanton said, "The President will issue commissions." This was done in no other state.[34]

Lane's ability to influence Lincoln came, in part, from his constant badgering of the president. Lincoln appears to have sometimes gone along with Lane just to get rid of him. Lincoln once told a Kansas governor: "He knocks at my door every morning. You know he is a very persistent fellow and hard to put off. I don't see you very often and have to pay attention to him."[35]

Lane offered bodyguards for Lincoln's trip to Washington for the inauguration. His Jayhawkers slept in the White House hallways following the battle at Fort Sumter. From 18 April to 27 April, fifty of Lane's men guarded the president against assassination. From the very beginning, Jim Lane was camped by Lincoln's door.[36]

33. Buice, "Civilized Tribes," p. 64.

34. Edwin M. Stanton to Lane, 23 August 1862, OR, 3:2, p. 444.

35. Edgar Langsdorf, "Jim Lane and the Frontier Guard," p. 25; Lloyd Lewis, "The Man the Historians Forgot."

36. Langsdorf, "Jim Lane," p. 25; Lane to Cameron, 27 April 1861, Mark W. Delahay Papers.

Lane embroiled Lincoln in the political quagmire of Kansas. Commissioner Dole accurately warned the president, "In Kansas they are purely political." When Lincoln entered office, Lane and Gov. Charles Robinson were in the midst of a struggle for power. Before it was over, Lincoln was drawn into the fight.[37]

Jim Lane's great obsession was to lead a military expedition against the South to shorten the war by an attack on the exposed flank of the Confederacy in Arkansas and Texas. Indian Office officials supported the scheme. W. G. Coffin, head of the Southern Superintendency, argued that it was workable if Lane could get "the propper [sic] authority from the President." If appointed brigadier general, Coffin believed that Lane "would be able to organize such a force as would strike terror into the secessionists in Arkansas and Texas."[38]

In June 1861 Jim Lane was in Washington agitating for his project. He succeeded in obtaining authorization to raise troops in Kansas—short of commanding an expedition. He was appointed brigadier general over the protest of Governor Robinson and his ally, Fred P. Stanton, who argued that Lane should at least resign his senate seat.[39] Lane, however, had secured a blank commission and did not accept the appointment officially. A month later, the adjutant general was still seeking his acceptance. Lane replied that he would accept as soon as the Kansas Brigade was organized. That date passed and Jim Lane kept the War Department dangling. He obviously hoped to keep a hold on both positions until he received assurances that he would command an expedition. Meanwhile, he campaigned to obtain Lincoln's support.[40]

On 29 August, Lane claimed that he had reports of six thousand Confederates advancing on Kansas. He initiated negotiations

37. Dole to Lincoln, 6 October 1863, Roll 60, Lincoln Papers, LC; Albert Castel, *A Frontier State at War: Kansas, 1861–1865,* p. 71; article in the *Weekly Western Argus,* Charles Robinson Papers.

38. Coffin to Dole, 3 June 1861, Roll 22, Lincoln Papers, LC.

39. Fred P. Stanton testimony before the Senate Judiciary Committee, 20 June 1861, Roll 196, M221, LR, SW, RG107, NA.

40. Lorenzo Thomas to Lane, 26 July 1861, Lane to Thomas, 28 June 1861, Roll 24, Lincoln Papers, LC.

with the southern Indians on his own, informing Commissioner Dole a month later. This move came too late to stop the Cherokees from allying with the Confederacy.[41]

On 9 October, Lane pressured Lincoln to establish a new military department, "to be composed of Kansas, the Indian country, and so much of Arkansas and the Territories as may be thought advisable to include therein." Lane wanted ten thousand troops for the new department and he had just the man to command it—Jim Lane. "I will cheerfully accept it, resign my seat in the Senate, and devote all my thoughts and energies to the prosecution of the War," he proclaimed.[42]

Lane had vocal allies in Superintendents Coffin and Mark Delahay. They called the Indian Territory "a strategic point of much importance" and pressed Lincoln for a new military department with Lane in command. "He is fearless, active, energetic and untiring in whatever he undertakes," they told Lincoln, "and has all the skill and experience necessary to constitute a prudent and successful commander." The two Indian officials blamed Governor Robinson for most of the charges against Lane and his old brigade. They reminded Lincoln that they were political supporters and that he should not be doing favors for their opponents.[43]

Thus far, Lincoln had refused to bend to the pressure. On 24 October, he told Gen. David Hunter not to worry about attacks from the South until spring. The War Department informed Lane that a request to raise an additional regiment of cavalry was denied. Lincoln did not intend to authorize a great Southern expedition—at least, not yet.[44]

In fact, the president had decided to rely on General Hunter in Kansas. Hunter's appointment to the Kansas command was one of the few positions Jim Lane had been unable to control. Hunter was an emotional, difficult man from Lincoln's home state of Illi-

41. Lane to Price, 29 August 1861, OR, 1:3, p. 465; Lane to Carruth, 30 August 1861, Roll 835, M234, LR, Southern Superintendency, OIA, RG75, NA.

42. Lane to Lincoln, 9 October 1861, OR, 1:3, pp. 529–30.

43. Coffin to Lincoln, 28 October 1861, Roll 28, Lincoln Papers, LC.

44. Lincoln to David Hunter, 24 October 1861, ibid.; Thomas A. Scott to Lane, 29 October 1861, Roll 46, M6, LS, SW, RG107, NA.

nois. But at this moment, he seemed safer to Lincoln than "Bloody Jim" Lane.[45]

Lincoln wanted Hunter to try diplomacy once more with the southern tribes. "I am directed by the President," Dole told Hunter on 16 November 1861, "to respectfully request the performance of you of the trusts herein indicated, involving, as you will perceive, some delicate and important matters." Lincoln was clearly worried about Albert Pike's recruiting activities. "It is this influence which the President is exceedingly anxious to counteract at once through you." The mission was to be "promptly done" to prevent the Indians from joining the Confederate forces. Lincoln had concluded that Hunter was "the most suitable person to do this." Jim Lane, by implication, was not.[46]

Hunter was instructed to deliver letters, including those that had gone undelivered the previous May. He succeeded in seeing some Indian leaders and promised them trips to Washington. It was too little, too late. Lincoln was tying to use words as a substitute for military action. Now, he was forced to take another look at the military option. That meant that Jim Lane's star was again on the rise.[47]

Lincoln Decides to Use Indian Troops

Jim Lane arrived back in Washington in November, prepared to push for his Southern expedition. He had added to his circle of powerful allies. They included Postmaster General Montgomery Blair; a lobbyist for New England textile interests, Edward Atkinson; and Benjamin F. Butler, commander of the Department of New England. The plan called for a two-pronged attack, with Butler landing on the Texas coast and another army marching southward from Kansas. This expedition lobby, coupled with the

---

45. Castel, *A Frontier State at War*, p. 78; Dudley Cornish, *The Sable Arm*, pp. 80–81.

46. Dole to Hunter, 16 November 1861, Roll 67, M21, LS, OIA, RG75, NA.

47. Dole to White Chief, Bob Deer, 16 November 1861, Dole to Hunter, 17 December 1861, ibid.

failure of Lincoln's Indian diplomacy, began to push the president toward military action.[48]

David Hunter was the one who suggested employing Indian troops in Kansas. On 27 November, he sought "authority to muster into the service a Brigade of Kansas Indians to assist the Creeks, Seminoles & Chickasaws in adhering to their loyalty."[49] This request may have helped convince policymakers that there was substance to Jim Lane's contention that a military force was needed.

Commissioner Dole also continued to support the use of troops in the Indian Territory. He was always Lincoln's favored advisor on Indian matters and later took credit for the decision to use Indian troops, much of which he deserved.[50]

The most decisive factor in that decision was the Indians themselves. By December 1861, thousands of Indian refugees were crossing into Kansas. The administration could no longer ignore the Indian Territory because Kansans would not allow it. They wanted to be rid of those extra Indians. Lincoln's previous decision to retake the Indian Territory coincided with the pressing need to relocate the refugees in their homes. The availability of these refugees as soldiers dovetailed with the need for troops to retake Indian country.

Stories reached Washington of the gallant fight of the refugees against the Confederates. Opothleyaholo appealed directly to Lincoln: "Now, Father, we ask you for all the help you can give us, send me 2 or 3 thousand men if you can spare them." Opothleyaholo had led four thousand Indians out of the Indian Territory. An agent reported to Dole that the Delawares wanted to help and were asking "why it is their Great Father in Washington delays sending them to assist their southern brethern." Another agent appealed to Dole, "Hurry up Lane."[51]

48. Castel, *A Frontier State at War*, p. 81; Ludwell Johnson, *The Red River Campaign*, pp. 9–11; Buice, "Civilized Tribes," p. 77.

49. Hunter to Thomas, 27 November 1861, Roll 29, Lincoln Papers, LC.

50. Dole to Smith, 5 June 1862, AR, CIA, 1862, p. 291.

51. T. Johnson to Dole, 31 December 1861, Opothleyaholo to Lincoln, G. W. Cullen [?] to Dole, 2 January 1862, Roll 59, M574, SF201, RG75, NA.

Jim Lane needed no hurrying. He had already persuaded Lincoln to authorize a Southern expedition that would utilize Indian troops. On 26 November, David Hunter was ordered to report on his resources for an expedition. On 4 December, General-in-Chief Henry Halleck told Hunter that a final decision had been made. Hunter was not happy. He had wanted an expedition with Indian troops, but he wanted to command it himself. He sensed the hand of Jim Lane in these communications. Hunter protested that an expedition was "altogether impracticable." He said he had only three thousand men and that the Confederates had ten thousand to the south and twenty thousand men in Missouri. Hunter was assured that sufficient force would be provided.[52]

Hunter was still upset, and he wrote Lincoln an angry letter. "I am very deeply mortified, humiliated, insulted, and disgraced," he told the chief executive.[53] His words drew an equally angry response from Lincoln. The president told the general that it was difficult to answer "so ugly a letter in good temper." Hunter was unwittingly playing into Jim Lane's hands. Lincoln told him:

> I am, as you intimate, losing much of the great confidence I placed in you . . . from the flood of grumbling dispatches and letters I have seen from you. . . . You constantly speak of being placed in command of only 3,000. Now tell me, is this not mere impatience? Have you not known all the while that you are to command four or five times that many? I have been, and am, sincerely your friend; and if, as such, I dare to make a suggestion I would say you are adopting the best possible way to ruin yourself.[54]

By 2 January 1862, Lincoln was ready to act. Simon Cameron informed Caleb Smith: "It is desired to receive into the U.S. Service 4,000 Indians from the borders of Kansas and Missouri. It is pro-

---

52. Hunter to Thomas, 26 November 1861, OR, 1:8, p. 379; Buice, "Civilized Tribes," p. 78; Hunter to Lane, 13 February 1862, Roll 32, Lincoln Papers, LC; Hunter to Thomas, 11 December 1861, OR, 1:8, p. 428; George B. McClellan to Hunter, 11 December 1861, OR, 1:8, pp. 428–29.

53. Hunter to Lincoln, 23 December 1861, Roll 30, Lincoln Papers, LC.

54. Lincoln to Hunter, 31 December 1861, OR, 1:53, p. 511.

posed to give them each a blanket, Army subsistence, and such arms as may be necessary to supply deficiencies."[55]

A triumphant Jim Lane wired the news to David Hunter on 3 January, "It is the intention of the Government to order me to report to you for an active winter's campaign. . . . They have also ordered you, in conjunction with the Indian Department, to organize 4,000 Indians." Lane and Dole were coming to Kansas to help.[56]

Hunter was furious. He was to "organize" the Indian troops with both Dole and Lane on the scene. This meant he would be a figurehead. Lane would command the soldiers, and Hunter could do little more than sign requisitions. A letter from the secretary of war confirmed this arrangement. It also revealed that Lane had falsely represented to Cameron that he was pursuing Hunter's wishes and had been authorized to command thirty thousand troops. In fact, Lincoln had never wanted to send more than ten thousand to fifteen thousand men.[57]

Nevertheless, the historic decision was made. Indians would serve in the Union army and would receive pay and benefits equal to that of white troops—"the same pay as other volunteers, whilst the chiefs will receive a higher remuneration." Death benefits were to be paid to the families of men who died while in service. This might have represented an extraordinary step toward Indian equality, just as the use of black troops in the Union army influenced the movement for citizenship for former slaves. Unfortunately, its great potential was never realized.[58]

55. Cameron to Smith, 2 January 1862, Roll 47, M6, LS, SW, RG107, NA; Smith to Dole, 3 January 1862, Roll 59, M574, SF201, OIA, RG75, NA.

56. Lane to Hunter, 3 January 1862, OR, 1:8, p. 482.

57. Cameron to Hunter, 3 January 1862, OR, 1:53, p. 512; Lincoln to the Secretary of War, 31 January 1862, OR, 1:8, p. 538.

58. Dole to W. W. Ross, Dole to H. B. Branch, 6 January 1862, Roll 67, M21, LS, OIA, RG75, NA.

IV. The Indian Expedition
"A Great Exhausting Affair"

THE SOUTHERN EXPEDITION project was in trouble from the outset. A week after acting to utilize Indian troops, Lincoln appointed Edwin Stanton to replace Simon Cameron as secretary of war.[1] Stanton was not enthusiastic about recruiting Indians into the army. Stanton, moreover, was to play a role in the larger quarrel over who was to command the expedition. Much of the responsibility for the resulting furor and subsequent delay of the expedition must rest with Lincoln. He consented to a patchwork arrangement that was bound to disintegrate. The situation demanded firm leadership and Lincoln did not provide it.

The Project Collapses

David Hunter received his detailed expedition orders on 24 January 1862. These were a blueprint for trouble. The adjutant general reminded Hunter that Jim Lane was the author of the plan and that Lane had promoted it claiming Hunter's approval. Lorenzo Thomas confirmed that Hunter was in command and that Lane would be subordinate to him. Thomas also stated, "If you deem it proper you may yourself command the expedition which may be undertaken"—words that had explosive potential. That was clearly not the way Jim Lane had interpreted the arrangement. Although someone might have misunderstood the president's intent, the wording almost surely reflected his wishes.[2]

1. Simon Cameron to Abraham Lincoln, 11 January 1862, Roll 31, Abraham Lincoln Papers, LC (for "Abbreviations in Footnotes," see p. vi).
2. Lorenzo Thomas to David Hunter, 24 January 1862, OR, 1:8, p. 525.

That statement gave David Hunter the opening he needed. He was determined not to let Jim Lane command that expedition. Lane was already on his way to Kansas. When he arrived in Leavenworth, the shocked senator found this proclamation in the press: "In the expedition about to go south from this department, called in the newspapers General Lane's Expedition, it is the intention of the major-general commanding the department to command in person, unless otherwise expressly ordered by the government."[3] Jim Lane's triumphant return to Kansas was turned into a farce. Lane was furious and sought to strike back.

While Hunter and Lane played their power games, the Indian refugees suffered. Superintendent Coffin estimated the number of refugees at ten to sixteen thousand and told Commissioner Dole, "They are in the most deplorable state of destitution, some of them are said to have starved and froze [sic] to death after their disastrous Battle."[4] They lacked provisions of all kinds. An army surgeon described their misery:

> It is impossible for me to depict the wretchedness of their condition. Their only protection from the snow upon which they lie is prairie grass and from the wind scraps and rags stretched upon switches. Some of them had personal clothing; most had but shreds and rags which did not conceal their nakedness, and I saw seven varying in age from three to fifteen years without one thread upon their bodies.[5]

There was little food, and disease took a heavy toll. "Why the officers of the Indian Department are not doing something for them I cannot understand," the surgeon complained. Eventually the Indian Office acted to provide aid, an action that Congress ratified in March 1862.[6] Lane was determined to use the condition of the Indian refugees in his struggle to attain command. The Indians felt their only

3. James H. Lane to John Covode, 27 January 1862, OR, 1:8, pp. 529–30.
4. W. G. Coffin to William P. Dole, 15 January 1862, Roll 59, M574, SF201, OIA, RG75, NA.
5. Joseph K. Barnes to A. B. Campbell, 5 February 1862, OR, 2:4, pp. 6–7.
6. Annie H. Abel, *The Slaveholding Indians*, 1:274. One of the best accounts of refugee problems is Edmund Danziger, "The Office of Indian Affairs and the problem of Civil War Refugees."

hope was to return to their homes with the help of the Union army. Now Jim Lane was telling them that his plan was in jeopardy. Opothleyaholo appealed to Lincoln, "Our object . . . is to beg that General Lane be placed in command of the expedition." The old Creek leader told the president that they trusted Lane. "General Lane is our friend. His heart is big for the Indian," he wrote. Opothleyaholo demanded that Lincoln act on behalf of the six thousand Indian women and children who were living without shelter or clothing in the midst of winter.[7]

The Lane-Hunter contest continued to dominate events and to threaten the proposed expedition. Hunter wired the War Department, demanding "discretion in attacking the South." Lane rallied his supporters. One observer concluded, "There is bitter feeling existing between Hunter and Lane which will have to be settled before anything is done with the army now collecting at Lear."[8]

An exasperated Lincoln finally attempted to break the deadlock. He had apparently learned of Jim Lane's plans for a thirty-thousand-man force and of his false representation of Hunter's wishes. Lincoln instructed the secretary of war:

> It is my wish that the expedition commonly called the "Lane Expedition" shall be as much as has been promised at the Adjutant-General's Office under the supervision of General McClellan and *not any more*. I have not intended and do not now intend that it shall be *a great exhausting affair*, but a snug, sober column of 10,000 or 15,000. General Lane has been told by me many times that he is under the command of General Hunter, and assented to it as often as told. It was the distinct agreement between him and me when I appointed him that he was to be under Hunter.[9]

Dole, who authored the compromise that produced this state of affairs, was in Kansas to help recruit Indian troops. The state

7. Opothleyaholo and Aluktustenuke to Lincoln, 28 January 1862, OR, 1:8, p. 534.

8. Hunter to Edwin M. Stanton, 29 January 1862, Edwin M. Stanton Papers; R. A. Cash to William Osborn, 30 January 1862, James H. Lane Collection.

9. Lincoln to the Secretary of War, 31 January 1862, OR, 1:8, p. 533.

was in an uproar and Commissioner Dole was upset with both Hunter and Lane. Dole said that Jim Lane had misled him on how "he could act in perfect harmony with Genl Hunter." He had always thought that Hunter would be content with a superior command and let Lane lead the expedition. It had all fallen apart. However, Dole remained hopeful. He told Lincoln that it was all worked out and that Hunter and Lane "are on their good behavior to each other."[10]

The very next day David Hunter demonstrated how poor Dole's judgment continued to be. The general wrote Lincoln, demanding that the president force Lane either to accept his commission or reject it. He accused Lane of opening his mail from the president. He alleged that Lane's real motives revolved around "the swarm of contractors who have accompanied his return to Kansas and the great number of schemes involving large expenditures which are said to have received his sanction."

Hunter's major allegation was that Lane was now trying to sabotage his own expedition project unless he could command it. Lane was not the only one who opened other people's mail. Hunter himself intercepted a telegram to Lane from Congressman John Covode of Pennsylvania. It read: "I have been with the man you name. Hunter will not get the money or men he requires. His command cannot go forward. Hold on. Do not resign your seat."

Hunter's charges might have been more credible had he not claimed that the adjutant general's communication of 24 January was "the first intimation I have ever had of the plan urged upon the President and the Secretary of War by Senator Lane."[11] In fact, Hunter had been notified by Lane himself on 3 January and probably knew of the expedition scheme much earlier.

Lincoln's 31 January attempt to break the Hunter-Lane deadlock failed. Instead, the pressure increased, especially from Jim Lane's numerous allies. On 6 February, the House of Representatives passed a resolution urging the president to appoint Lane to

10. Dole to Lincoln, 3 February 1862, Roll 32, Lincoln Papers, LC.
11. The "man you name" may have been Secretary of War Stanton; Hunter to Lincoln, 4 February 1862, ibid.

command the expedition. Joseph Medill of the Chicago *Tribune* lectured the president on his political responsibilities, "If you would listen to the wishes of the 850,000 noble men who voted for you in the West, you would never think of letting Lane's expedition fall through." Medill claimed that Lane's army could establish a free state in Texas and "spread terror and panic among the rebels." He scolded, "Mr. Lincoln, for God's sake and your country's sake rise to the realization of our awful national peril."[12]

Jim Lane's trump card was Secretary of War Edwin Stanton. Caleb Smith lamented that the "Secretary of War is unwilling to put Indians in the Army." That was a certain way to thwart Hunter's plans—deny him the Indians so essential to the expedition. Lincoln had run out of patience. Smith informed Commissioner Dole on 6 February that Lincoln was going to see Stanton "and settle it today."[13]

On 10 February, Lincoln turned his anger on Hunter and Lane:

> My wish has been and is to avail the Government of the services of both General Hunter and General Lane, and, so far as possible, to personally oblige both. General Hunter is the senior officer and must command when they serve together; though in so far as he can, consistently with the public service and his own honor, oblige General Lane, he will also oblige me. If they cannot come to an amicable understanding, General Lane must report to General Hunter for duty, according to the rules, or decline the service.[14]

Jim Lane had lost the game. He tried once more to move Hunter, insisting that Hunter go along with the original arrangement and let Lane command the expedition. Hunter's response left no room for negotiation. He intended to command the column himself. An angry Jim Lane left for Washington to resume his Senate seat. He is reported to have muttered all the way about the

12. Resolution of the House of Representatives, 6 February 1862, Joseph Medill to Lincoln, 9 February 1862, ibid.

13. Caleb B. Smith to Dole, 6 February 1862, Roll 4, M606, LS, ID, OSI, RG48, NA.

14. Lincoln to Hunter and Lane, 10 February 1862, OR, 1:8, p. 551.

man in the White House being a "d——d liar, a demagogue, and a scoundrel." As Lane saw it, Lincoln was guilty of "leaving him before the public in the light of a braggart, a fool and a humbug."[15]

David Hunter should not have been too smug about his triumph over Jim Lane, whom he considered representative "of the scum thrown to the surface by political troubles." Lincoln was not happy with him either. In March 1862, Lincoln ordered a reorganization that placed the Department of the Mississippi, which included Kansas, under General Halleck. Hunter was transferred to the East. The Indian expedition was canceled. Lincoln had never really been convinced of the project's military value. He now decided it was expendable.[16]

Despite his setback, Jim Lane did not give up. He actually secured an order from Lincoln to rescind the new appointment in Kansas and place his own man in command. This only touched off a new furor and demanded new compromises because, although Lane succeeded in disposing of Hunter, he did not succeed in replacing him with his choice. Lane was not giving up. He still intended to be both a United States senator and the military boss in Kansas.[17]

The Project Is Revived

The Southern expedition had languished for two months. It appeared to be defunct. However, Lincoln had demonstrated a tendency to waver if someone could convince him that a combination of military and political necessities demanded a change of direction. Several factors forced Lincoln to reconsider.

First, the Confederates demonstrated the military utility of Indian soldiers during the Battle of Pea Ridge (Elkhorn Tavern).

15. Lane to Hunter, 13 February 1862, Roll 32, Lincoln Papers, LC; Hunter to Lane, 13 February 1862, Roll 32, Lincoln Papers, LC; Albert Castel, *A Frontier State at War: Kansas, 1861–1865*, pp. 80–81.

16. Hunter to Lincoln, 14 February 1862, Roll 32, Lincoln Papers, LC; Hunter to Stanton, 15 August 1862, Stanton Papers; Castel, *A Frontier State at War*, p. 81.

17. E. A. Hitchcock to Henry Halleck, 22 March 1862, OR, 1:8, pp. 832–33; Castel, *A Frontier State at War*, p. 83.

It took place in Arkansas, on 6–8 March, and Gen. Samuel Curtis won a victory that was costly to the Union forces. One thousand, three hundred-eighty-four Northerners died at Pea Ridge. Despite their victory, Union officers were impressed with "the hordes of Indians, cavalry, and infantry that were arrayed against us." The legends of Indian atrocities in this battle spread across the country. A congressional investigation revealed that 3,000 Indians had fought for the Confederates and engaged in scalpings and other atrocities. Pea Ridge pushed Union leaders to reconsider the plan for a Southern expedition.[18]

A second major factor was the Indian refugees. Kansans wanted to get rid of them, and a removal bill was introduced in Congress in March 1862. Congressmen were complaining about the costs of providing for the estimated 7,600 Indians. The refugees continued to live in terrible conditions. An agent described the Creeks as destitute of food and clothing. In the two months they had camped in Kansas, 240 Creeks had died and their grand old leader, Opothleyaholo, was near death. More than a hundred frozen limbs had been amputated. Many Indians were naked and hungry. Much of the food they were allotted had already been rejected by the military at Fort Leavenworth because it was spoiled.[19]

Jim Lane, as always, played his part in reversing Lincoln's decision to cancel the expedition. On 17 March, he introduced in the Senate a resolution to require the commissioner of Indian affairs "to inquire as to the propriety and expediency of extending the southern boundary of Kansas to the northern boundary of Texas, so as to include within the boundaries of Kansas the territory known as the Indian Territory." Whatever Commissioner Dole's position on this wild scheme, he was certainly Lane's ally on the issue of a Southern expedition. He had been its early advocate and

18. Abel, *Slaveholding Indians*, 2:13–36; Report of Samuel R. Curtis, OR, 1:8, pp. 199, 206; Curtis to John W. Noble, OR, 1:8, pp. 206–7; Curtis was promoted to major general as a reward for his victory.

19. Smith to Cyrus B. Aldrich, Roll 4, M606, LS, ID, OSI, RG48, NA; Resolution of the House of Representatives, 28 May 1862, Roll 20, M825, LR, ID, OSI, RG48, NA; George W. Collamore to Dole, 21 April 1862, Roll 835, M234, LR, Southern Superintendency, OIA, RG75, NA; also found in OR, 2:4, pp. 11–13.

once again urged its revival. Caleb Smith accepted the commissioner's recommendation and forwarded it with his approval, to the secretary of war and the president.[20]

Lincoln changed his mind again. On 19 March 1862, the adjutant general transmitted the news to the commander of the Department of Mississippi:

> It is the desire of the President, on the application of the Secretary of the Interior and the Commissioner of Indian Affairs, that you should detail two regiments to act in Indian country, with a view to open the way for friendly Indians who are now refugees in Southern Kansas to return to their homes and to protect them there. Five thousand friendly Indians will also be armed to aid in their own protection and you will please furnish them with necessary subsistence.[21]

Officials differed on just how many Indians to arm. Dole mentioned the figure of two thousand in a 21 March communication to Halleck. Smith said it was "the wishes of the President" that "two or three thousand" Indians be included in the expedition. They were also uneasy concerning the use of Indian troops in the expedition, perhaps remembering the horror stories from Pea Ridge. Halleck's orders carefully limited their duties, "These Indians can be used only against Indians or in defense of their own territory and homes."[22]

The new expedition was to be much less spectacular than Jim Lane's original scheme. Lane was not too disappointed; things were going his way. With his influence, the Kansas legislature had impeached Governor Robinson for conspiring with Robert S. Stevens to obtain forty-eight thousand dollars in governmental funds. He persuaded the War Department to delay funds due Kansas for

20. U.S., Congress, Senate, *Congressional Globe,* resolution introduced by James H. Lane, 37th Cong., 2d sess., 17 March 1862, pt. 2:1246; Smith to Stanton, 14 March 1862, Roll 4, M606, LS, ID, OSI, RG48, NA.

21. Thomas to Halleck, 19 March 1862, OR, 1:8, p. 624.

22. Dole to Halleck, 21 March 1862, Roll 67, M21, LS, OIA, RG75, NA; Smith to Halleck, 21 March 1862, Roll 4, M606, LS, ID, OSI, RG48, NA; Halleck to J. W. Denver, 5 April 1862, OR, 1:8, p. 665; Jay Manoghan, *Civil War on the Western Border,* p. 252.

organizing troops until he approved their release. He flattered Lincoln and worried aloud to the president about a possible coup.[23] Most important, Lane used all these connections to select the next military commander in Kansas. Jim Lane at last had achieved his goal of becoming both a senator and military boss in Kansas.

In April 1862, Lane secured the appointment of James G. Blunt as brigadier general and, on 2 May, the War Department restored Kansas as a separate military department with Blunt in command. Historians have disagreed over Blunt's character. Edmund Danziger calls Blunt "a decisive and gifted soldier." Albert Castel finds him "coarse and unscrupulous" and says there were reports he had "a worse reputation than Lane himself." Castel maintains, "Blunt was to all intents and purposes merely Lane in a different body and under a different name." Castel is probably correct. Lane was in control and in position to obtain the political and financial fruits of the situation. On 16 May 1862, Commissioner Dole wrote General Blunt concerning final arrangements for the expedition and expressed his desire "that the expedition shall start immediately." The letter was endorsed with the words, "I fully concur." The signature was "J. H. Lane."[24]

The Expedition Is Launched—and Aborted

The great Southern expedition became a reality, more than six months after Lincoln first authorized it. Even then, it was not launched until 28 June 1862. Instead of being the grand project Jim Lane had envisioned to turn the tide of war for the Union, its aims were to repossess the Indian Territory and return the refugees to their homes. In addition, the original scheme had called for ten thousand or more men; the new project provided for only two thousand whites and three thousand Indian soldiers. Lane was not in-

23. Lane (et al.) to Edwin M. Stanton and Salmon P. Chase, 6 April 1862, Charles Robinson Papers; Lane to Lincoln, 20 April 1862, Roll 21, Lincoln Papers, LC.

24. Edmund Danziger, "Civil War Refugees in Kansas," p. 268; Castel, *A Frontier State at War*, p. 83, Dole to J. H. Blunt, 16 May 1862, Roll 48, M21, LS, OIA, RG75, NA.

terested in commanding this meager force, so Col. William Weer was appointed field commander.[25]

The Northerners were luckier than they deserved to be. The Confederates were forced to concentrate their troops and resources farther east, and their alliance with the Cherokees was growing strained. After the Confederate forces were defeated at Pea Ridge, Albert Pike moved his headquarters two hundred miles north of the border of the Cherokee nation, leaving the Indian Territory virtually unprotected. As a result, retaliation against Stand Watie's raids into Missouri cost the Cherokees dearly. Plundering was common, even by Southern whites. To add insult, the Cherokee soldiers were not receiving their promised pay, arms, or provisions. John Ross was disturbed at all this and complained to Confederate officials only days before the Northern invasion began.[26]

Ross soon received word that Union forces were returning. He was enticed with hints that he could return to his old Northern loyalties. However, the olive branch bore some thorns. On 5 July 1862, the Union Congress passed an act allowing the president to abrogate treaties with any tribe "in actual hostility to the United States." The Cherokees did not have much time to make amends. General Blunt was confident "that a large majority of the Cherokees are loyal, and that whenever Ross and the other leading men of the nation are satisfied that we are able to hold the country they will cooperate with us." Blunt reported many desertions by Indians in the Confederate army as the expedition moved southward. Another source confirmed that slaves belonging to Indians were being enrolled in the army as "wooly-headed" Indians. John Ross was taken prisoner in July, a symbolic end to Cherokee resistance.[27]

The Indian System and business-as-usual corruption that accompanied it were returning to Indian country. The traders were al-

25. Abel, *Slaveholding Indians*, 2:126; *The American Annual Cyclopedia and Register of Important Events of the Year 1862*, 2:539.

26. John Ross to Thomas C. Hindman, 25 June 1862, OR, 1:13, p. 950.

27. Coffin to Ross, 16 June 1862, Roll 37, Lincoln Papers, LC; James A. Phillips to Ross, 26 June 1862, OR, 1:13, p. 450; U.S., Congress, *Congressional Globe*, 37th Cong., 2d sess., 5 July 1862, pt. 4:394; Blunt to Stanton, 21 July 1862, OR, 1:13, p. 486; *American Annual Cyclopedia*, p. 539.

ready there because Blunt permitted them to accompany the expedition. The general saw this as perfectly proper, "as they are much in need of a market for their stock and various kinds of merchandise."[28]

The progress of the Northern forces did not continue. On 18 July 1862, Col. F. Salomon led a mutiny against Colonel Weer, arrested him, and began a retreat back to Kansas. Salomon blamed the lack of success on Weer's inefficiency and failure to stay close to supplies and medical care. There is some indication that the underlying issue concerned the unwillingness of whites to fight with Indian troops. After the mutiny, the Indian troops found themselves abandoned to defend Indian country alone. Embarrassed Indian agents pleaded with them to hold on and protect property from plunderers, despite the desertion of the whites.[29]

General Blunt called Salomon's retreat "utterly unjustifiable and disgraceful." It made a difficult situation even worse. The army not only failed to return the refugees from Kansas, two thousand additional refugees followed the soldiers' retreat into Kansas. The Indian troops broke up and returned to their families. The Indians had lost faith in the government, according to Blunt, "They claimed that the government had failed in its promises, made to them." Only with difficulty was he able to persuade Indian soldiers to join Union forces on campaigns in Missouri and Arkansas. Once again, Blunt promised to return them to their homes as soon as possible.[30]

Despite federal blunders, the tribes in Indian country found Southern whites equally unreliable. The Confederates had neither the will nor the strength to hold the Indian Territory, even in the face of the Northern retreat. On 31 July, Albert Pike resigned his command and complained bitterly at the lack of support for his forces. Pike had the same problem as Union commanders—white

28. Blunt to Stanton, OR, 1:13, p. 486.
29. F. Salomon to expedition commanders, 18 July 1862, OR, 1:13, pp. 475-76; E. H. Carruth, H. W. Martin to R. W. Furnas, 25 July 1862, AR, CIA, 1862, p. 305.
30. AR, CIA, 1862, p. 182; Blunt to Smith, 21 November 1862, Roll 4, Lincoln Papers, LC.

troops were reluctant to fight with Indians and field commanders refused to force them to do it. Pike urged the tribes to remain loyal to the Confederacy. By his own admission, he could neither pay their soldiers nor protect their homes. Empty phrases were his only remaining weapons.[31]

Lincoln's indecision and the political infighting in Kansas had made a bad situation worse in Indian country. Money, time, and lives were lost in a manner characterized by ineptitude on the part of everyone concerned. For the Indian refugees, circumstances had worsened and almost no one seemed to care what happened to them. The only man who could transform the situation was the man who had already changed his mind so often—Abraham Lincoln. John Ross knew that. He also knew what Jim Lane had long ago discovered. The way to move Lincoln was to see him in person.

31. Albert Pike to the Five Tribes, 31 July 1862, OR, 1:13, pp. 869–71.

V. Lincoln and the Refugees "A Multitude of Cares"

BY SEPTEMBER 1862 the situation in Kansas had plagued the Lincoln administration for nearly a year. It was obviously not Lincoln's only problem. Lincoln later told John Ross that this was a time of "a multitude of cares."[1] Indeed, it was. September was an uncertain time in the Civil War for the Northern forces. The Union army had achieved some success in the West, especially in the Mississippi Valley. However, the war on the eastern front was not reassuring. Robert E. Lee had outmaneuvered Lincoln's army and was making it look foolish in Virginia. The Union army had been humiliated at Second Bull Run on 29–30 August. Lincoln had failed to find adequate leadership for his army, and the squabbles among his generals had reached the point of absurdity. Radicals in his own party were critical of Lincoln's conduct of the war and were calling for the abolition of slavery and the use of black troops in the war effort. On top of all this, Indian affairs were demanding an extraordinary amount of attention due to a massive Indian war that broke out in Minnesota in August. The Lincoln government was in serious trouble.

John Ross Visits Lincoln

John Ross chose this time to meet with the president in Washington. He did so with the blessings of General Blunt, Mark Delahay, and Jim Lane. Blunt admitted to the president that Ross was

1. Abraham Lincoln to John Ross, 25 September 1862, Roll 42, Abraham Lincoln Papers, LC (see "Abbreviations in Footnotes," p. vi).

going to Washington "at my suggestion." Delahay gave Lincoln no graceful exit from a confrontation with the Cherokee leader:

> I have assured him that you would be very glad to see him at Washington, and that you will afford him and the loyal people of the Nation every reasonable protection in your power, assuring him that you feel a deep interest in the restoration of peace and order in his beautiful country.[2]

Delahay was certain he could count on Lincoln "to extend to him all kindness and good will."[3] With these two men backing the project, Jim Lane had to be the prime mover. The foxy senator was once again backing Lincoln into a corner.

On 11 September, Lincoln informed Caleb Smith: "I will see Mr. Ross at 9 A.M. to-morrow, if he calls." Lincoln was apparently irritated about the meeting and gave the Cherokee leader a fairly cool reception. They met and Lincoln asked Ross to reduce his requests to writing.

The issue was the loyalty of the Cherokees to the Union cause. Ross tried to explain to Lincoln that he had been left with no choice but to ally with the Confederacy and had rejoined the North as soon as it was feasible. The withdrawal of the Indian expedition left his people in an impossible situation, Ross told the president. He requested protection and a presidential proclamation to his people "in accordance with the views you entertain on this subject and which will enable me to make assurances in behalf of the Government in which they can confide." Ross argued that the government could not hold the Cherokees responsible for disloyalty when the administration had violated solemn treaty obligations to protect them.[4] Lincoln told Ross he would investigate the alleged treaty violations.

On 25 September, Lincoln wrote Ross that his "multitude of

2. Mark W. Delahay to Lincoln, 21 August 1862, Roll 40, Lincoln Papers, LC.

3. James G. Blunt to Lincoln, 13 August 1862, Roll 39, ibid., also found in OR, 1:13, pp. 565–66.

4. Lincoln to Caleb B. Smith, 11 September 1862, Roy P. Basler, ed., *Collected Works of Abraham Lincoln,* 5:415; Ross to Lincoln, 16 September 1862, Roll 41, Lincoln Papers, LC.

cares" had kept him from his promised examination of the treaty relations between the government and the Cherokees. "This letter, therefore, must not be understood to decide anything upon these questions," Lincoln cautioned. He was carefully noncommittal. He promised the Cherokees only "the protection which can be given them consistently with the duty of the government to the whole country."[5] Thus far, John Ross had gotten nowhere with Lincoln.

Caleb Smith's report on the treaty question apparently convinced Lincoln that Ross's complaints were justified. Smith informed Lincoln that the 1835 treaty promised that the government would "protect the Cherokee Nation from domestic strife and foreign enemies."[6] Clearly, the Lincoln administration had not met that obligation.

Nevertheless, Lincoln had no intention of doing anything at the moment. He made a token gesture. On 10 October 1862, he wired Gen. Samuel Curtis:

> I believe some Cherokee Indian Regiments, with some white forces operating with them, now at or near *Fort-Scott,* are within your Department, & under your command. John Ross, principal Chief of the Cherokees, is now here, an exile; and he wishes to know, and so do I, whether the force above mentioned, could not occupy the Cherokee country, consistently with the public service. Please consider and answer.[7]

Curtis responded that he was already conducting a military operation that would ultimately affect the Indian Territory and said, "I expect to make rebels very scarce in that quarter pretty soon." This vague promise satisfied Lincoln and pacified Ross, who had been persistent in his requests to the president for a month. In fact, the

5. Lincoln to Ross, 25 September 1862, Roll 42, ibid., also found in Basler, ed., *Collected Works,* 5:439; Gary E. Moulton, "Chief John Ross During the Civil War," pp. 322–33.

6. Smith to Lincoln, 29 September 1862, Roll 42, Lincoln Papers, LC; Smith to Lincoln, 29 September 1862, Roll 4, M606, LS, ID, OSI, RG48, NA.

7. Lincoln to Samuel Curtis, 10 October 1862, Basler, ed., *Collected Works,* 5:456; Curtis had been appointed commander of the Department of the Missouri the previous month.

Indian Territory was not cleared of Confederate forces until 1864.[8]

Ross had done all he could. Three days later, he wrote Commissioner Dole and thanked him for "the friendly interview with which I have been honored by yourself and the President of the United States." Ross was running out of money, and he was forced to plead for his family, calling on "the justice and magnanimity of the govt for relief" in the form of a "sum of money." Ross was granted an appropriation and was much criticized for accepting it.[9] It is conceivable that the Lincoln administration found this an easy way to silence him.

Broken Promises and Kansas Politics

Back in Kansas, the refugees continued to be the pawns of power politics. Promises to return them to their homes were broken again and again. Their living conditions were reported to be intolerable while white opportunists profited from their misery. Lincoln refused to do anything to change the situation.

The refugees became the focus of contention almost as soon as the aborted expedition returned to Kansas in mid-1862. The old tension between the military and the Indian Office surfaced in a dispute between General Blunt and Superintendent Coffin. Coffin was in Washington when the expedition arrived in Kansas with a new crop of refugees. Blunt recognized their needs and ordered Indian officials to provide for them. Although he had no official jurisdiction, Blunt justified exceeding his authority on the grounds that it was essential to assure the Indians that there would eventually be another expedition. Blunt charged that the refugees were being victimized by "a clique of mercenary and unscrupulous speculators who were resolved upon robbing the Indians and the govern-

8. Curtis to Lincoln, 10 October 1862, OR, 1:13, p. 723; Kenny A. Franks, "The Confederate States and the Five Civilized Tribes: A Breakdown of Relations," pp. 441, 453–54.

9. Ross to William P. Dole, 13 October 1862, Roll 99, M234, LR, Cherokee Agency, OIA, RG75, NA; Gary E. Moulton, "John Ross and W. P. Dole: A Case Study of Lincoln's Indian Policy," pp. 420–22; Moulton, "Chief John Ross," pp. 325–27.

ment, of every dollar they could; and the longer the former could be kept in Kansas, the greater the profits." Blunt hinted that Indian Office personnel were profiting from the corruption. He was apparently implicating Coffin when he charged "that some individuals, holding positions as Agents and Superintendents, have had their pockets well lined with the profits from contracts."[10]

Coffin exploded in anger over Blunt's actions and charges. He held no respect for the general whose Southern expedition had been such a spectacular failure. His correspondence to Blunt dripped sarcasm, "I have no doubt you will discharge your duty, *ably, faithfully* and I trust *successfully* and I hope you will allow me to attend to *mine*."[11]

When there were political fights in Kansas, Jim Lane was never far away. During this conflict, he was in the state recruiting troops, some of which Secretary of War Stanton threatened not to commission. The reason was that Lane was recruiting blacks as well as Indians, and citizens were complaining to Lincoln about Lane's "tri-colored brigade." Lane's ally, Mark Delahay, continued the propaganda that was designed to distract from Blunt's and Lane's failures. He echoed Blunt's charges of corruption and mailed President Lincoln copies of Coffin's advertisements for supplies for the refugees.[12]

The power of the Lane faction was demonstrated by the fact that Blunt did not fully surrender control of the refugees. He openly appealed in the newspapers for charitable contributions to feed and clothe them. He issued orders to steal enemy food for them. Indian agents bitterly complained of "a constant effort on the part of some Military officers and some of them high in authority to prejudice the Indians against the Indian department and all its employees."

---

10. Blunt to Smith, 21 November 1862, Roll 835, M234, LR, Southern Superintendency, OIA, RG75, NA.
11. W. G. Coffin to Blunt, 28 September 1862, Roll 42, Lincoln Papers, LC.
12. Edwin M. Stanton to James H. Lane, 23 August 1862, Correspondence of the Kansas Governors, 1861–1865; Hamilton R. Gamble to Lincoln, 9 September 1862, Roll 41, Lincoln Papers, LC; Dudley Cornish, *The Sable Arm*, pp. 74–75; Delahay to Lincoln, 16 November 1862, Roll 44, Lincoln Papers, LC.

Coffin protested this agitation but the Lincoln administration did nothing about it.[13]

Lincoln Refuses to Return the Refugees

Caring for the refugees was a comparatively minor issue. The big argument revolved around returning them to the Indian Territory. The military, led by Blunt, wanted immediate removal. Indian Office officials advocated removal only if there was adequate protection against additional violence and suffering. Lincoln supported the civilians on this particular issue.

General Blunt strongly dissented from this policy. He badly needed to rebuild his damaged reputation after the failure of the Southern expedition. In September 1862, Blunt ordered preparations for a new expedition, but Lincoln refused to authorize them. Blunt believed he had compelling reasons for action. He claimed that the Indian Territory was virtually under Union control and that the Indians could hold it by themselves. Furthermore, the refugees wanted to go back and they could provide for themselves there. Finally, Blunt argued that the refugees needed to be removed from the clutches of the profiteering contractors in Kansas. These arguments met a stony silence at the White House. Despite his lack of authority, Blunt continued to promise the refugees that they would soon go home.[14]

The refugee leaders agreed with Blunt. Anything would be better than the suffering they were enduring in Kansas. Cherokee leaders were especially bitter. They told Superintendent Coffin that the "Great Father at Washington" had betrayed them by failing to provide promised protection and provisions. Whatever the expense, they complained, "is all this to be counted with the lives of Cherokee

13. Blunt to the Humane and Philanthropic Citizens of Kansas, 2 December 1862, Blunt to John A. Foreman, 2 December 1862, Roll 44, Lincoln Papers, LC; H. M. Martin to Coffin, 20 December 1862, Coffin to B. S. Henning, 28 December 1862, Roll 99, M234, LR, Cherokee Agency, OIA, RG75, NA.

14. Blunt to George A. Cutler, 13 September 1862, Roll 41, summary of Blunt's correspondence on Kansas Indians, 13 September 1862, Blunt to Pascopa and Singleton, 23 September 1862, Roll 41, Lincoln Papers, LC.

women and children." They had little respect for a Lincoln government that made promises in order to keep their loyalty and then delivered nothing, "We know, all great and magnanimous Governments make no accounts of cost; that *they may be just,* or fulfil[l] a promise."[15]

John Ross begged Commissioner Dole for help during the winter of 1862–1863. Ross said many of his people were dying, and he feared many more deaths, "principally women and children." Inadequate as the aid to the Indians had been, it was also expensive. Commissioner Dole admitted to an economy-minded Congress in December that the funds spent to maintain subsistence for the refugees had already reached $193,000. Both finances and the refugees' miserable circumstances seemed to support the argument for an early return to the Indian Territory.[16]

Nevertheless, Indian officials steadfastly opposed Blunt's plan to take the refugees home. The issue was military protection. Underlying that was the old problem of using white soldiers in an Indian cause. Blunt wanted the refugees to return to Indian Territory without substantial military escort and expected the Indians to fend for themselves. Mutiny by white soldiers had ruined one expedition, and he did not want to risk another humiliation. Secretary Smith and Commissioner Dole argued that this policy would be inhumane. On 26 November 1862, Smith once again relayed Dole's request to the War Department for the organization of an Indian brigade "with a view to the recovery and protection of the Indian country south of Kansas." Smith concurred, "It is deemed by the Department a matter of great importance to recover the possessions of the Indian country and restore to their homes the loyal Indians who have been forcibly expelled."[17]

Smith and Dole had good reasons for fearing for the safety of the refugees. The secretary of the interior learned in May 1863 that

15. Coffin to Dole, 10 November 1862, Cherokee Refugees to Coffin, 31 October 1862, Roll 99, M234, LR, Cherokee Agency, OIA, RG75, NA.

16. Ross to Dole, 5 January 1863, ibid.; AR, CIA, 1862, p. 182.

17. Smith to Stanton, 26 November 1862, Roll 4, M606, LS, ID, OSI, RG48, NA.

an attempt to move Indian refugees out of Missouri had been a disaster. Twelve hundred to thirteen hundred people and their provisions had been piled into twenty-six wagons. They arrived in Indian Territory without food, a "frightful number having died on the way."[18] The Cherokees who had stayed in Indian Territory were as miserable as their brothers in Kansas. An agent called their condition "the most pitiable imaginable." Stand Watie, with his ragged band of seven hundred Indians, had raided and stolen most of the federal goods given to the Cherokees during the winter. "The women and children have been still more exposed to sickness and death than the men," reported the agent, "and great numbers have died." In January 1864, the Cherokee Executive Council protested to Union military authorities concerning their lack of protection. Cherokee soldiers had been used to defend Union territory other than Indian Territory, and when Cherokees refused and returned to protect their own homes, the army designated them "deserters."[19]

This situation demonstrated Lincoln's actual policy toward the refugees. It was one of temporizing and exploitation. Civilian and military authorities agreed that there were powerful arguments for taking the refugees home. The rub was the need for military protection, and Lincoln would not provide the military aid. He intended to exploit Indian soldiers as long as possible in the Civil War effort. Despite the complaints of the Cherokee Executive Council, General Blunt could inform Gen. John M. Schofield in November 1862, "The Indian regiments are fast filling up with recruits."[20] These soldiers were not used to return the refugees or protect their own homes. Perhaps they were promised something more in order to obtain their service. In any event, Indian men understood only too well that Union soldiers at least got to eat on a somewhat regular basis.

White Kansans were not happy with this policy either. They

18. William S. Phillips to the Secretary of the Interior, 15 May 1863, ibid.

19. Justin Harlan to Coffin, 8 August 1863, AR, CIA, 1863, pp. 331–33; Executive Council of the Cherokee Nation to William A. Phillips, Roll 99, M234, LR, Cherokee Agency, OIA, RG75, NA.

20. Blunt to John M. Schofield, 9 November 1862, OR, 1:13, p. 786.

wanted the refugees returned, and Jim Lane was their champion. Lane moved to break the logjam by introducing legislation for removal of the Indians (including Indians who had lived in Kansas before the refugees had arrived) in December 1862. He managed to get a bill passed by the Senate in early 1863.

Lincoln began to feel the pressure, although he gave ground reluctantly. John Ross went to Washington to see him again in the autumn of 1863. Lincoln granted General Blunt permission to come to Washington to discuss the return of the refugees to Indian Territory. Some of the Indian "Home Guards" journeyed to the capital to represent the Cherokees in these negotiations, although the War Department petulantly refused to pay their salaries while they were off duty.[21] Despite this flurry of activity, Lincoln procrastinated and months passed before he reached a decision.

The Refugees Go Home

In 1864, Jim Lane was ready to force Lincoln's hand. On 3 March, Lane introduced a bill to remove the refugees from Kansas. He appealed to his colleagues on a blatantly financial basis. The senator said that the government was spending sixty thousand dollars a month on ninety-two hundred Indians. On 21 March, Lane pushed the Senate Indian Committee into recommending to the secretary of the interior that the refugees be immediately moved. His legislation passed Congress, along with an act to extinguish the title to lands belonging to native Kansas tribes. The Kansas congressional delegation did not attempt to hide the selfish motivation behind this legislation, "Those tribes occupy central positions, holding large tracts of productive country in the very heart of our state." They called the removal "an act of justice to the Indians and to the people of Kansas."[22]

21. Dole to Ross, 19 November 1863, Roll 72, M21, LS, OIA, RG75, NA; Lincoln to Stanton, 9 January 1864, Basler, ed., *Collected Works,* 7:119; E. R. S. Canby to the Secretary of the Interior, 10 January 1864, Roll 99, M234, LR, Cherokee Agency, OIA, RG75, NA.

22. U.S., Congress, Senate, *Congressional Globe,* 38th Cong., 1st sess., 3 March 1864, p. 921; Senate Indian Affairs Committee to the Secretary of the Interior,

By the time Jim Lane had finished his congressional handi-work, Lincoln was left with no alternative. On 3 May, Congress appropriated sixty-two thousand dollars to move the refugees to Indian country.[23] On 14 May, the Senate confronted the president in a resolution:

> Resolved, that the President of the United States be requested to communicate to the Senate the reasons, if any exist, why the refugee Indians in the State of Kansas, are not returned to their homes.[24]

Lincoln replied that he had not returned them because of fears for their safety.[25] The game was over and Jim Lane had won. Lincoln capitulated and ordered the refugees moved to Indian Territory.

Superintendent Coffin supervised the removal of five thousand refugee Indians in June 1864. It took nearly a month. The Indians arrived too late to plant crops. Coffin was concerned about the lack of military protection and the fact that there were fifteen thousand destitute people in Indian Territory, "dependent upon the government for their support." He predicted that the government would have to support them at least one more year. Throughout 1864, Indian officials had to almost beg for funds to feed and clothe the Indian population. In October, Lincoln recognized the need as "so great and urgent" that he authorized $200,000 of clothing and food on credit and asked the Congress to appropriate the money after the fact.[26]

Meanwhile, Lincoln continued to exploit the Indians as pawns in the struggle with the South. Commissioner Dole instructed Coffin in November 1864, "Tell the Indians of Kansas that the Great

---

21 March 1864, Lane, J. C. Pomeroy, Wilder to John P. Usher, 12 April 1864, Roll 21, M825, LR, ID, OSI, RG48, NA.

23. Usher to Stanton, 24 May 1864, Roll 4, M606, LS, ID, OSI, RG48, NA; Dole to Coffin, 15 June 1864, Kansas Governors (Thomas Carney), 1861–1865.

24. Resolution of the Senate to the President, 14 April 1864, Roll 21, M825, LR, ID, OSI, RG48, NA.

25. Lincoln to the Senate, 14 May 1864, Basler, ed., *Collected Works*, 7:341.

26. Coffin to Dole, 24 September 1864, AR, CIA, 1864, pp. 447–51; Usher to Lincoln, 22 August 1864, Usher to Lincoln, 1 October 1864, Roll 5, M606, LS, ID, OSI, RG48, NA; Lincoln to William T. Otto, 1 October 1864, Basler, ed., *Collected Works*, 8:34.

Father takes them by the hand as his friends, and that he is glad to know that they have set their faces against those who would lead their young men astray."[27]

The Lincoln administration's policy toward the southern tribes had benefited no one. Lincoln failed to exploit any military advantage in the Indian Territory early in the Civil War. Then he allowed Jim Lane to talk him into a disastrous Southern expedition. Time, lives, and funds were lost, and petty politics dominated while the refugees suffered. Lincoln changed his mind frequently and the government exploited Indian troops to aid in the Union military effort rather than allowing them to defend their homes. Finally, as the result of mismanagement, when the refugees were escorted to Indian Territory, their reward for loyalty to the Union cause was destitution.

The callous disregard for the residents of Indian Territory continued beyond Lincoln's death. The government defaulted on interest due on Cherokee trust funds. When the Cherokees applied for the back interest, they learned that the money was already reserved for contractors who provided services to the refugees. After much negotiation, the secretary of the interior authorized a fifty-thousand-dollar payment to the tribe. Simultaneously, a large sum was sent to Superintendent Coffin who, it was alleged, paid it to contractors for services never delivered. To add insult, the secretary suddenly reversed himself and suspended payment on the fifty thousand dollars.

In spite of Lincoln's abandonment of their cause, the Cherokee leaders continued to place faith in the White House after Andrew Johnson assumed office, "Our trust is in your wisdom and sense of justice to protect us from wrong and oppression."[28] That trust in the "great father" was destined to be even more severely tested for the Natives farther north in the Republican state of Minnesota.

27. Dole to Coffin, 7 November 1864, Roll 75, M21, LS, OIA, RG75, NA.
28. Lewis Ross to Andrew Johnson, 5 June 1864, Roll 1, M825, LR, ID, RG48, NA.

VI. Indian Affairs in Minnesota
"A System of Wholesale Robberies"

IN 1862 TWO SENATORS from Minnesota told Abraham Lincoln just how they intended to use the Indian System to benefit their region. Their purpose was to promote a candidate for the position of secretary of the interior on the basis of his experience in Indian affairs. For the peoples of Minnesota and the Northwest, this position was crucial, "The peoples of that vast region [are] more dependent upon the action of that Department than any other of the Government."[1]

A Case Study in Corruption

Minnesota provides an excellent case study of the Indian System in operation. It, more than any other state, involved Lincoln directly in the tragic legacy of that System.

Minnesota politicians were among Lincoln's early supporters in his quest for the presidency. The Republican State Central Committee invited Lincoln to the state in 1859. Congressman Cyrus Aldrich and Gov. Alexander Ramsey both supported Lincoln for the presidential nomination.[2]

Ramsey, a native Pennsylvanian, had skillfully used the "pathway to power" inherent in the Indian System. He had served as an Indian agent and as territorial governor. His cooperation in the 1851 treaty negotiations between the Sioux and Henry H. Sibley

1. Henry M. Rice and Morton Wilkinson to Abraham Lincoln, 10 December 1862, Roll 45, Abraham Lincoln Papers, LC.
2. Minnesota Republican State Central Committee to Lincoln, 25 July 1859, Roll 4, Cyrus B. Aldrich to Lincoln, 28 July 1860, Roll 8, Alexander Ramsey to Lincoln, 7 July 1860, Roll 7, all in Lincoln Papers, LC (for "Abbreviations in Footnotes," see p. vi).

became a public scandal. Congress investigated Ramsey in 1853, and witnesses alleged that he had mishandled $450,000 of Indian money. Nevertheless, Ramsey's political career was not damaged. He was elected mayor of St. Paul in 1855, joined the new Republican party shortly after its organization, and became its first candidate for governor of Minnesota. He lost his first campaign for governor to Sibley but was successful in 1859. When Lincoln became president, Ramsey hoped to be appointed to the cabinet.[3]

Sen. Morton Wilkinson was another major figure in Indian affairs in the Lincoln years. A native New Yorker, Wilkinson moved to Minnesota in 1847. He was elected to the Senate in 1859. By 1861, Wilkinson had learned the value of the Indian System to his state. The great patronage prize was the Northern Superintendency. One observer predicted a "big fight" for that job among men from Wisconsin, Indiana, Michigan, and Ohio—"All want it." Wilkinson intended to have his own man in that position. He selected Clark W. Thompson, a campaigner and presidential elector as well as a banker and railroad speculator. Wilkinson made all the right moves. He manipulated his ally, Secretary of State William Henry Seward, threatening to withdraw support from Lincoln if he did not get his way. Thompson himself went to Washington to lobby for the position. Wilkinson eventually succeeded, in part because he was willing to trade some offices to other states for the superintendent's position.[4]

Thompson did not end his business activities when he entered office. He continued to be active in railroad speculation. He apparently retained his interest in the St. Paul banking firm, Thompson Brothers.[5] In July 1862 his brother, Edward Thompson, was at

3. Biographical information from Alexander Ramsey Papers; R. W. Clellan to George W. Manypenny, 11 April 1853, M. Sweetser to William K. Sebastion, n.d., Roll 10, M574, SF85, OIA, RG75, NA; Aldrich to Lincoln, 23 December 1861, Roll 12, Aldrich and Wilkinson to Lincoln, 28 January 1861, Roll 15, Lincoln Papers, LC.

4. A. T. C. Pierson to Clark W. Thompson, 10 February 1861, Wilkinson to William H. Seward, 15 March 1861, Box 1, Clark W. Thompson Papers.

5. The evidence of Thompson's continued financial activities are found in a number of letters in Box 1, Thompson Papers; W. S. Washburn enigmatically informed Thompson (6 March 1862) that "the child is born"—possibly referring to

the Sioux Agency. "I have been here sometime waiting for the payment seeing the sights," he wrote Clark Thompson. Those annuity payments were supervised by the superintendent, and it is reasonable to surmise that Thompson was frequently involved in blatant conflicts of interest.[6]

Thompson did not neglect his political duties. He recommended appointments to the patronage jobs under his jurisdiction, and he was flooded with applications from the party faithful. Congressman Cyrus Aldrich reminded Thompson of his political obligations: "Clark, keep your ears open & your eyes peeled. . . . Write us occasionally, & give us the 'points.' "[7]

Thompson demonstrated only minimal concern for the Indians he supervised. His first annual report complained of illegal timber cutting and whiskey sales that were detrimental to the Natives. His main preoccupations, however, were with business transactions and the disbursement of Indian funds. The demands of the Civil War were causing difficulty for Thompson concerning annuity payments on which those transactions were dependent. By September, one agent complained: "What in hell is the trouble. . . . Is there any money coming this fall or is Uncle Samuel busted."[8]

Money for Minnesota

Despite the war, Indian money found its way to Minnesota. Claims were big business in the state. Processing claims from Minnesota and other parts of the Northern Superintendency always kept the Indian Office busy. Sen. Henry Rice demonstrated how a congressman could use the System when, in early 1861, he claimed

---

state legislative activity related to land speculation. He had many dealings with T. B. Stoddard concerning railroads, an example of which is a letter dated 8 December 1862, from Stoddard to Thompson.

6. Thompson Brothers to Thompson, 21 April 1862, Edward Thompson to Thompson, 26 July 1862, I. C. H. C. Burbank Co. to Thompson, 28 January 1862 (a bill cosigned by Thompson Brothers), all in Box 2, Thompson Papers.

7. Aldrich to Thompson, 20 June 1861, Box 1, Thompson Papers.

8. Thompson to William P. Dole, October 1861, C. E. Mix to Thompson, 27 August 1861, S. E. Webb to C. G. Wykoff, 9 September 1861, all in ibid.

$24,000 for supervising the removal of some Indians.[9] Thomas Galbraith, the Santee Sioux agent, presented Thompson with $52,000 in claims in January 1862. Galbraith suggested that the Indian Office cooperate in helping them perpetrate a little fraud while processing the claims. "The *biggest* swindle please[s] them best if they but have a *share* in [it]," the agent assured the superintendent. Galbraith told Thompson to "riddle" his report as he saw fit. He was sure that the assistant commissioner of Indian affairs, Minnesotan Charles Mix, "would aid you & I think old Mix would easily go in."[10]

Business in claims was matched by the business in contracts in Minnesota. Contracts were let on bid, but Thompson found ways to circumvent the regulations. Senator Wilkinson, in late 1861, informed Thompson that he wanted to penalize newspapers that were politically disloyal by giving printing contracts to friendly papers. He instructed Thompson to give them to the St. Paul *Pioneer & Democrat* if at all possible. If this proved too difficult to accomplish, Wilkinson suggested manipulating the bid process so his chosen paper could secure the contract.[11]

Special arrangements for contracts were numerous in the Northern Superintendency. Assistant Commissioner Mix wrote Thompson about a friend who "has a little business transaction with you."[12] Cyrus Aldrich promoted O. D. Webb for a contract for pork and flour for the Sioux and Chippewa in November 1861. Aldrich called Webb an "active and devoted Republican" and "deserving of and entitled to a share of the 'spoils,' and if you can consistently

9. Resolution of the House of Representatives, 18 February 1861, Roll 20, M825, LR, ID, OSI, RG48, NA.

10. Thomas Galbraith to Thompson, 31 January 1862, Box 2, Thompson Papers. An example of claims is found in Mix to Dole, 18 July 1862, Roll 764, M234, LR, St. Peter Agency, OIA, RG75, NA. There are a great number of claims from the Minnesota Indian war mentioned in communications in M606, LS, ID, OSI, RG48, NA. Minnesota's congressmen were nearly always kept informed.

11. William R. Snider to Thompson, 8 December 1861, Box 1, Thompson Papers; Thompson's papers contain many contract bids. See January 1862, Box 2, Thompson Papers. Also there is much such information in the records of the Northern Superintendency, Roll 599, LR, OIA, RG75, NA.

12. Mix to Thompson, 29 June 1861, Box 1, Thompson Papers.

give him the contract he desires, you will greatly oblige him and his many friends."[13] Senator Wilkinson also had friends who wanted contracts. Wilkinson wrote Thompson on behalf of E. C. Wells, who sought a contract for plows for the Indians. Although Wilkinson was anxious for party reliables to benefit, he preferred to preserve the appearance of regularity and cautioned Thompson, "I should like to see him get the contract in the proper way, if possible."[14]

The corruption common among all traders was prevalent in Minnesota. When the Republican regime took over Indian affairs, a whole new team of traders sought licenses. An ugly struggle ensued between the "old" and "new" traders. The Indian Office was reluctant to order a wholesale turnover of licenses, but C. B. Hensley suggested that Thompson avoid standard procedure by issuing a "temporary permit" to A. T. Hawley. The permit would enable Hawley "to monopolize the orders issued by the Agent this winter, which comprise all the trade of any value for the year to come." Hensley called this "a pretty little game."[15] The fight between the old and new traders continued, but the power of the System was on the side of the newcomers. On 19 May 1862, the secretary of the interior ordered, "All trading by the old traders will be interdicted."[16]

As elsewhere, agents were at the center of corruption in Minnesota. S. E. Webb worried aloud that too many people knew too much about the fraudulent activities of previous agents. Webb had other concerns. There was a girl at his agency who was being paid for a teaching job but had never done any teaching. That was not what upset Webb. His problem was that she was too virtuous, "hard hearted," and refused to "offer to contribute to his relief."[17]

13. Aldrich to Thompson, 12 November 1861, ibid.

14. Wilkinson to Thompson, 11 July 1861, ibid.

15. C. B. Hensley to Thompson, 30 November 1861, Box 1, Hensley to Thompson, 20 May 1862, Box 2, Thompson Papers; James B. Hubbell and Alpheus T. Hawley to Dole, n.d., Roll 935, M234, LR, Winnebago Agency, OIA, RG75, NA.

16. William Windom to Caleb B. Smith, 31 May 1862, Roll 20, M825, LR, ID, OSI, RG48, NA.

17. Webb to Thompson, 2 July 1861, Box 1, Thompson Papers.

The scandals in Minnesota matched those in other locales. Agent Balcombe at the Winnebago Agency was accused of misusing annuity funds. An investigation elicted testimony that Balcombe had told one man "that he intended to make money out of his Agency and that the only reason why he accepted so small an appointment as Winnebago Agent was for the purpose of making money." A month after that investigation ended, Balcombe was still on the job and Clark Thompson approved a $100,000 appropriation request from the agent and passed it on to Commissioner Dole. Thompson called the charges against Balcombe "mainly general in character" and claimed that the accusers were mostly traders who had been refused licenses by the agent. Thompson was correct about the identity of the accusers. In Minnesota, it was sometimes difficult to tell the old crooks from the new ones.[18]

Minnesota's congressmen did their duty in funneling Indian money to their constituents in their home state. For example, in July 1862, Morton Wilkinson introduced a bill to appropriate fifty thousand dollars of Winnebago funds for "improvements" on the reservation. Wilkinson claimed the Indians desired these improvements. The Indian Committee routinely approved the bill as a typical courtesy due a fellow committee member. On the Senate floor, Sen. John Sherman of Ohio questioned the expenditures, but Wilkinson managed to refute objections with generalities. In a letter to Clark Thompson shortly thereafter, Wilkinson revealed the real reason for the appropriation, "It will give Balcombe a chance to employ our friends this fall."[19]

Minnesota Gets Investigated

Indian officials in Minnesota did not like investigations. They particularly disliked the one that was launched during the first year of Lincoln's administration. It started innocently enough. Cyrus

18. Depositions by John Pulkey, Henry Foster, Simeon Laquere, 8 March 1862, Thompson to Dole, 18 April 1862, Thompson to Dole, 21 April 1862, all in Roll 935, M234, Winnebago Agency, OIA, RG75, NA.
19. Wilkinson to Thompson, 21 July 1862, Box 2, Thompson Papers.

Aldrich and Sen. James Doolittle of Wisconsin recommended George E. H. Day as a special commissioner "to use and recommend such measures as will be most likely to promote peace between the Indians and the whites."[20] Their purpose was to appease the Indians while the North fought the Civil War. Day was appointed to the post on 10 August 1861. Cyrus Aldrich had made a serious mistake. George Day did not intend to be just a pacifier; he was determined to expose the corruption in the Northern Superintendency.[21]

Commissioner Dole received his first warning in a message from Day on 31 August, "Superintendent Thompson informed me that there were no contracts nor vouchers nor books from which I could learn anything in relation to disbursements or other transactions of his superintendency." Apparently, Thompson was not cooperating with the investigation.[22]

In October, Day said he had facts "showing voluminous and outrageous frauds upon the Indians." The basis for the system of fraud was the "blank voucher." Day was astounded at what he found, "Had the most skillful rogues in the [world] been employed to get up a safe mode of swindling . . . no more perfect system could have been devised." Day urged Dole to institute new accounting methods immediately in order to "save this honest Republican Administration with honest Abraham Lincoln at its head and an honest man whom I now address, from the charge of *dishonesty* especially toward the poor ignorant Indians." Day discovered that more than one hundred Winnebagos had died from disease and many more were ill. A physician, Dr. Townsend, was being paid four thousand dollars a year and had never even visited the Indians.[23]

20. Aldrich and James Doolittle to Dole, received 2 August 1861, Roll 57, M234, LR, Central Superintendency, OIA, RG75, NA. There is much on George E. H. Day's activities in Roll 59, M574, SF201, OIA, RG75, NA.

21. Dole to Day, 10 August 1861, Roll 66, M21, LS, OIA, RG75, NA.

22. Day to Dole, 31 August 1861, Roll 59, M574, SF201, OIA, RG75, NA.

23. Day to Dole, 1 October 1861, Roll 599, M234, LR, Northern Superintendency, OIA, RG75, NA; Day to Dole, 3 September 1861, Roll 59, M574, SF201, OIA, RG75, NA.

Because Day began to fear the consequences of his investigation, he asked Dole to send him secret letters so that clerks in the Indian Office would not intercept his mail and pass on the information to dishonest agents. The investigator fully expected that his revelations would "bring down upon my head the wrath & indignation of many men of influence."[24]

The Investigator Runs into Trouble

Day's fears were well placed, but he should have worried more about the intentions of the commissioner of Indian affairs. Commissioner Dole was getting nervous about the consequences of this investigation. On 8 November 1861, Dole wrote Day an unusual letter in his own handwriting, suggesting that Dole agreed with Day that their correspondence should remain private. Dole did not like what Day was doing. "It was not the intention of your appointment to institute an investigation into the acts of all the employees of the Indian service past & present," the commissioner informed the investigator; he informed Day that he was not to be a "spy." Dole continued, "Our agents are honest & faithful"—a statement the commissioner knew very well to be false.[25]

Day refused to limit his investigation. In answer to Dole's reprimand for having investigated too many past deeds, Day replied that it was necessary to investigate some past actions in order to understand the present. He charged that Clark Thompson's predecessor as superintendent had spent between $100,000 and $200,000 in personal expenditures during four years when he only earned $2,000 a year in salary. The superintendent had managed this through an alliance with St. Paul merchants and through kickbacks from Indian funds spent with those merchants.[26]

Dole had personal cause to be anxious. A few days later, Day wrote concerning a man named Morrison who was illegally cut-

---

24. Day to Dole, 3 September, 7 October 1861, Roll 59, M574, SF201, OIA, RG75, NA.
25. Dole to Day, 8 November 1861, ibid.
26. Day to Dole, 20 December 1861, ibid.

ting timber on Indian land. The man carried written authorization signed with the name of William P. Dole. Dole denied the authenticity of the authorization but Day no longer trusted the commissioner. He replied that he had seen the authorization. He wondered aloud whether Morrison "would not have contracted this . . . if he had not had authority to lumber."[27]

Commissioner Dole evidently threatened to suspend Day's pay if he did not cease making charges. Day had an answer, "If not allowed any pay for my services over the 100 days I have proof enough to satisfy the *nation* & *Congress* too of the fraudulent transactions & robberies committed by the Indian officers." He called the Indian System a *"system* of *wholesale robberies"* and demanded that Dole introduce reforms. Day threatened that if the Lincoln administration did nothing, he would appeal to the public, "the people, the hearts of honest people of the nation who will *demand* in *thunder tones* that the *remnants* of the *owners* of this national domain shall not be *robbed* & defrauded of the little miserable pittance granted them by Congress or by treaties."[28]

Clark Thompson denied Day's charges. Day saw that he was getting nowhere with the Indian Office. So he went over Dole's head to Lincoln. He reiterated his charges to the president: "The whole system is defective and must be revised." The investigator requested expense money to travel to Washington so he could discuss the situation with the president.[29]

In January 1862, Day implicated Assistant Commissioner Charles Mix in fraud. Mix and the former superintendent had contracted to supply pork at sixteen dollars to nineteen dollars per barrel and had instead delivered spoiled meat and bones worth only three dollars per barrel. Day found the fraud had been perpetrated by using blank vouchers. "I have the proof," Day told Dole.[30]

27. Day to Dole, 20 December 1861 (a separate letter from the one above), and 23 January 1862, ibid.
28. Day to Dole, 20 December 1861, ibid.
29. Thompson to Dole, 28 December 1861, 18 February 1862, Roll 59, M574, SF201, OIA, RG75, NA; Day to Lincoln, 1 January 1862, Roll 31, Lincoln Papers, LC.
30. Day to Dole, 28 January 1862, Roll 59, M574, SF201, OIA, RG75, NA.

George E. H. Day had gone too far, and he knew it. "I have incurred the displeasure of the whole *band*—yes *army* of men who have [fed] upon the poverty of the Indians."[31] Lincoln apparently did not answer his letter. The commissioner, the assistant commissioner, the superintendent, and numerous agents and merchants had reason to be angry with him. They turned to a classic tactic for discrediting an opponent. They accused Day of the same crime he was charging against them.

On 4 February 1862, Clark Thompson wrote Dole concerning Day's allegations and suggested that matters "could be more fully explained by a personal interview than by any other means." Thompson's trip to Washington produced results. On 4 April, Dole gave Day's expense accounts to Thompson to inspect. Thompson, still in Washington, announced that the accounts appeared to lack proper forms and vouchers and might contain overcharges. "It appears that Mr. Day has charged for his board while at home a portion of the time," Thompson told the commissioner. He made other ambiguous references to "the peculiarities of this bill."[32]

Day was possibly guilty of dishonesty himself. It is also conceivable that he was the victim of a conspiracy among dishonest Indian officials. The pattern in the Indian bureaucracy would tend to support the latter, but no conclusive evidence is available. In any event, Day's charges were ignored by Lincoln and other responsible officials. Day was resigned to doing legal work for the Winnebagos in an attempt to regain funds fraudulently taken from them.[33]

Tragedy Ahead in Minnesota

George E. H. Day learned the hard lesson of the institutionalized corruption of the Indian System. Any challenge to its normal

---

31. Ibid.

32. Thompson to Dole, 4 February 1862, Roll 599, M234, LR, Northern Superintendency, OIA, RG75, NA; Dole to Thompson, 4 April 1862, Roll 68, M21, LS, OIA, RG75, NA; Thompson to Dole, 15 April 1862, Roll 599, M234, LR, Northern Superintendency, OIA, RG75, NA.

33. Day to Smith, 26 May 1862, Roll 20, M825, LR, ID, OSI, RG48, NA.

operation would be met aggressively in Minnesota or elsewhere. Like Henry Rector of Oregon, Day discovered that attempting to uncover corruption could result in more trouble for the exposer than the profiteers.

Lincoln would have been well advised to listen to the charges of corruption in Minnesota. Day was not alone in his concern. On 2 January 1862, missionaries Thomas Williamson and Stephen Riggs warned the Minnesota congressional delegation that the situation in Minnesota was critical. Indian timber was being cut. Indians were stealing horses. The discrimination against Indians in claims for damages was leading to retaliation. Whites and Indians were harassing each other and stealing property. In particular, "the Indians are greatly cheated by the traders." The churchmen accused government officials of complicity, saying they "have aided the traders in getting pay for goods that many of the Indians say they already paid for." The Sioux were hungry and could not even afford to buy provisions from the disreputable traders. Continuation of these circumstances was inevitably going to lead to trouble. Riggs and Williamson pronounced a grave warning: inaction would guarantee a "collision with the Indians on our frontiers."[34]

Six months later, a crisis in Minnesota proved the stark accuracy of Bishop Whipple's description of the Indian System: "It commences in discontent and ends in blood."[35]

34. Thomas Williamson and Stephen Riggs to the Minnesota Congressional Delegation, Roll 764, M234, LR, St. Peter Agency, OIA, RG75, NA.
35. Henry Benjamin Whipple to Dole[?], 2 November 1863, Box 40, Letterbook 4, Henry Benjamin Whipple Papers.

VII. Rebellion in Minnesota "A Most Terrible and Exciting Indian War"

THE DATE WAS 21 AUGUST 1862. Secretary of War Edwin Stanton read a telegram from the governor of Minnesota: "The Sioux Indians on our western border have risen, and are murdering men, women, and children." Several white settlers had been killed in an incident on 17 August, near Acton, Minnesota. The Sioux, fearing reprisal, launched what one historian has called a "preventive war."[1]

The roots of the conflict went back to 1851. The treaty negotiated that year cost the Santee Sioux twenty-four million acres of land. The Sioux were awarded $1,410,000 in annuities, but whites were permitted to levy claims amounting to around $400,000. Settlers continued to crowd in upon the new reservations and, in 1858, the Sioux had to sign away another million acres. The sale of these lands brought in funds designated for advancing the "civilization" of the Indians. However, $96,000 of Lower Sioux money was nearly all absorbed by claims, leaving only $880.58. The Indian System in Minnesota had always been extraordinarily corrupt, and it was making life more difficult for the Indians every year.

More immediate factors entered into the situation that resulted in war. Many Minnesotans of fighting age were away with the Union army, so the whites were vulnerable. More important, the Sioux were virtually starving due to a crop failure and a delay in the arrival of annuities made matters worse. The hungry Sioux

1. Alexander Ramsey to Edwin M. Stanton, 21 August 1862, OR, 1:13, p. 590; Robert Huhn Jones, *The Civil War in the Northwest*, pp. 23–24.

waited at their agencies for nearly two months. The money arrived the day after the war began.[2]

Circumstances were not ameliorated by the political leadership in Minnesota. The governor was Alexander Ramsey, a man who skillfully used the Indian System as a means to attain wealth and power. His top military commander was Henry Hastings Sibley, the former governor and Indian trader. Officials in the Indian agencies were closely linked to these men. To make matters worse, 1862 was an election year and Alexander Ramsey wanted to be a United States senator. This guaranteed that the governor would not deal lightly with an Indian rebellion.

On 14 July, Agent Thomas Galbraith found himself surrounded by five thousand hungry Sioux demanding food from warehouse stores intended for them. Galbraith refused and detailed soldiers to guard the provisions. He reported to Superintendent Thompson that the Indians "are getting clamorous for food." On 4 August, the Sioux forced Galbraith to yield some provisions. Other promises to provide food were broken. An angry confrontation took place on 15 August. Negotiations were abruptly terminated when trader Andrew Myrick said: "So far as I am concerned, if they are hungry let them eat grass or their own dung."[3]

This set the stage for the inevitable incident. On 17 August, four young Sioux men discovered some chicken eggs on a farm near Acton, Minnesota. They argued over whether to steal them. Taunts of cowardice escalated into an incursion into the farmer's house, demands for food, and the death of five white settlers.[4]

Abraham Lincoln knew nothing of these events, although he was not ignorant of the corruption in the Minnesota Indian system. The president was destined to be involved immediately. Governor Ramsey learned of the warfare on 19 August. By the next day, there were reports that five hundred whites had already died. On

2. Henry Benjamin Whipple, "The Duty of Citizens Concerning the Indian Massacre," Box 39, Letterbook 3, Henry Benjamin Whipple Papers; Kenneth Carley, *The Sioux Uprising of 1862*, pp. 12–14, see pp. 32–33 on Sibley's career.

3. Thomas Galbraith to Clark W. Thompson, 19 July 1862, Clark W. Thompson Papers; Dee Brown, *Bury My Heart at Wounded Knee*, p. 40.

4. Carley, *The Sioux Uprising*, pp. 16–17.

21 August, Ramsey notified the War Department.[5] Minnesota's secretary of state, John H. Baker, described a fearful situation:

> A most frightful insurrection of Indians has broken out along our whole frontier. Men, women, and children are indiscriminately murdered, evidently the result of a deep-laid plan, the attacks being simultaneous along our whole border.[6]

A Confederate Conspiracy?

The effect of this news in Washington was electric. The Minnesota war compounded the problems of an administration already haunted by military defeat and frustrated by manpower shortages. Especially ominous was the possibility of "a deep-laid plan." It was during these months that the Lincoln administration feared the existence of a Confederate conspiracy in the northwest.[7] In December 1862, Caleb Smith was certain one existed, "I am satisfied the chief cause is to be found in the insurrection of the southern states," and he reported that "southern emissaries" had been at work among the Sioux.

Smith reached this conclusion in part because of rumors that the English were about to intervene on behalf of the Confederacy. In Minnesota, English traders from Canada were reported to have engaged in conspiracy with the Sioux. Smith connected this with

5. Ramsey to Oscar Malmros, 19 August 1862, *Minnesota in the Indian and Civil Wars*, 2:165; Ramsey Diary, 19 and 21–22 August 1862, Roll 39, vol. 36, Alexander Ramsey Papers; Ramsey to Stanton, 21 August 1862, OR, 1:13, p. 590 (for "Abbreviations in Footnotes," see p. vi). An indication of the lack of concern in the administration over the Indians' situation occurred a month earlier, Commissioner Dole and John G. Nicolay, Lincoln's personal secretary, had been sent to Minnesota to negotiate a treaty with the Chippewas. John Hay, another secretary, teased Nicolay: "If in the wild woods you scrouge an Indian damsel, steal her moccasins while she sleeps and bring them to me." Hay's desire for moccasins was stimulated by the president's new footwear. "The Tycoon [Lincoln] has just received a pair gorgeously quilled, from an Indian Agent who is accused of stealing. He put them on & grinned. Will he remember them on the day when Caleb [Smith] proposes another to fill the peculating donor's office? I fear not, my boy, I fear not."

6. J. H. Baker to C. P. Wolcott, 21 August 1862, OR, 1:13, p. 590.

7. Caleb B. Smith to Abraham Lincoln, 12 February 1863, Roll 4, M606, LS, ID, OSI, RG48, NA.

the *Trent* affair, in which two Southern emissaries to Great Britain were arrested by Union naval forces. Some reports claimed that Indian warriors were given orders in English. Secretary Smith found it significant that Confederate prisoners of war were being paroled to the North on the condition that they could not be used against the Indians. The Sioux agent, Thomas Galbraith, insisted that "rebel sympathizers" were responsible for instigating the violence in Minnesota.[8]

Washington authorities found it safer to assume the worst. Lincoln was more cautious than his subordinates, but even he spoke of his "suspicions." He told the Congress, "Information was received . . . that a simultaneous attack was to be made upon the white settlements by all the tribes between the Mississippi river and the Rocky mountains." It was not until 12 February 1863 that Caleb Smith concluded, "I have not been able to discover any satisfactory and conclusive evidence of a pre-meditated design on the part of the Indians."[9]

Given the circumstances, the Lincoln administration's fearful reaction was understandable. They could not know with certainty. They had seen how far the Confederacy would go to gain the aid of the southern Indians. John Ross was on his way to Washington to witness to that. For all Lincoln knew, a new front had been opened in the War for the Union.

"Attend to the Indians"

The Minnesota war demanded men and supplies needed in the South. The Third Minnesota Volunteer Regiment, which had surrendered in Tennessee and been paroled, was quickly ordered into action in Minnesota. The news reaching the War Department dampened hopes for a quick end to the Indian war. From Wyoming came rumors of a wider war, "Indians, from Minnesota to Pike's Peak,

---

8. AR, SI, 1862; Galbraith to William P. Dole, 28 January 1863, AR, CIA, 1863, p. 401.

9. LAM, 1862, p. 2; Smith to Lincoln, 12 February 1862, Roll 4, M606, LS, ID, OSI, RG45, NA.

and from Salt Lake to near Fort Kearney, committing many depredations."[10]

On 25 August 1862 Governor Ramsey wired that the war was worsening, "The panic among the people has depopulated whole counties." Then, Ramsey made the one request guaranteed to upset the War Department—he demanded an extension on the draft deadline for Minnesota's quota of 5,360 men.[11]

Lincoln desperately needed soldiers for the Union army. On 4 August, the president had issued an order to call up 300,000 militia. The Minnesota contingent was not large, but its leaving might set a dangerous precedent for other states that were also reportedly suffering from the spreading Indian war.[12]

Commissioner William P. Dole immediately endorsed Ramsey's request for a draft extension. Secretary Stanton refused the request, so Ramsey promptly appealed to Lincoln. "Half the population of the State are refugees," he told the president. He demanded a one-month extension. Lincoln's response bluntly swept away the legal niceties: "Attend to the Indians. If the draft can *not* proceed, of course it *will* not proceed. Necessity knows no law. The government cannot extend the time."[13]

Lincoln eventually regretted the blanket authority he gave Minnesotans to "attend to the Indians." However, he was in a crisis situation. The day of his reply to Ramsey, Lincoln read a joint telegram from Nicolay, Dole, and Sen. Morton Wilkinson: "We are in the midst of a most terrible and exciting Indian war. Thus far the massacre of innocent white settlers has been fearful. A wild

10. Henry Halleck to Ramsey, 23 August 1862, Roll 13, Ramsey Papers; James Craig to Stanton, 23 August 1862, OR, 1:13, p. 592.

11. Ramsey to Stanton, 25 August 1862, Roll 13, Ramsey Papers.

12. Stanton to ?, 8 August 1862, Edwin M. Stanton Papers; General Order No. 99, AGO, 9 August 1862, Order by Secretary of War Stanton, 14 August 1862, Roll 40, Abraham Lincoln Papers, LC; C. P. Buckingham informed Governor Ramsey on 9 August 1862 that Minnesota had 2,681 troops due to fill its portion of the 300,000 troops being called up, Roll 13, Ramsey Papers. The number of 5,360 comes from a letter from Ramsey to Stanton, 25 August 1862, OR, 3:2, p. 457.

13. Stanton to Ramsey, 26 August 1862, Roll 13, Ramsey Papers; Ramsey to Lincoln, 27 August 1862, Roll 40, Lincoln Papers, LC, also found in OR, 1:13, p. 597; Lincoln to Ramsey, 27 August 1862, Roy P. Basler, ed., *The Collected Works of Abraham Lincoln*, 5:396, also found in OR, 1:13, p. 599.

panic prevails in nearly one-half the state."[14] Nicolay reported fighting along a two-hundred-mile front and estimated white deaths at several hundred. Lincoln's secretary put his own prestige behind Ramsey's requests for weapons, including howitzers, equipment for twelve hundred cavalry and five thousand to six thousand guns. Such communications moved the irreverent John Hay to write Nicolay and inquire, "Where is your scalp?"[15]

On 26 August, Governor Ramsey called for the creation of a new military department in the northwest. Word came from Nebraska that "the hostilities are so extensive as to indicate a combination of most of the tribes and suggest the propriety of some action by the War Department." Secretary of State Seward was informed on 29 August that "secession agents" were conspiring with the Chippewas of the northwest.[16]

All this was happening at a crucial moment in the war with the South. On 29-30 August, the Union forces under Gen. John Pope were defeated at Second Bull Run (Second Manassas). Robert E. Lee was at the peak of his success, the Union armies were in disarray, and it appeared that Lincoln might even have trouble defending Washington against an attack. In this context, the Indian war took on an exaggerated significance. The Minnesota war demanded attention, not only because of its potential drain on men and supplies, but because civilians were dying in that staunchly Republican state. Lincoln needed support from the northern states in the Union, and he could ill afford to ignore the bloodshed in Minnesota. Furthermore, at that moment, the Indian war appeared to many in the administration to be part of a great Confederate movement to win the war.

14. Morton Wilkinson, Dole, John G. Nicolay to Lincoln, 27 August 1862, OR, 1:13, p. 599.

15. Nicolay to Stanton, 27 August 1862, OR, 1:13, p. 599; John Hay to Nicolay, 29 August 1862, Tyler Dernett, ed., *Lincoln and the Civil War in the Diaries and Letters of John Hay*, p. 44.

16. Ramsey to Halleck, 26 August 1862, OR, 1:13, p. 597; Smith to Halleck, 28 August 1862, Roll 4, M606, LS, ID, OSI, RG48, NA; Joshua Giddings to William H. Seward, 29 August 1862, Roll 599, M234, LR, Northern Superintendency, OIA, RG75, NA.

Black Troops and an Indian War

With the coincidence of the crises, Lincoln made the momentous decision to enlist Negro troops into the Union army. As late as 6 August 1862, Lincoln publicly rejected this step.[17] His change of mind is usually attributed to the lag in recruitment and setbacks in the South. The additional factor of the Minnesota Indian war must also have been a consideration. Lincoln and the War Department were led to believe that the Indian war was a big one. The president's call for three hundred thousand militia in August illustrates the North's desperate need for soldiers. Alexander Ramsey's request for a draft extension and the decision to employ black soldiers must also be viewed in this context.

The decision to use black troops was actually reached in a cabinet meeting on 22 July 1862 and was tied to the movement for emancipation that culminated in the famous proclamation of 1 January 1863. After much discussion, Lincoln decided to hold the announcement until an opportune moment. Although he immediately issued an order permitting the use of Negroes for military labor,[18] the president continued to refuse to authorize the enlistment of black soldiers. Gen. David Hunter was denied permission in early August. On 6 August, Hunter's old enemy, Jim Lane, wired Stanton: "I am receiving negroes under the late act of Congress. Is there any objection?" Stanton referred the request to Halleck who informed Lane that Lincoln had not authorized the recruitment of black troops. Lane again requested authority to enlist them, but Stanton confirmed on 23 August that the president was unyielding. "He has not given authority," he told Senator Lane.[19]

The significant date was 25 August. That is the day that Secre-

17. New York *Tribune*, 5 August 1862, reprinted in Basler, ed., *Collected Works*, 5:356; see Dudley Cornish, *The Sable Arm*, pp. 50–55, and Benjamin Quarles, *Lincoln and the Negro*, pp. 153–55; OR, 3:2, p. 346; James H. Lane to Stanton, 6 August 1862, OR, 3:2, p. 311.

18. Notes on Cabinet Meeting, 22 July 1862, Executive Order of 22 July 1862, Stanton Papers.

19. Halleck to Stanton, 6 August 1862, Stanton Papers; Stanton to Lane, Roll 49, M6, LS, SW, RG107, NA.

tary Stanton authorized Gen. Rufus Saxton to organize black soldiers.[20] It is the same day that Governor Ramsey sought an extension of the draft and that Gen. James Craig wired Halleck about the worsening situation in Wyoming, "I am satisfied rebel agents have been at work among the Indians." Ramsey's telegram concerning the draft was one of three he sent to the harried secretary of war on 25 August. Stanton also heard from Nebraska, "Our frontier people are becoming much alarmed at the news of Indian hostilities in different parts of the country."[21] These messages constitute only part of a flood of messages that attest to the significance of the Indian war on 25 August.

The authorization to Rufus Saxton came four days before the Second Bull Run, nearly three weeks after Lincoln publicly rejected such a course, and only two days after Jim Lane had been denied authorization. The importance of troop maneuvers in the South cannot be minimized, but the most dramatic new military action that occurred between 6 and 25 August was the Minnesota Indian war. That war takes on special significance in light of the administration's suspicion of a Confederate conspiracy in the northwest. Dudley Cornish attributes Lincoln's refusal to sanction David Hunter's August project to Lincoln's belief that Hunter was not the right man for the job.[22] That explanation could also fit Jim Lane. It is more important, however, to look at military events. Cornish cites McClellan's failure in the peninsular campaign and the defeat at Second Bull Run as the important military influences on the black troop decision. Second Bull Run did not occur until after the 25 August decision. News of the Indian war (21 August) and Ramsey's request for a draft extension (25 August) make a powerful circumstantial case for the Indian war's impact on the decision to use black soldiers in the Union army.

---

20. Stanton to Rufus Saxton, 25 August 1862, Stanton Papers, also found in OR, 1:14, p. 377.
21. Craig to Halleck, 25 August 1862, OR, 1:13, p. 596; OR, 3:2, pp. 456–57; A. Saunders to Stanton, 25 August 1862, OR, 3:2, pp. 457–58.
22. Cornish, *The Sable Arm,* p. 81.

Lincoln Finds a General

Governor Ramsey's request for a new military department of the northwest (26 August) was denied by General-in-Chief Henry Halleck. Halleck was overruled by Lincoln. The defeat at the Second Bull Run may have affected this decision. A disgruntled, defeated Gen. John Pope blamed his defeat on Gen. George McClellan. Because Pope was a friend of both Stanton and Mary Todd Lincoln, Lincoln had to reassign him to an important position, but he would have to be transferred from his position in the South because "there was an army prejudice here against him."[23]

On 4 September, Lincoln met with John Pope. The president was forced to listen to Pope read a long and vitriolic document detailing his grievances against McClellan. Pope demanded that Lincoln publish his report.[24] Lincoln had heard enough and he decided to get rid of this troublesome general.

Military rivalries were not the only reasons for reassigning Pope. Reports from the northwest concerning the Indian war continued to be discouraging. Gov. William Jayne of Dakota Territory repeated the same old refrain, "A general alarm prevades all our settlements." Jayne raised the specter of "a few thousand people at the mercy of 50,000 Indians should they see proper to fall upon us."[25]

The decision was made on 5 September. McClellan informed Halleck, the "President has directed that General Pope be relieved and report to the War Department." Lincoln was creating the Department of the Northwest sought by Ramsey, and Pope was going to command it. Pope was angry. He demanded that Stanton tell him "the meaning of the order" and inquired whether it was the result of "the treachery of McClellan and his tools." Pope felt humiliated and later complained of his "sacrifice" in a series of bitter letters to Halleck.

23. Ramsey to Halleck, 29 August 1862, OR, 1:13, p. 605, also found in Roll 13, Ramsey Papers; Welles Diary, 8, 10 September 1862, Howard K. Beale, ed., *The Diary of Gideon Welles,* pp. 116, 120.

24. John Pope to Lincoln, 5 September 1862, Roll 41, Lincoln Papers, LC.

25. William Jayne to Blunt, 3 September 1862, OR, 1:13, p. 613.

Although Stanton's reply to Pope was carefully worded to avoid the squabble with McClellan, it must be taken at face value. "The Indian hostilities . . . require the attention of some military officer of high rank, in whose ability and vigor the Government has confidence," he told the general. Stanton continued, "You cannot too highly estimate the importance of the duty now intrusted to you." Stanton was confident that Pope could "meet the emergency."[26]

Lincoln obviously had dual purposes—to separate bickering generals and to meet a military need. The latter was not contrived, as Pope discovered when he arrived in Minnesota. Lincoln had adopted Alexander Ramsey's view that the Indian war was not merely a state concern, "This is not our war, it is a National War."[27]

While General Pope prepared to leave for Minnesota, the war went forward, and so did the corruption that lay at its root. A whole new set of contractors was seeking contracts for rifles and other war materials.[28] It was an election year, and there was no moratorium on politics. John C. Hicks, who supported Alexander Ramsey's bid for the Senate, tied the contest directly into the Indian war. Hicks blamed the war on the fact that "the Indians have been outraged by dishonest men in high places in the Government." Hicks meant "the Aldrich faction," led by Congressman Cyrus Aldrich, who also sought the Senate seat. Hicks charged this faction with profiting financially and politically on the Indian situation. He alleged that Commissioner "Dole was trying to avoid an investigation." Hicks forecast "the greatest fraud ever perpetrated upon the ballot box" by "the Aldrich clique."[29]

The war news continued to be bad. Newspapers reported that, in Minnesota, "the massacre does not seem confined to one locality,

26. George B. McClellan to Halleck, 5 September 1862, OR, 1:12, pt. 3, p. 811; Stanton to Pope, 6 September 1862, OR, 1:13, p. 617; Pope to Stanton, 5 September 1862, Stanton Papers; OR, 1:12, pt. 3, pp. 816–26; David Donald, ed., *Inside Lincoln's Cabinet: The Civil War Diaries of Salmon P. Chase*, p. 121.

27. Ramsey to Lincoln, 6 September 1862, Roll 41, Lincoln Papers, LC.

28. William Haywood to Ramsey, 25 August 1862, H. M. Eastman to Ramsey, 27 August 1862, Roll 9, Ramsey Papers.

29. John C. Hicks to Ramsey, 4 September 1862, Roll 13, Ramsey Papers.

but spread over a vast area." The Boston *Journal* reported that John Ross and fifty Cherokees had passed through Chicago on their way to see the president of the United States. The two theaters of Indian concern were converging. Ross was not the president's only visitor in September 1862. Episcopal Bishop Henry Whipple was on his way, and Governor Ramsey urged Whipple to use his influence with his cousin, General Halleck, to secure a regiment of cavalry for Minnesota. On 6 September, Ramsey informed Lincoln, "I have accepted the generous offer of Senator Wilkinson to visit you." Wilkinson was already pursuing Lincoln about Minnesota's need for arms, supplies, and provisions for refugees.[30]

The fears of a wider Indian war did not abate in early September. Gov. Samuel Kirkwood of Iowa reported, "I have reliable information that Yankton Indians on our western border, north of the Missouri River, have joined with the hostile Indians in Minnesota, and threaten our whole northwestern border." Kirkwood predicted a "terrible massacre" unless there was immediate action. Nebraska officials reported "Nebraska settlers by hundreds fleeing." On 16 September, Nebraskans discovered "A combined effort on the part of the unfriendly Indians is meditated against the entire region." Caleb Smith endorsed the report, telling Stanton, "The statements of the agent are corroborated by other information which has been communicated to this Department." The situation seemed to be getting out of hand even with the tribes in Minnesota that were still peaceful. John G. Nicolay informed the White House that negotiations with the Chippewas had broken down and he feared "open hostility in a day or two."[31]

30. Carl Schurz to Lincoln, 29 August 1862, Roll 40, Lincoln Papers, LC; Ramsey to Lincoln, 6 September 1862, *Minnesota*, 2:224, also found in the Ramsey Journal, Roll 2, vol. 6, Records of the Territorial Governors, Minnesota Historical Society, St. Paul; Ramsey to Whipple, 9 September 1862, Box 3, Whipple Papers.
31. Samuel J. Kirkwood to Stanton, 8 September 1862, OR, 1:13, p. 620; A. S. Paddock to Stanton, 9 September 1862, OR, 1:13, p. 621; B. F. Sushbaugh to Charles E. Mix, 13 September 1862, Smith to Stanton, 16 September 1862, OR, 1:13, pp. 644–45; Nicolay to Hay [?], 8 September 1862, Roll 95, Lincoln Papers, LC. These reports proved to be quite inaccurate. George A. S. Crooker told Lincoln that this was all a giant hoax, cooked up among Ramsey, Henry M. Rice, and Chippewa Chief Hole-in-the-Day. The plot was hatched, he claimed, so that "their

These predictions of doom never came to fruition. Many of these reports reflected the white mentality toward Indians rather than the actual situation. However, responsible officials in Washington had no way to evaluate the information and were forced to consider the possibility of a frontierwide conflict. By mid-September 1862, Gen. John Pope joined the ranks of the panic mongers.

Pope arrived in Minnesota on 16 September. That evening, Pope wired Halleck, sounding as though he had spent weeks on the scene. He predicted "a general Indian war all along the frontier, unless immediate steps are taken to put a stop to it." He found "panic everywhere in Wisconsin and Minnesota" and prophesied the loss of half the populations of those states.[32]

Militarily, Pope planned no mere holding action. He ordered Colonel Sibley to destroy Indian farms and food.

> It is my purpose utterly to exterminate the Sioux if I have the power to do so and even if it requires a campaign lasting the whole of next year . . . They are to be treated as maniacs or wild beasts, and by no means as people with whom treaties or compromises can be made.[33]

Sibley was pleased to have a commander who felt this way about Indians. Sibley thought the Sioux were "devils in human shape" and "miserable wretches." He told Governor Ramsey, "My heart is steeled against them, and if I have the means, and can catch them, I will sweep them with the besom of death." Sibley was pleased with the extermination policy for personal reasons. His first

---

coffers can be once more filled." In the Crooker scenario, William Dole played the fool to this conspiracy. Dole was squired around St. Paul for two weeks of sightseeing, then hauled around the countryside in search of the allegedly hostile Chippewa. In the final scene, Dole and his party were surrounded by Hole-in-the-Day's men and a mock confrontation was played out. (If true, Crooker's account could explain Nicolay's frantic letter.) Ramsey then rode to the rescue, Rice was nominated a commissioner along with other cronies, and an agreement made that was so extravagant that, if approved, Crooker claimed, "the nation will have to go into liquidation." Crooker to Lincoln, 7 October 1862, Roll 42, Lincoln Papers, LC.

32. Pope to Halleck, 16 September 1862, OR, 1:13, p. 642.

33. Pope to Henry H. Sibley, 17 September 1862, OR, 1:13, pp. 648–49; Pope to Sibley, 28 September 1862, OR, 1:13, pp. 685–86.

communication to Pope concerned a promotion in rank which he thought he could obtain by carrying out the general's wishes. On 29 September, Sibley was promoted to brigadier general. The man who had profited from Indians in trade and politics now reaped new rewards by killing large numbers of them.[34]

Meanwhile, Pope's communications to the War Department were frantic. "I am doing all I can, but have little to do it with," he complained. Pope called it a war of "formidable proportions." He demanded supplies that, in Stanton's view, constituted "an immense expenditure of money and material needed elsewhere." Halleck tried to restrain Pope, telling him, "Your requisitions . . . are beyond all expectations." The general's demands could not be met without depriving troops elsewhere.[35]

Pope's tone grew more hysterical. "You do not seem to be aware of the extent of the Indian outbreaks," he told Halleck. Pope claimed that fifty thousand people were refugees and that "the whole of Minnesota west of the Mississippi and the Territories of Dakota and Nebraska will be entirely depopulated." Never one to understate, Pope continued:

> You have no idea of the wide, universal and uncontrollable panic everywhere in this country. Over 500 people have been murdered in Minnesota alone and 300 women and children now in captivity. The most horrible massacres have been committed; children nailed alive to trees and houses, women violated and then disemboweled— everything that horrible ingenuity could devise. It will require a large force and much time to prevent everybody leaving the country, such is the condition of things.[36]

Halleck replied that he could not provide everything Pope wanted "but all that is possible will be done."[37]

34. Sibley to Ramsey, 24 August 1862, *Minnesota,* 2:198; Sibley to Pope, 19 September 1862, OR, 1:13, p. 650; Stanton to Sibley, 29 September 1862, Roll 11, Henry Hastings Sibley Papers.

35. Pope to Stanton, 22 September 1862, Stanton to Halleck, 23 September 1862, OR, 1:13, p. 658; Halleck to Pope, 23 September 1862, OR, 1:13, p. 663.

36. Pope to Halleck, 23 September 1862, OR, 1:13, pp. 663–64.

37. Halleck to Pope, OR, 1:13, p. 669.

Prisoners to Fight Indians

Lincoln's desperate need for soldiers led to the organization of black troops. That same problem led to another expedient, the attempt to use Union prisoners paroled by the Confederates against the Indians in Minnesota. Gov. David Tod of Ohio suggested this on 9 September 1862. Stanton called the idea "excellent" and promised action. Orders were issued within a week. By 20 September, there were twenty thousand paroled Union soldiers at Annapolis, Maryland. Lincoln instructed Stanton to get them "to the seat of the Indian difficulties . . . with all possible dispatch." These soldiers were to relieve troops in Minnesota who would then be sent to fight in the South. "Arm them and send them away just as fast as the Railroad will carry them," ordered the president.[38]

Lincoln's scheme to use paroled prisoners did not reckon with the morale of the soldiers. By 22 September, the project was in trouble. The soldiers at Annapolis complained that an assignment in the West was "very distasteful to them." Some called it a violation of the terms of their parole whereby they could not be used again against the South. Many deserted to their homes. Nevertheless, Stanton ordered the adjutant general to proceed with preparations. The secretary of war promised General Pope ten thousand men from among the former prisoners.[39]

General Pope waited impatiently. On 25 September, he demanded of Stanton: "When will the paroled troops begin to arrive?" Pope also complained that he had no cavalry and "it is impossible to follow mounted Indians on foot." He warned Halleck: "Do not misunderstand the facts. It is not only the Sioux with whom we have to deal. All the Indians—Sioux, Chippewas, and

38. David Tod to Stanton, Stanton to Tod, 9 September 1862, OR, 2:4, p. 499; Halleck to Schofield, 16 September 1862, OR, 1:13, pp. 640–41; Lincoln to Stanton, 20 September 1862, Basler, ed., *Collected Works*, 5:432.

39. Lorenzo Thomas to Stanton, 22 September 1862, OR, 2:4, pp. 546–47; Stanton to Thomas, 24 September 1862, OR, 2:4, p. 550; Pope to Halleck, 23 September 1862, OR, 1:13, pp. 663–64.

Winnebagoes, are on the verge of outbreak along the whole frontier."[40]

The soldiers simply refused to go to Minnesota. Gen. Lewis Wallace reported from Ohio that when he went to organize the men to fight Indians, "nearly the whole body protested." Wallace had to give up. The same was true of prisoner camps in Illinois where it proved impossible to send troops to General Pope because the men were in "a state of sure mutiny."[41] As a result, the prisoner-soldiers were not sent to Minnesota.

The whole affair irritated Lincoln. He was especially upset because in October the Confederates had begun to parole Union soldiers on the stipulation that they could not be used against the Indians. This supported the perception of the Minnesota war as part of a Confederate conspiracy. Lincoln threatened not to accept such parolees and "send the prisoners back with a distinct notice that we will recognize no paroles given our prisoners by the rebels as extending beyond a prohibition against fighting them." Eventually, however, the government determined that employing the prisoners against Indians would violate the cartel agreed upon for their exchange.[42] The parolees won their victory. Regardless of legalities, Lincoln was unable to force unwilling men to fight Indians. Indian warfare stirred patriotism only in Minnesota.

Corruption as Usual in Minnesota

It was truly a time of "a multitude of cares."[43] Lincoln had problems in the South, in Minnesota, and with his troops. September 1862 was also a month of great pressure for the emancipation of slaves as a war measure. Lincoln selected 22 September, just following a marginal victory at Antietam, to announce his preliminary

40. Pope to Stanton, 25 September 1862, OR, 1:13, p. 668; Pope to Halleck, 25 September 1862, OR, 1:13, pp. 668–69.
41. Lewis Wallace to Thomas, 28 September 1862, OR, 2:4, pp. 569–71; Daniel Tyler to Thomas, 3 October 1862, OR, 2:4, p. 621.
42. Lincoln to Halleck, Halleck to Lincoln, 3 October 1862, OR, 2:4, p. 593; Thomas to Stanton, 11 October 1862, OR, 2:4, p. 621.
43. Lincoln to Ross, 25 September 1862, Roll 42, Lincoln Papers, LC.

Emancipation Proclamation. The Minnesota Assembly was among the many state legislatures to praise this action.[44]

Minnesotans were actually more concerned about Indians than slaves. That same legislature showered the president with memorials for compensation to pay for damages done by Indians. On 23 September, the Assembly called on Lincoln to remove the relatively innocent Winnebagos from Minnesota. Governor Ramsey supported that demand. The Presbyterian Synod of St. Paul petitioned the president to remove the Indian tribes and suggested taking them to Indian Territory.[45] Those who issued calls for justice for blacks did not extend their open-mindedness to Indians, since exploitation of Indians translated into money and power. Procedures were already under way to establish a claim commission that would bring more of the Indians' money to Minnesota.[46]

The politics of Indian affairs did not adjourn during the war. Alexander Ramsey wrote in his diary on 24 September concerning his efforts to "induce the Legislature to elect a U States Senator in H. M. Rice's place." Ramsey wanted to be that senator. Rice, in turn, was trying to get General Pope's job, and he was supported in that quest by Secretary of the Interior John Usher. Benjamin Wade, a prominent radical senator from Ohio, also supported Rice, telling Lincoln that Rice was a man "who the Indians fear and respect."[47] Symbolic of the central concerns of Minnesota politicians was a letter to Lincoln on 7 October 1862. It was marked "private." The Minnesotans asked Lincoln to allow Union soldiers to leave the

44. A number of resolutions calling for emancipation can be found in Roll 41, Lincoln Papers, LC; for the Resolution of the Minnesota General Assembly, 29 September 1862, see Roll 42, Lincoln Papers, LC.

45. Memorial from the Minnesota General Assembly to Lincoln, 18 September 1862, Memorial from Minnesota Assembly, 23 September 1862, Roll 41, Lincoln Papers, LC; Ramsey to Smith, 8 October 1862, Roll 20, M825, LR, ID, OSI, RG45, NA; Memorial of the Presbyterian Synod of St. Paul to Lincoln, 29 September 1862, Roll 599, M234, LR, Northern Superintendency, OIA, RG75, NA.

46. Rice to Dole, 30 September 1862, Roll 599, M234, LR, Northern Superintendency, OIA, RG75, NA.

47. Ramsey, 24 September 1862, vol. 36, Ramsey Papers; John P. Usher to Smith [?], 1862, Lincoln Papers, Minnesota Historical Society; Lincoln to Stanton, 9 October 1862, Benjamin F. Wade to Lincoln, 30 September 1862, Basler, ed., *Collected Works*, 5:455.

army in order to vote in their own state. Otherwise the Republicans could not carry the state. The man in the White House was also interested in politics. They could count on his help.[48]

Lincoln did not realize until it was too late that this politicking and corruption in Indian affairs lay at the root of the bloodshed. Bishop Whipple, in his September visit, impressed the president with his recitation of the evils of the Indian System. On 8 October, another Minnesotan, George A. S. Crooker, sent Lincoln an enlightening letter via Secretary of State Seward.[49]

Crooker was merciless in his condemnation of the Minnesota Indian System. "The cohesive power of public plunder cements rogues together stronger than party or any other ties," Crooker proclaimed to Seward. He described St. Paul as a city of "40 thieves of every known color and political creed and no matter what administration may be in power some of the band are always right and therefore the same men always rule." Crooker said he was contacting the president in order "to lay bare the conduct of a set of villains whose work not only cost a large sum of money but has deluged our western border in blood."

Crooker believed the war's causes to be obvious. There was no conspiracy caused by the Confederates. The main factor was "the wretched condition of the tribes." Crooker cited their starvation, the delay of annuity funds, and the "rapacious robberies of, the Agents[,] Traders and Goverment [sic] officials who always connive together to steal every dollar of their money that can be stolen."

Crooker claimed that there were never more than five hundred Indians fighting at any time. Little Crow probably had only about two hundred fifty warriors left by October. "These 200 or 300 Indians form the grand army that Gen. Pope gravely demands 25,000 men and all the necessary munitions and paraphernalia and pomp of Western warfare to crush out." However, continued Crooker,

48. Wilkinson, William Windom, Cyrus B. Aldrich, Donnelly to Lincoln, 7 October 1862, Roll 42, Lincoln Papers, LC.

49. Crooker to Seward, 8 October 1862, Crooker to Lincoln, 7 October 1862, Roll 42, Lincoln Papers, LC, also found in the Lincoln Papers, Minnesota Historical Society.

Minnesota Indians would not be exterminated because "the *dead Indian* draws no money from the government."

Many of Crooker's charges were intemperate but there was much in what he said. If Lincoln had listened a year earlier to another eccentric complainer, George E. H. Day, the Minnesota Indian war might have been avoided. Crooker was right about the exaggerated requests for men and material for the war. The constant reports that the Chippewas and Winnebagos were in revolt were either erroneous or intentionally falsified. Lincoln's reaction to these charges is not known.

By early October, it was clear that the panic over the Indian war had been out of proportion to the reality. General Sibley was fast subduing the Sioux, forcing surrender in the name of "your Great American Father" and telling those who raised white flags they would be treated as "friends." Upon surrender, however, these "friends" became prisoners of war. By 3 October, Sibley had twelve hundred captives, almost a thousand of whom were women and children. On 28 September, he set up a military commission to try his war criminals. By 3 October, the commission had tried twenty to thirty Indians. The administration of justice was obviously neither unbiased nor unhurried. General Pope would have preferred to forget the ritual, "We have and can have troops enough to exterminate them all, if they furnish the least occasion for it."[50]

On 9 October, Pope informed the government, "The Sioux War may be considered at an end."[51] Bishop Whipple's maxim that the Indian System "ends in blood" perfectly fit Minnesota. The war was not really over for Lincoln or the Sioux. Due to the trials being conducted by General Sibley, Lincoln was destined to become more deeply embroiled in Minnesota Indian affairs than ever. The man who had ordered, "attend to the Indians," was going to have to attend to them himself. Abraham Lincoln was going to have to decide whether to sanction the greatest official mass execution in American history.

50. Sibley to Ta-Tanka-Nazin, 24 September 1862, *Minnesota,* 2:250; Special Order No. 55, 28 September 1862, Roll 11, Sibley Papers; Sibley to Pope, 3 October 1862, OR, 1:13, pp. 707–8; Pope to Sibley, 6 October 1862, Roll 483, M619, LR, AGO, RG94, NA.
51. Pope to Halleck, 9 October 1862, OR, 1:13, p. 722.

VIII. Lincoln and the Sioux Executions: "I Could Not Afford to Hang Men for Votes"

"THE SIOUX WAR IS AT AN END," reported Gen. John Pope. Those words should have brought relief to Abraham Lincoln. However, Pope's communications of 9 and 10 October unveiled a new problem, "We have about 1,500 prisoners—men, women, and children—and many are coming every day to deliver themselves up." For Pope, the results of the military trials were foreordained, "Many are being tried by military commission for being connected in late horrible outrages and will be executed."[1]

General Pope Plans Executions

Pope's plan for executing Indians was not a sudden notion. He and Sibley had begun to discuss the hangings as soon as it was evident they could win the war. A week before the fighting ended, Pope wrote Sibley, "I altogether approve of executing the Indians who have been concerned in these outrages." There was a problem, "I don't know how you can discriminate now between Indians who say they are and have been friendly, and those who have not." Pope would not bother his conscience too much about that. "I distrust them all," he said. He thought all should be kept as prisoners and "all who are guilty whatever the number should in my judgement

---

1. John Pope to Henry Halleck, 9 October 1862, OR, 1:13, p. 722; Pope to Halleck, 10 October 1862, OR, 1:13, p. 724 (for "Abbreviations in Footnotes," see p. vi).

be hung." Women and children were to be included among the prisoners. Any Indian who left his reservation was to be shot on sight.[2]

Pope had plans for the Indians exempted from execution. "I shall keep and feed for the winter such as are not hung and shot for their crimes, so that with the sanction of Congress obtained this winter they can all be removed beyond the limits of this state, in the spring." Pope wanted "a final settlement with all these Indians." The first step to that settlement was to hang a large number. "Do not allow any false sympathy for the Indians to prevent you from acting with the utmost rigor," he told Sibley. "Be assured I will sustain you in whatever measures you adopt to effect the object."[3]

Henry Sibley knew that a blood sacrifice was expected, and he would provide it, although he was not altogether comfortable with that assignment. Most of the "prisoners" he was herding toward Fort Snelling were women and children. He could not avoid being in contact with the "poor wretches," and he called them "objects of pity." As the trials progressed at the rate of thirty to forty per day, Sibley lamented that he had to pass judgment on each individual. "This power of life, and death, is an awful thing to exercise," he confided to his wife, "and when I think of more than three hundred human beings are subject to that power lodged in my hand, it makes me shudder." These private qualms did not keep Sibley from his "duty," and he pronounced most of his male prisoners guilty.[4]

Lincoln Inherits a Problem

On 14 October, Lincoln's cabinet was informed of the events in Minnesota. The secretary of war read Pope's report aloud. Gideon

2. Pope to H. H. Sibley, 2, 10 October 1862, Roll 483, M619, LR, AGO, RG109, NA.
3. Pope to Sibley, 7, 10 October 1862, ibid.
4. Sibley to his wife, 17 October 1862, Roll 11, Henry Hastings Sibley Papers; Sioux Trial Transcripts, Military Commission, U.S. Army.

Welles disliked it immediately, "I was disgusted with the whole thing; the tone and opinions of the dispatch are discreditable." The cabinet was apparently disturbed over the plan to execute large numbers of the Sioux. "The Indian outrages have, I doubt not, been horrible," Welles confided to his diary, but, "what may have been the provocations we are not told." Welles perceived ulterior motives, "The Winnebagoes have good land which white men want and mean to have."[5]

Welles was not the only one who was worried. So was Abraham Lincoln. The president moved quickly to prevent any wanton slaughter. He dispatched Assistant Secretary of the Interior John P. Usher to Minnesota to help restore peace. He wrote to Sen. Henry M. Rice of Minnesota, an old friend of Bishop Henry Whipple, and urged him to aid and advise Usher. On 17 October, a chastened Pope informed Sibley, "The President directs that no executions be made without his sanction."[6]

Minnesota politicians were not only concerned with carrying out the executions; they were also determined to remove the Indians and take charge of Indian-related funds. On 20 October, Alexander Ramsey pressured Lincoln to remove the Indians from Minnesota. He called the war a "sudden and terrible blow." He said the whites of his state had learned "to regard this perfidious and cruel race with a degree of distrust and apprehension which will not tolerate their presence of their neighborhood in any number or in any condition." The Sioux were "assassins" and "ravishers of . . . wives and sisters and daughters." Therefore, the governor proclaimed, "the Sioux of Minnesota have forfeited all claims for the protection of the Government."

Ramsey's removal objective was not limited to the Sioux. Gideon Wells had been right about the hunger for Winnebago land. Ramsey's reason for expelling the Winnebagos was racist, "It is enough to say the Winnebagoes are Indians." It did not matter that

5. Welles Diary, 14 October 1862, Howard K. Beale, ed., *The Diary of Gideon Welles,* 1:171.

6. Abraham Lincoln to Henry M. Rice, 16 October 1862, Henry Mower Rice Papers; Pope to Sibley, 17 October 1862, Roll 483, M619, LR, AGO, RG109, NA.

they had not fought in the war. Minnesotans would not tolerate them in the state.[7]

Governor Ramsey developed a network to influence the president on these matters. Congressmen were not his only friends in Washington. Most important, he had an ally high in the government, John P. Usher. Usher shared private information with Ramsey's agents.[8] Richard Shute worked on the problem of getting the government to pay the cost of the war. Shute quickly found that "the President & Sec. of War are anxious that Govt shall assume & at once pay our Sioux War expenses." Stanton assured Shute that Minnesotans could count on the money one way or another. Shute believed that John Usher's report would be the key, "for I think this report will greatly influence the Government in its action."[9] It turned out that only an appropriation by Congress could pay the war expenses, but Shute was able to assure Ramsey that, once approved by Congress, the payment would be made quickly. The heads of departments and the president all wanted the matter given "prompt and thorough attention."[10]

Ramsey also sought compensation to Minnesota citizens for losses in the war. He personally pressed Lincoln on this issue, and Lincoln referred it to the secretary of the interior. Richard Shute told Ramsey that he had been promised that a claims commission would be appointed. Ramsey wrote Caleb Smith on 12 November asking that the commission be set up, and Smith replied that it would have to wait until John Usher returned from Minnesota and made his report.[11]

Ramsey's motivation in all these matters was highly political.

7. Alexander Ramsey to Lincoln, 20 October 1862, Roll 20, M825, LR, ID, OSI, RG48, NA.

8. A. S. H. White to Ramsey, 7 October 1862, Roll 13, Alexander Ramsey Papers.

9. Richard Shute to Ramsey, 1 November 1862, ibid.

10. Shute to Ramsey, 4 November 1862, Roll 13, Ramsey Papers; Shute to Ramsey, 5 November 1862, Roll 2, Ramsey Papers.

11. Ramsey to Lincoln, 22 October 1862, Roll 2, Ramsey Papers, also found in *Minnesota in the Indian and Civil Wars*, 2:282–83; Ramsey to Caleb B. Smith, 12 November 1862, Smith to Ramsey, 13 November 1862, Roll 13, Ramsey Papers.

He wanted to be a United States senator, and the Minnesota legislature had not yet made its decision. On the day the war ended, 9 October, Ramsey worried to his diary about his contest with Aldrich.[12] The governor may have seen that he could use the Indian war to win the contest on the basis of who could do the most for Minnesota in Indian affairs. Clark Thompson, superintendent of the Northern Superintendency, was being pressured to help Aldrich. One Aldrich supporter complained that Thompson was not delivering, "Aldrich promised to do something for us financially in this country to help us carry the election . . . and I have heard nothing from any one." That was because Aldrich was in faraway Washington and Alexander Ramsey was in St. Paul where he could make Thompson his ally. In the midst of the senatorial contest, Ramsey recorded in his diary, "Saw C. W. Thompson Esq. Ind. Supt. on political subjects."[13]

While political maneuvering went forward, so did the politically explosive trials of the Sioux. Henry Sibley felt the pressure. "I see the press is very much concerned, lest I should prove too tender-hearted," he wrote. Sibley was determined that the number of executions "will be sufficiently great to satisfy the longings of the most blood-thirsty." Sibley fulfilled his promise. By 5 November the trials were over. At 7:40 P.M. on 8 November 1862, Sibley presented the government with a list of 303 Sioux men condemned to death. Minnesotans were prepared to stage a mass execution of unprecendented scope.[14]

Abraham Lincoln rejected the projected slaughter. On 10 November, he wired Pope, "Please forward, as soon as possible, the full and complete record of these convictions." He specifically instructed the general to include any materials that might discriminate as to which of the condemned were the most guilty. He

12. Ramsey Diary, 9 October 1862, Roll 39, vol. 36, Ramsey Papers.
13. Charles H. Lee to Clark W. Thompson, 23 October 1862, Box 2, Clark W. Thompson Papers; Ramsey Diary, 12 December 1862, Roll 39, vol. 36, Ramsey Papers.
14. Sibley to his wife (extracts), 20 October 1862, Roll 11, Sibley Papers; Dee Brown, *Bury My Heart at Wounded Knee*, p. 59.

ordered "a careful statement" prepared by Pope concerning the verdicts.[15]

Pope's response was anything but "careful." He replied, "The only distinction between the culprits is as to which of them murdered most people or violated most young girls." Pope threatened Lincoln with the defiant assertion that prohibiting the executions would result in mob action—a standard warning of the pro-execution forces:

> The people of this State . . . are exasperated to the last degree, and if the guilty are not all executed I think it nearly impossible to prevent the indiscriminate massacre of all the Indians—old men, women, and children.

Lincoln could not have been comfortable as he read Pope's accounts of the exhibition of mutilated war victims in various towns and of the daily funerals for Minnesota's dead. Especially serious was the revelation that Pope's soldiers were "in full sympathy with the people on this subject." About fifteen hundred women, children, and old men were among Pope's prisoners, "and I fear that so soon as it is known that the criminals are not at once to be executed that there will be an indiscriminate massacre of the whole."[16]

Alexander Ramsey reinforced the potent argument he and General Pope had apparently agreed upon. On the day that Lincoln requested the trial records, Ramsey wired Lincoln: "I hope the execution of every Sioux Indian condemned by the military court will be at once ordered. It would be wrong upon principle and policy to refuse this." Ramsey continued, "Private revenge would on all this border take the place of official judgement on these Indians."[17]

Lincoln and his lawyers were apparently shocked by what they found in the trial transcripts. The trials had become shorter and shorter as they progressed, averaging only ten to fifteen minutes

15. Lincoln to Pope, 10 November 1862, Roy P. Basler, ed., *The Collected Works of Abraham Lincoln*, 5:493.

16. Pope to Lincoln, 11 November 1862, OR, 1:13, p. 788.

17. Ramsey to Lincoln, 10 November 1862, OR, 1:13, p. 787.

per case. The lack of evidence against the accused was manifest. Indians who honestly admitted their involvement in battles had condemned themselves. Hearsay evidence and a denial of due process and counsel were characteristic of General Sibley's trial proceedings.

In case number 388, a lone witness stated, "I saw the prisoner . . . and he stated to me that he was wounded at the Fort, and that he there fired one shot." The court immediately sentenced the prisoner to death without letting him speak in his own defense.

Case number 389 was typical. After he was asked if he was involved in a battle, the prisoner replied: "I saw nothing, but fired. I fired twice." On those few words, the military tribunal acted, "And thereupon the case being closed, the commission was cleared and proceeded with their finding and sentence." Moments later, the sentence was pronounced: "Guilty of the charge."

Lincoln's lawyers recommended pardon in many such cases. They tried to distinguish between cases in which there were eyewitnesses to rape or murder and those in which the accused was apparently only involved in battle. It was not an easy task. They labored for over a month, seeking just criteria for selecting Indians deserving of the death sentence.

In the end, even some of those selected for execution must have caused some uneasiness among the transcript evaluators. Number 327 claimed he fired only at horses. The lone witness against him said he saw the prisoner in a situation "where the Indians killed an old man and 2 girls." The Indian replied, "I was there, but I don't know who shot them." He was condemned to death.

Case number 333 remained condemned on hearsay evidence. A Mrs. Robertson testified, "I heard prisoner say he was out at Green Lake and killed some one with an axe." The prisoner replied that he struck the man only after he was dead.

Slowly, case by case, the number of the condemned was reduced. Abraham Lincoln was apparently a torn man. If he failed to execute any Indians, he risked losing support in a key northern state. If he executed many, he could be charged with injustice that might well offend foreign nations that were considering alliance with the Confederacy. Lincoln, therefore, put off a decision as long as possible.[18]

The Struggle Begins

Ramsey and Pope offered the politically sensitive Lincoln an easy way out of his dilemma. Pope tried the strategy on the president on 12 November, "I would suggest that if the govt be unwilling at so great distance to order the execution of the condemned Indians the criminals be turned to the State Govt to be dealt with."[19] In other words, the governor could assume the responsibility and, in his Senate race, receive the credit in his home state. Lincoln eventually found this option quite attractive.

Lincoln was pressured to execute the Indians by many other persons. Thaddeus Williams, a doctor from St. Paul, wrote a long and emotional letter to Lincoln, filled with racist stereotypes about "lurking savages" and "savage cruelty and demonic hatred."[20] Williams's letter was a vivid reflection of the emotions set loose by the Indian war in Minnesota:

> Mr. President, if a being in the shape of a human, but with that shape horribly disfigured with paint & feathers to make its presence more terrible, should enter your home in the dead hours of night, & approach your pillow with a glittering tomahawk in one hand, & a scalping knife in the other, his eyes gleaming with a thirst for blood, you would spring from your bed in terror, and flee for your life; . . . there you would see the torch applied to the house your hands had built . . . your wife, or your daughter, though she might not yet have seen twelve sweet summers (nay, do not start, the scene is real, & has been enacted nearly 400 times in Minnesota . . .) ravished before your eyes, & carried into a captivity worse than death.

Williams depicted many such scenes and then turned the question on the president. Would Lincoln not also seek revenge?

18. Sioux Trial Transcripts.

19. Pope to Lincoln, 12 November 1862, Abraham Lincoln Papers, Minnesota Historical Society.

20. Thaddeus Williams to Lincoln, 22 November 1862, Roll 44, Abraham Lincoln Papers, LC, also found at the Minnesota Historical Society.

Next morning, suppose I told you Brig. Gen. Sibley had captured them all; that a commission had tried them by the rules of human justice, found them guilty & condemned them to die the death of the murderer, . . . would you sign the death warrant? Aye, if you had to do it with your own heart's blood.

Williams sketched visions of horror, claiming they were real, not imagined. They were, he told Lincoln, the genuine experiences of

> 400 *human beings, butchered,* their entrails torn out, & their heads cut off & put between their lifeless thighs, or hoisted on a pole; their bodies gashed & cut to strips, & nailed or hung to trees; mothers with sharp fence rails passed through them & their unborn babes; children with hooks stuck through their backs & hung to limbs of trees—these are the shadows which flit in the backgrounds of the picture, and cry, not *only* for *justice* but for *vengeance.*

The hideous recitation closed with the allegedly true story of twenty-three Indians raping a young girl. Despite the wild tone of the letter, Williams ended with the same conclusion, using almost the same language as Ramsey and Pope:

> Not only does *justice* require the blood of these savages, but *vengeance will have it.* The people of this state . . . are so exasperated against the Indians that if the authorities do not hang them, *they will.*

Newspapers expressed the same sentiments. The Stillwater, Minnesota, *Messenger* openly attacked the president, "We ask you, Abraham Lincoln, has crime become a virtue?" In direct challenge to Lincoln, the editorial writer threatened mob rule:

> We tell you, Abraham Lincoln, that the remaining twenty thousand men of Minnesota will never submit to such ingratitude and wrong. We tell you plainly and soberly, if these convicted murderers are dealt with more leniently than other murderers . . . the people of the State will take law and vengeance in their own hands, and woe to any member of the hated race that shall be found within our borders.

The editorial writer demanded extermination of the Indians and warned Lincoln that the bloodshed to come would surpass even that of the war for the Union, "DEATH TO THE BARBARIANS! is the sentiment of our people."[21]

Lincoln was confronted by more than crank letters and editorials. Even eminent citizens and churchmen called for blood. Stephen Riggs had been a missionary among the Sioux for a quarter century. Riggs did not ask Lincoln for executions on the same scale as the more rabid Indian haters, but the clergyman advanced a similar pragmatic argument:

> Knowing the excited state of this part of the country—the indignation which is felt against the whole Indian people in consequence of these murders and outrages—this indignation being often unreasonable and wicked, visiting itself on the innocent as well as the guilty—knowing this I feel that a great necessity is upon us to execute the *great majority* of those who have been condemned by the Military Commission.

Riggs, however, suggested that Lincoln be flexible in his approach to the problem. He maintained that discrimination was possible concerning "various grades of guilt from the man who butchered women and children to the man who simply followed with a party for the purpose of taking away spoils from the homes of settlers who had fled." Some clemency could be exercised. Riggs even identified specific Sioux men who should be pardoned. Excepting these, he concluded, "Justice requires it [the mass execution] should be done."[22]

Riggs also argued in the public press in favor of flexibility. He called the trials inadequate and contended that some of the Sioux "were guilty only to the extent of taking property." Bishop Henry Whipple read Riggs's opinions and leaped at the chance to extend somewhat the possibilities for clemency, "It seems to me that there is a broad distinction be[t]ween the guilt of men who went through

---

21. W. C. Dodge to Lincoln, 20 November 1862, Roll 20, M825, LR, ID, OSI, RG48, NA.

22. S. R. Riggs to Lincoln, 17 November 1862, Roll 44, Lincoln Papers, LC.

the country committing fiendish violence, massacring women &
babes with spirit of demons & the guilt of timid men who received
a share of the plunder or who under threat of death engaged in
some one battle where hundreds were engaged."[23] Whipple expressed this view both in newspapers and to Lincoln. Neither Riggs
nor Whipple dared suggest pardoning all the condemned. They
made only a stopgap effort to save some lives.

Meanwhile, Bishop Whipple was busily organizing his own
lobby against the executions. His attempt to influence Lincoln had
begun when he visited the president in September 1862, long before
the trial verdicts were announced. The churchman found Lincoln
receptive to his message. Lincoln reportedly told a friend that
Bishop Whipple's arguments had shaken and disturbed him. Lincoln even pledged an eventual reform of the Indian System. Following this initial success, Whipple kept the pressure on Lincoln.[24]
On 12 November, he wrote Senator Rice and asked him to deliver
another letter to the president:

> We cannot hang men by the hundreds. Upon our own premises
> we have no right to do so. We claim that they are an independent
> nation & as such they are prisoners of war. The leaders must be
> punished but we cannot afford by an wanton cruelty to purchase a
> long Indian war—nor by injustice in other matters purchase the
> anger of God.[25]

The bishop's position was not popular in Minnesota. He found
himself under fire no matter how moderate his pronouncements.
He tried to explain, "As to the condemned, I have had no desire
to find fault with the court or shield the really guilty." However,
how could justice be done when thirty or forty men were tried
in six to seven hours? Whipple protested that he wanted the guilty
punished: "The law of God & man alike require it. The stern
necessities of self protection demand it." He also wanted "the

23. Henry Benjamin Whipple to the Editor of the *Pioneer*, n.d., Box 40, Letterbook 3, Henry Benjamin Whipple Papers.
24. Henry B. Whipple, *Lights and Shadows of a Long Episcopate*, pp. 136–37.
25. Whipple to Rice, 12 November 1862, Box 40, Letterbook 4, Whipple Papers.

strictest scrutiny lest we punish the innocent." Whipple believed that the real blame lay not with individuals but with the Indian System and its corruption. "I believe God will hold the nation guilty," he said.[26]

Commissioner William P. Dole was perhaps the most influential opponent of the mass executions. On 11 November, Caleb Smith sent Lincoln a letter from Dole (who was still in Minnesota) and endorsed his "humane views."[27]

Dole was no sentimental reformer, but he could not stomach the proposed executions of the Sioux. Dole admitted that the Sioux had committed "most horrible and atrocious crimes," and he understood the emotions of the Minnesotans. However, "I cannot reconcile it to my sense of duty to remain silent," he told the secretary of the interior. The Indians about to be slaughtered had peaceably surrendered with the impression that they would be safe. The execution hysteria, Dole believed, "partakes more of the character of revenge than the infliction of deserved punishment. . . . It is contrary to the spirit of the age, and our character as a great magnanimous and Christian people."

Dole's opinions reflected the abivalent racism and humaneness that was typical of Indian officials of the era. He called Indians "a wild, barbarous, and benighted race" and portrayed them as superstitiously obeying their leaders. He contended that because of this alleged blind obedience, only the leaders should be punished. Rank-and-file Indians were not responsible.

Dole's judgments meshed with those of Riggs and Whipple. The president could take a middle road. Dole did not blame Pope or Sibley for the decisions that had been reached during the trials, "They could not do otherwise, but their sentence may be modified by the President." The commissioner begged Smith to act to "prevent the consummation of an act which I cannot believe would be otherwise than a stain upon our national character, and

26. Whipple to the Editor of the *Pioneer*, n.d.; Whipple, "The Duty of Citizens concerning the Indian Massacre," n.d., Box 40, Letterbook 3, Whipple Papers.

27. Smith to Lincoln, 11 November 1862, Dole to Smith, 10 November 1862, Roll 43, Lincoln Papers, LC.

a source of future regret." Smith took the matter to Lincoln, who was going to have to make a decision.

Lincoln Moves Toward a Decision

By late November 1862, both sides were well organized. The pressures to execute the Sioux grew daily. On 24 November, General Pope wired Lincoln, "Organizations of inhabitants are being rapidly made with the purpose of massacring these Indians." Pope foresaw "serious trouble" and demanded an early decision. Pope was not just inventing tales. He had reports that agitation was increasing at Camp Lincoln, where the Indians were confined. Sibley reported an assault by two hundred men and he warned of "a fearful collision between the United States forces and the citizens."[28]

Bishop Whipple did his best to counter these influences. Whipple was not only trying to obtain pardons, he was also attempting to use the situation to convince the president to implement a wholesale reform of the Indian System. The bishop promoted memorials and petitions, one of which was signed by the Episcopal bishops and delivered by Senator Rice to Lincoln on 26 November. Rice had a "long interview" with the president that day. The executions, Indian System reform, and the intrigues of Minnesota congressmen were integral to that discussion. Rice made a hopeful report to Whipple.[29]

The Minnesotans favoring executions skillfully coordinated their efforts. Ramsey and Pope met regularly in late November. On 28 November, Ramsey wired Lincoln, "Nothing but the speedy execution of the tried and convicted Sioux Indians will save us from scenes of outrage." He also offered Lincoln the escape from

28. Pope to Lincoln, 24 November 1862, Lincoln Papers, Minnesota Historical Society, also found in *Minnesota,* 2:290; Sibley to Elliott, 6, 8 December 1862, *Minnesota,* 2:290–91.

29. Episcopal Bishops to Lincoln, 20 November 1862, Roll 44, Lincoln Papers, LC; Rice to Lincoln, 26 November 1862, Roll 44, Lincoln Papers, LC, also found in Box 3, Whipple Papers; Rice to Whipple, 27 November 1862, Box 3, Whipple Papers.

responsibility that Pope had proposed earlier, "If you prefer it turn them over to me & I will order their execution."[30]

That same day, Sen. Morton S. Wilkinson and Congressman Cyrus Aldrich met with Lincoln with the executions the topic of discussion. The president promised to report a decision after he delivered his annual message to Congress on 1 December. The Minnesotans left nothing to chance. 1 December was the day that Congressman William Windom of Minnesota introduced a resolution, quickly passed, to have the Committee on Indian Affairs investigate the "mode" of removing all the Indians from the state of Minnesota.[31]

The execution problem haunted Lincoln. He made the necessary bow in his annual message, telling Congress, "The State of Minnesota has suffered great injury from this Indian war." He reported on the number killed and on the atrocities. He noted that Minnesotans wanted the Indians removed from the state, although he made no clear recommendation. Lincoln even raised "for your especial consideration" the idea of remodeling the Indian System—an apparent victory for Bishop Whipple. But he said not one word about the proposed executions.[32]

Everyone was puzzled at the president's silence, and he hadn't satisfied either side of the controversy. Joseph Scattergood wired Commissioner Dole on behalf of Philadelphia Quakers: "Has the President revoked the sentence of the Court Martial upon the three hundred Minnesota Indians?" Other Quaker groups presented memorials. Bishop Whipple may have suspected things were about to break. He cautioned Senator Rice "not to add to the excitement especially as the President has not as yet definitely acted."[33]

30. They met on both 21 and 22 November; Ramsey recorded that Pope had left town on 23 November, implying another meeting or communication, Ramsey Diary, Roll 39, vol. 36, Ramsey Papers; Ramsey to Lincoln, 28 November 1862, Roll 44, Lincoln Papers, LC.

31. New York *Tribune*, 29 November 1862, reprinted in Basler, ed., *Collected Works*, 5:493; U.S., Congress, House, *Congressional Globe*, 37th Cong., 3d sess., 1 December 1862, pt. 1:3.

32. LAM, 1862, p. 2.

33. Joseph Scattergood to William P. Dole, Thomas Evans to Dole, 1 December 1862, Roll 599, M234, LR, Northern Superintendency, OIA, RG75, NA; Rice to Whipple, 4 December 1862, Box 3, Whipple Papers.

Lincoln was not just being coy. He gave every sign of being a troubled man. On 1 December, the date of his annual message, he sought legal advice from Judge Advocate General Joseph Holt, "I wish your legal opinion whether if I should conclude to execute only a part of them, I must myself designate which, or could I leave the designation to some officer on the ground?" Was Lincoln considering the Pope-Ramsey proposition for shifting the responsibility? Lincoln's use of the word *designate* was significant. His lawyers had gone over the trial transcripts and had some information as to the degrees of guilt. Lincoln apparently believed that the situation demanded a blood sacrifice if emotions were to be calmed. Yet he was considering leaving to local authorities the responsibility of designating who would die. Judge Holt, however, gave Lincoln no option, "The power cannot be delegated."[34]

Lincoln moved reluctantly toward a decision. Gideon Welles said the president had made up his mind by 4 December, "The members of Congress from Minnesota are urging the President vehemently to give his assent to the execution of three hundred Indian captives, but they will not succeed." Lincoln had chosen the middle road. He was going to sanction the execution of thirty-nine of the three hundred and three condemned prisoners. Welles reflected the president's exasperation:

> When the intelligent Representatives of a State can deliberately besiege the Government to take the lives of these ignorant barbarians by wholesale, it would seem the sentiments of the Representatives were but slightly removed from the barbarians they would execute. The Minnesotians are greatly exasperated and threaten the Administration if it show clemency.[35]

Welles was correct. Minnesota's congressmen were threatining because they had heard that Lincoln had decided "to pardon or reprieve a large majority of the Indians in Minnesota who have been formally condemned for their participation in the brutal massacre

34. Lincoln to Joseph Holt, 1 December 1862, Basler, ed., *Collected Works,* 5:537–38; Holt to Lincoln, 1 December 1862, Roll 44, Lincoln Papers, LC.
35. Welles Diary, 4 December 1862, Beale, ed., *Gideon Welles Diary,* p. 186.

of our people." Wilkinson and Aldrich made one last desperate attempt to reverse the decision. They angrily wrote the president, "We *protest against the pardon* of these Indians." They again warned that if the president did not execute the prisoners, Minnesotans would do it themselves.[36]

Morton Wilkinson was probably the author of that letter. It bore a remarkable resemblance to a speech he made on the floor of the Senate on 5 December.[37] There the private threats were converted into legislative rhetoric and action. Wilkinson introduced a resolution demanding that the president of the United States account to the Senate concerning the Minnesota war and the projected execution of the Sioux prisoners. Since Lincoln had not publicly announced his decision, Wilkinson apparently hoped that senatorial pressure might still change his mind.

Wilkinson launched into a speech punctuated with some of the same tales of atrocity that had been recited in his letter to Lincoln. He spoke with disdain of the Quakers who urged mercy for Indians and worried aloud over committees visiting the president seeking clemency for the condemned. Wilkinson told the Senate he was fearful that such people "have so wrought upon the President as to shake his purposes and render him doubtful as to what he ought to do." Wilkinson's speech left the president an opening to change his mind. His private letter had protested what he already believed to be a decision. His public oration referred only to a "doubtful" president.

The Minnesota senator spared no rhetorical device as he described innocent farmers slain in their fields by Indians.

> They then went, from the murdered bodies of the men, into the houses where the women and children were; they murdered the little children, and they took the mothers and daughters into captivity.

36. Morton Wilkinson and Cyrus B. Aldrich to Lincoln, [?] December 1862, Reserve Item, Edward Duffield Neill Papers, also found in *Senate Executive Document 7*, pp. 2–4.

37. U.S., Congress, Senate, *Congressional Globe*, 37th Cong., 3d sess., 5 December 1862, pt. 1:13.

As one who had been on the scene, Wilkinson could cloak his allegations in apparent authenticity. "I wish to state a few facts," he said, and he described to the Senate the details of the rape of a thirteen-year-old girl. The senator excoriated the military trials, contending that Colonel Sibley "ought to have killed every one of the Indians as he came to them."

Wilkinson capped his argument by repeating the warnings of Ramsey and Pope—the threat of mob action.

> The result will be this: either the Indians must be punished according to law, or they will be murdered without law. The people of Minnesota will never consent that they shall be turned loose in their midst. They have always been a law-abiding, law-loving, law-respecting people. I want the people of my state to be so still; but, sir, I tremble at the result; I dread the consequences in that state of turning these murderers, these violaters of our women, loose among our people. The matter is in the hands of the President of the United States, and it is for him to say whether our people shall be protected under the forms of law, or whether they must without law protect themselves.

Wilkinson made plain his own sentiment, "I could not stop it if I wished to do so." The Wilkinson resolution passed the Senate.

Rumors of possible leniency were met with protest in Minnesota as well as in Washington. Citizens of St. Paul petitioned the president, saying they had heard "with fear and alarm . . . reports of an intention on the part of the United States government to dismiss without punishment the Sioux warriors captured by our soldiers; and further, to allow the several tribes of Indians lately located upon reservations within this State to remain upon the reservations." The petitioners told the president, "Against any such policy we respectfully but firmly protest."[38]

Other Minnesotans were not so respectful. At 4:00 A.M. on 6 December 1862, Governor Ramsey was roused from his sleep with a report from Sibley that citizens had attempted to attack the Indian prisoners being held at Mankato. Ramsey immediately

38. Memorial to Lincoln, n.d., *Senate Executive Document 7*, p. 5.

issued a proclamation ostensibly designed to temper lynch-mob emotions and pleading with his people to obey the law and abstain from violence.[39]

Ramsey also used the proclamation to pressure Lincoln. He proclaimed, "Our people indeed have had just reason to complain, of the tardiness of executive action." In addition, he promised his constituents that Lincoln would go ahead and execute the condemned Sioux. Although Ramsey may not have known of Lincoln's decision to drastically limit the number of hangings, it is also possible that he lied when he claimed that "the Agent sent out by the Government gave the assurance upon his departure that he would spare no effort to procure an order to that effect." Ramsey apparently referred to John Usher as the "agent" sent by Lincoln. Usher did make some promises, but there is no evidence that he made one like that. The governor continued, "No official intimation has been received that the President contemplates any other course." Ramsey's language was carefully chosen. By 6 December, he may not have had official notice, but he probably had heard the same unofficial message that had led to Morton Wilkinson's speech the day previous. The governor was trying to put Lincoln on the spot. Thanks to Ramsey's fallacious claims, Minnesotans would think Lincoln had gone back on his word.

Ramsey's proclamation warned:

> Whatever may be the decision of the President it cannot deprive the people of Minnesota of their right to justice or exempt the guilty Indians from the doom they have incurred under our local laws. If he should decline to punish them the case will then clearly come within the jurisdiction of our civil courts. In a month the State Legislature will assemble and to them it may be safely left to provide for the emergency.[40]

Ramsey wasted his words. Lincoln had accepted the challenge, because that same day, the president forwarded to Sibley the list

---

39. Ramsey Diary, 6 December 1862, Roll 39, vol. 36, Ramsey Papers; Proclamation of 6 December 1862, Roll 45, Lincoln Papers, LC.

40. Proclamation of 6 December 1862, Roll 45, Lincoln Papers, LC.

of names of the thirty-nine men from the original three hundred and three that were to be executed.[41]

Lincoln's defense of his decision was typically pragmatic. On 11 December, he responded to Wilkinson's Senate resolution in measured tones. He said he had listened to various opinions, sent for the records, and had them studied carefully. He made a special bow to the protest letter from the Minnesota congressmen and enclosed a copy for the senators to read. One statement of the president's response denoted the tightrope Lincoln had attempted to walk between the poles of opinion:

> Anxious to not act with so much clemency as to encourage another outbreak on one hand, nor with so much severity as to be real cruelty on the other, I ordered a careful examination of the records of the trials to be made, in view of first ordering the execution of such as had been proved guilty of violating females.

In one statement, Lincoln had appeased almost everyone. The president found the records designated only two Indians guilty of rape. He had further attempted to distinguish those who participated in "massacres" from those in "battles" (a discrimination suggested earlier by Riggs and Whipple) and thereby reduced the number of death sentences. The thirty-nine were to be executed on 19 December.[42]

Henry Sibley was humiliated over the reversal of his decisions. He predicted "a war of races which will extend along the whole frontier & be attended with an incalculable loss of human life." He believed the Indians "should all be hung as a great example which would strike terror into all Indians on the continent and save hundreds and perhaps thousands of lives." In January 1863, Sibley sent Lincoln more evidence, maintaining, "There are still on the list many who are even more guilty, than some of those who have been hung." Months later, Sibley was still trying to convince Lincoln to execute fifty more prisoners.[43]

41. Lincoln to Sibley, 6 December 1862, Basler, ed., *Collected Works,* 5:542–43.
42. Lincoln to the Senate, 11 December 1862, Basler, ed., *Collected Works,* 5:550–51.
43. Sibley to Whipple, 7 December 1862, Box 3, Whipple Papers; Sibley to John P. Usher, 19 December 1862, Roll 483, M619, LR, AGO, RG109, NA; Sibley

Lincoln was determined to conclude the matter of the executions. He also made sure that Sibley watched his step. He had John Nicolay notify Sibley concerning a Robert Hopkins (also known as Chas-kay-don), whose name was similar to one of the condemned, "The President desires to guard against his being executed by mistake before his case shall be finally determined." It was another way to remind Sibley to do his duty with care.[44]

On 10 December, John Usher was given the task of calming the disgruntled General Sibley. Usher told Sibley that the evidence presented during the trials had been unsatisfactory. He urged Sibley to explain to others "the difficulty in which the President is involved in this unlucky business." Usher called on Sibley to prevent violence. The balance of the letter dealt with another matter— how Lincoln would accommodate the Minnesotans if they cooperated with him.[45]

Trading Lives for Land and Money

The outlines of the bargain had been apparent for some time. Indian removal was its nucleus. Other facets included the disposition of the remaining prisoners, payment of the cost of the war, compensation for damages, and a key political appointment.

On 9 December, Senator Wilkinson reported to Governor Ramsey, "I have done all in my power to induce our President to have the law executed in regard to your condemned Indians." While only thirty-nine Indians were to be executed, the president had made some concessions. The prisoners not executed would not be released but would be held for further disposition. More important, "if the people be patient, we will be able . . . to dispose of those condemned, and will also succeed in removing the Sioux and Winnebago Indians from the State."[46]

---

to Lincoln, 7 January 1863, Roll 47, Lincoln Papers, LC; Sibley to Lincoln, 16 February 1863, Roll 49, Lincoln Papers, LC, also found in Lincoln Papers, Minnesota Historical Society.

44. John G. Nicolay to Sibley, 9 December 1862, Roll 96, Lincoln Papers, LC.
45. Usher to Sibley, 10 December 1862, Roll 4, M606, LS, ID, OSI, RG48, NA.
46. Wilkinson to Ramsey, 9 December 1862, *Minnesota*, 2:291.

Usher described the trade-off to Sibley in his 10 December letter. "The views which I expressed to you concerning the future disposition of the Indians of your State, seem to meet with reasonable approval here," meaning that Lincoln would cooperate in Indian removal. Moreover, Usher sweetened the proposition with the promise of a "reasonable compensation for the depredations committed." Sibley suggested $2 million as "reasonable."[47] Indian lives would be traded for land and money.

John Usher received his reward. Caleb Smith retired as secretary of the interior, and Minnesotans Henry M. Rice, Cyrus Aldrich, and William Windom all promoted Usher for that job. Rice's letter to Lincoln praised Usher for "the great judgement and skill exercised . . . in the judicious measures he has adopted and has in view in regard to the management of Indian Affairs in the North West." Minnesotans knew where their interests lay. As Rice put it in his recommendation, "The people of that vast region [are] more dependent upon the action of that Department than any other of the Government." They would feel safe with John Usher in the secretary's chair and, by January, Usher had the job.[48]

Despite the concessions Lincoln granted Minnesotans, his actions on the executions were politically dangerous. The situation had arisen simultaneously with the Radical Republicans' campaign to unseat Secretary of State William Seward. Historians have traditionally focused on the Republican caucuses of 16–17 December 1862, at which Seward was the major topic of conversation. At the 16 December meeting, Morton Wilkinson harangued his colleagues about "a cause lost" and "the country ruined." Wilkinson was talking about Seward but the secretary of state was not the only thing on his mind that day.[49]

47. Usher to Sibley, 10 December 1862, Roll 4, M606, LS, ID, OSI, RG48, NA; Sibley to Usher, 19 December 1862, Roll 483, M619, LR, AGO, RG109, NA.

48. Rice to Wilkinson, 10 December 1862, Roll 45, Lincoln Papers, LC; Windom and Aldrich to Lincoln, n.d., Usher to Windom, 18 December 1862, Smith to Usher, 6 January 1863, all John P. Usher Papers.

49. Browning Diary, 16 December 1862, James G. Randall and Theodore C. Pease, eds., *The Diary of Orville Hickman Browning*, p. 597; T. Harry Williams, *Lincoln and the Radicals*, pp. 208–9.

It was also a key day for the consummation of the bargain between the government and the Minnesotans. That day, Morton Wilkinson took the floor of the Senate to introduce a bill to compensate Minnesotans for losses in the Indian war—a bill that, by the time it was passed, carried a $1.5 million price tag. Wilkinson also introduced bills to remove the Sioux and Winnebagos from Minnesota. Simultaneously, Aldrich and Windom introduced similar bills in the House. On 18 December, Aldrich produced a bill to indemnify the state for its expenses in the Indian war. The bargain was being acted out in the Congress.[50]

Caleb Smith also confirmed the details of the bargain in a letter to Cyrus Aldrich dated 16 December.[51] As the legislative bills already reflected, one tribe would not be moved—the Chippewas. Smith's stated reason was that the Chippewas did not live close to whites. That tribe had long been a special interest of Bishop Whipple, and it is reasonable to surmise that this was a concession to the eloquent churchman. The following year, the bishop was placed on a board of visitors to supervise the implementation of a new treaty for the Chippewas.[52] In this Lincoln bargain, there was a little something for everyone.

The government needed no special rationale for moving the Sioux, due to their primary role in the war. The Winnebagos were another matter. Caleb Smith admitted, "The Winnebagoes are without fault sufficient to justify any substantial complaint." However, whites hated them simply because they were Indians, so they would have to be removed for their own protection. Smith did not foresee that the removal would leave the Winnebagos destitute. In any event, he intended to give them no voice in the matter: "The treaty of April 15, 1859, provides that former treaties may be modified and changed by the President with the assent of Congress." That loophole made negotiation unnecessary, and the Win-

50. U.S., Congress, Senate, *Congressional Globe*, 37th Cong., 3d sess., 16 December 1862, pt. 1:100; Thompson to Dole, 20 January 1863, Roll 764, M234, LR, St. Peter Agency, OIA, RG75, NA; U.S., Congress, House, *Congressional Globe*, 37th Cong., 3d sess., 16 December 1862, pt. 1:104, 130.

51. Smith to Aldrich, 16 December 1862, Roll 4, M606, LS, ID, OSI, RG48, NA.

52. Usher to Whipple, 9 May 1863, Box 3, Whipple Papers.

nebagos and the Sioux could be summarily removed from the state of Minnesota.[53] These arrangements soothed the Minnesotans. The day after Christmas, Morton Wilkinson informed Governor Ramsey, "Our Indian matters look well."[54]

On 15 January 1863, Ramsey defeated Aldrich for the Senate seat. Ramsey's Indian policies had been politically productive. He was, as one newspaper put it, "one of the men on whom the country in her darkest hours can rely with the most unflinching confidence." Through Ramsey's efforts, the state was able to present a bill of $350,000 for the cost of the war to Minnesota. On 16 February 1865, Congress passed a relief act to indemnify those who had suffered losses during the war.[55] Indian money continued to flow to Minnesota.

The Executions

The time drew near for the executions. General Sibley begged Lincoln for an extension beyond 19 December to prepare for possible lynch mobs. "Combinations exist embracing thousands of citizens pledged to execute all the Indians," he warned. Lincoln granted a one-week extension, to 26 December.[56]

For the thirty-nine, the time grew short. One clergyman appealed to Sibley to tell the men their fate and let them make their peace with their maker.[57] Sibley instructed his chaplain, Stephen Riggs, to inform the men:

> Their Great Father in Washington, after carefully reading what the witnesses testified to in their several trials, has come to the conclusion that they have each been guilty of wantonly and wickedly murdering his white children. And for this reason he has directed

53. Smith to Aldrich, 16 December 1862, Roll 4, M606, LS, ID, OSI, RG48, NA.
54. Wilkinson to Ramsey, 26 December 1862, Roll 13, Ramsey Papers.
55. Ramsey to Rice, 19 January 1863, Roll 14, Ramsey Papers; Rice to the Secretary of the Interior, 5 June 1863, Roll 21, M825, LR, ID, OSI, RG48, NA.
56. Sibley to Lincoln, 15 December 1862, Roll 45, Lincoln Papers, LC; Lincoln to Sibley, 16 December 1862, Basler, ed., *Collected Works*, 6:6.
57. Ravoux to Sibley, 17 December 1862, Roll 483, M619, LR, AGO, RG109, NA.

that they each be hanged by the neck until they are dead, on next Friday; and that order will be carried into effect on that day, at ten o'clock in the forenoon.

Riggs then urged the men to appeal to the Prince of Peace for mercy—a mercy they were not to receive from the United States Government at Christmastime.[58]

On 26 December, the condemned Indians were executed. At the last moment, one more man was pardoned. Sibley telegraphed Lincoln: "I have the honor to inform you that 38 Indians and half-breeds ordered by you for execution were hung yesterday at Mankato, at 10 A.M. Everything went off quietly and the other prisoners are well secured." A large crowd had been present, but there was no violence. Evidence later indicated that a prisoner who was not among the condemned had been executed by mistake.[59]

Arguments have raged since as to whether Lincoln acted humanely or whether he could have prevented bloodshed altogether. Those favoring the humanity of the decision can argue that Lincoln acted in an atmosphere of hatefulness. Without him, all of the three hundred three probably would have been executed. On the other hand, Lincoln still ordered the largest official mass execution in American history in which guilt of the executed cannot be positively determined. He also acquiesced in concessions to Minnesotans that resulted in further injustice to the Indians. Nevertheless, viewed in context, Lincoln's actions were relatively humanitarian. By the time the problem reached Lincoln's desk, no ideal decision was possible. Given the demands of the War for the Union, there may have been very little else he could do.

Following the 1864 election, Sen. Alexander Ramsey visited the White House and talked politics with Lincoln. The president noted that he carried Minnesota only by seven thousand votes

58. Sibley [?] to Riggs, [?] December 1862, ibid.
59. Sibley to B. O. Selfridge, 27 December 1862, Roll 483, M619, LR, AGO, RG109, NA; Whipple to Sibley, 7 March 1863, Box 40, Letterbook 3, Whipple Papers.

compared to ten thousand in 1860. Ramsey replied "that if he had hung more Indians, we should have given him his old majority." Lincoln failed to appreciate the humor of the remark. "I could not afford to hang men for votes," he said.[60]

60. Ramsey Diary, 23 November 1864, Roll 39, vol. 36, Ramsey Papers, also in Abraham Lincoln Collection, Blue Earth County Historical Society.

IX. Lincoln and Removal
"A Disagreeable Subject"

LINCOLN WANTED TO FORGET the whole affair in Minnesota, just as he had forgotten the refugees in Kansas. In March 1863, Alexander Ramsey asked Lincoln about the Indian prisoners he had not hung. Lincoln "said it was a disagreeable subject but he would take it up and dispose of it."[1] Lincoln's reluctance to finish the matter had already resulted in many deaths from disease and starvation among the men, women, and children still confined in Minnesota prison camps.

Money and Military Action

Part of the unfinished business had to do with the claims for damages by Minnesota citizens. A commission was set up in response to legislation passed by the Congress on 16 February 1863. In March, the secretary of the interior reported that $1,370,374 had been paid out in relief and damage claims. Traders and merchants received $208,000 of that amount. Much of this money was undoubtedly for reparations. However, the claim judgments were made in great haste. Although John Usher admitted that many claims were difficult to evaluate, he wanted the benefit of the doubt given to claimants. As a result, Minnesota received a massive infusion of federal money.[2]

Another problem concerned subsequent military actions against the Indians. In some respects, the war of 1862 merged into the wars with plains Indians in the 1860s and 1870s. The region was

1. Ramsey Diary, 25 March 1863, Roll 39, vol. 36, Alexander Ramsey Papers.
2. John P. Usher to the Speaker of the House, *House Executive Document 58.*

the scene of almost continual guerrilla warfare. A sizable military force was kept in Minnesota for the winter of 1862. In early 1863, a new expedition was launched on what can be described in modern terms as a "search and destroy" mission. It had two prongs, one commanded by Henry Sibley in Minnesota and the other by Gen. Alfred Sully, who moved out from Sioux City.

Little Crow, leader of the insurrection, was scalped and mutilated on 3 July 1863. The expeditions chased the retreating Indians into Dakota Territory, the scene of most of the warfare during 1863. The military claimed that eight thousand to ten thousand Indians were driven out of Minnesota. Sibley boasted to Bishop Whipple, "The Indians have been badly beaten, demoralized, and have sent me messages desiring peace on any terms."[3]

Even that was not enough for the Minnesotans. Expeditions were sent out in 1864, 1865, and 1866. The 1864 expedition pursued Indians beyond the Missouri River as far west as the Yellowstone River. The Indians, whatever their tribe, could find no resting place.[4] These expeditions were hardly justifiable militarily. Their aim was to destroy as many Indians as possible, regardless of their misdeeds or origins.

These missions were clearly sanctioned by the United States Government. Alexander Ramsey noted in his diary that he visited with General Halleck "in reference to Sully & Indian campaign."[5] There can be no doubt that Lincoln knew about and permitted the expeditions. Ramsey personally sought Lincoln's permission to let troops cross the Canadian border in pursuit of retreating tribesmen. Lincoln and Seward even asked the British government for authority to cross the border.[6]

3. *Minnesota in the Indian and Civil Wars*, 1:748–52; Kenneth Carley, *The Sioux of 1862*, p. 70; Henry H. Sibley to Henry Benjamin Whipple, 13 October 1863, Box 3, Henry Benjamin Whipple Papers.

4. *Minnesota*, 1:753.

5. Ramsey Diary, 13 January 1864, Roll 39, vol. 36, Ramsey Papers.

6. Alexander Ramsey to Abraham Lincoln, 22 May 1863, Roll 53, Abraham Lincoln Papers, LC, a copy is available at the Minnesota Historical Society; Lincoln to the Senate, 29 January 1864, Roy P. Basler, ed., *The Collected Works of Abraham Lincoln*, 7:160.

The Winnebago Removal

The Winnebagos had not been involved in the 1862 war. Thus, they demonstrate the impact of Lincolnian policies most vividly. Minnesotans wanted to be rid of the Winnebagos because they wanted Winnebago land and simply because they were Indians. Morton Wilkinson called for removal, "Humanity requires it; the welfare of the Indians as well as the peace of the whites demand it." By 21 February 1863, the Winnebago removal bill passed both houses of Congress.[7]

By late June 1863, nearly two thousand Winnebagos had been shipped from their homes and growing crops to Crow Creek in Dakota Territory. The Winnebagos protested this injustice, but they had no choice. Tribal leaders bowed to the inevitable and told Lincoln, "The Winnebagoes now, as ever heretofore, are willing to obey the commands of their Great Father the President, and anxious to please him in every way possible."[8]

The indignities were only beginning for the Winnebagos. The removal trip was a miserable affair. John Williamson, the son of missionary Thomas Williamson, described the conditions on the boats. They were overcrowded, women and children were dying, and there was no doctor or medicine available. Williamson reported that twenty-four Winnebagos died en route to Dakota.[9]

On arrival at Crow Creek, the Winnebagos discovered they had given up good land for inferior soil. Williamson observed, "I think the land is too barren." General Sully complained to the secretary of the interior:

7. Petition for Winnebago Removal (quoting a letter from Morton Wilkinson to Judge Cleveland), 21 January 1863, Roll 936, M234, LR, Winnebago Agency, OIA, RG75, NA; U.S., Congress, Senate, *Congressional Globe*, 37th Cong., 3d sess., 11 February 1863, pt. 1:868 (for "Abbreviations in Footnotes," see p. vi).

8. Edmund Danziger, "Indians and Bureaucrats: Administering the Reserve Policy during the Civil War" (Ph.D. diss.), p. 153; Winnebago Chiefs to Lincoln, contained in a letter from Sibley to R. O. Gelfridge, 23 May 1863, Roll 936, M234, LR, Winnebago Agency, OIA, RG75, NA.

9. John Williamson to Thomas S. Williamson, 25 May, 3 June 1863, Roll 1, Thomas S. Williamson Papers.

The land is poor, a low sandy soil. I don't think you can depend on a crop of corn even once in five years, as it seldom rains here in the summer. There is no hunting in the immediate vicinity, and the bands of Sioux near here are hostile to them.[10]

The Winnebagos had to cope not only with their natural surroundings but also with the profiteers of the Indian System. Because they could not be self-sufficient with farming, they depended upon the usual government contracts for goods and services. By 9 June, predating the Winnebagos' arrival at Crow Creek, Williamson reported an incredible situation in the Winnebago camp. There were thirteen hundred Indians, only one hundred and sixteen of whom were males fifteen years or older. Camped around them were nearly six hundred white people. Why were they there? Williamson said, "They all live one way or another from the Governmental appointments."[11]

Finally, the Winnebagos endured military brutality. Williamson found that the soldiers were "a very reckless sort of people." An example concerned a stolen horse. The soldiers rode out to find the thief and killed seven Indians without knowledge of their guilt or innocence. According to Williamson, "The general order over here is to take no prisoners."[12]

Gen. Alfred Sully was no Indian sympathizer; he had led some of the bloodiest expeditions against them. Nevertheless, the situation of the Winnebagos moved this hardened soldier. Sully protested to his superiors, "I feel it to be my duty as a Christian and a human being to make known the sufferings of these poor human beings, though they are only Indians." Sully was outraged at the secretary of the interior, who instructed him to furnish troops to protect the Winnebagos when they hunted buffalo. The trouble was that the Winnebagos had no horses. "*Afoot* it is impossible to hunt buffalo," the general stormed.[13]

10. Alfred Sully to the Secretary of the Interior, 16 July 1863, Roll 599, M234, LR, Northern Superintendency, OIA, RG75, NA.

11. J. Williamson to T. Williamson, 9 June 1863, Roll 1, Williamson Papers.

12. J. Williamson to T. Williamson, 18 June 1863, ibid.

13. Sully to J. F. Heline, 21 November 1863, Roll 499, M234, LR, Northern Superintendency, OIA, RG75, NA.

In the meantime, Minnesotans were quite satisfied to divide the spoils of the Indian removal. The government appointed Morton Wilkinson to make the arrangements for distributing Winnebago land. Wilkinson nominated the appraisers and John Usher continued his happy relationship with the senator by summarily approving those nominations. Among the firms authorized to finance the land sales was Thompson Brothers of St. Paul, Clark Thompson's old firm. Wilkinson supervised everything, including advertising. Lincoln placed his official approval on the whole transaction. On 23 August 1864, Lincoln signed the order for sale of fifty-four thousand acres of Winnebago land.[14]

The Sioux Prisoners

The Winnebagos suffered in removal, but the Sioux situation was worse. Among the concessions Lincoln had granted to the Minnesotans was the continued incarceration of the remaining prisoners. This left 329 prisoners at Mankato, including 49 acquitted in the military trials but, for some reason, never released. The circumstances of these prisoners were miserable.[15]

Missionaries protested to Lincoln concerning the condition of the prisoners. Henry Sibley denied their claims and urged Lincoln to execute fifty more of the men. This is the "disagreeable subject" Senator Ramsey brought up with Lincoln in March 1863.[16] Bishop Whipple heard of this and wrote an angry letter to Sibley, "Your official report to Genl Pope states explicitly that these men came

14. William P. Dole to Wilkinson, 13 June 1863, Roll 71, M21, LS, OIA, RG75, NA; Wilkinson to Usher, 25 September 1863, Roll 936, M234, LR, Winnebago Agency, OIA, RG75, NA; Dole to Thompson Brothers, 13 July 1864, Roll 74, M21, LR, OIA, RG75, NA; Wilkinson to Dole, 27 July 1864, Roll 937, M234, LR, Winnebago Agency, OIA, RG75, NA; Dole to Wilkinson, 9 August 1864, Roll 74, M21, LS, OIA, RG75, NA; Order for Sale of Land by the President, 23 August 1864, Basler, ed., *Collected Works,* 7:515.

15. Wilkinson to Ramsey, 9 December 1862, *Minnesota,* 2:291; I. R. Brown and G. D. Redfield to Sibley (Sibley enclosure to Lincoln), 7 January 1863, Roll 47, Lincoln Papers, LC.

16. Ramsey Diary, 25 March 1863, Roll 39, vol. 36, Ramsey Papers; Sibley to Lincoln, 16 February 1863, Roll 49, Lincoln Papers, LC, also found in the Abraham Lincoln Papers, Minnesota Historical Society.

to you under a flag of truce." "Officers have told me privately that the trial was conducted with such haste as to forbid all justice," he continued. The bishop confronted the general with evidence that one innocent man had been executed by mistake on 26 December. "The civilized world cannot justify the trial by a military commission of men who voluntarily came in under a flag of truce," Whipple angrily proclaimed. Sibley denied the charges and lied, "There were no such flags, strictly speaking, used." Sibley was unrepentant, "If I had not received the Presidents orders to the contrary, I should have executed these Indians as fast as convicted."[17]

Lincoln refused to execute more Indians. He did, however, make one more concession to the Minnesotans. Sibley pleaded with him, "I beg of you, Mr. President, to issue immediate instructions to have those of the condemned men who are not to be capitally punished, removed without delay from the state." Lincoln ordered the prisoners taken to Davenport, Iowa.[18]

Bishop Whipple attempted to get something done for the prisoners in Davenport. Whipple told Usher, "To incarcerate them in an ordinary prison under restraints of solitary confinement must end in early death." The bishop said that two hundred had learned to read while in prison, and he urged that a reform school be established to prepare them for their eventual release.[19] However, the bishop had little influence with the secretary of the interior.

Thomas Williamson also pressed Lincoln concerning the prisoners. One of his letters was endorsed by George E. H. Day, the investigator who had warned Lincoln of Minnesota's corruption in 1861. Fifteen of the prisoners had died in prison at Mankato. By April 1864, fifty-two more died—more than had died on the gallows.[20]

17. Whipple to Sibley, 7 March 1863, Box 40, Sibley to Whipple, 11 March 1863, Box 3, Letterbook 3, Whipple Papers.

18. Sibley to Lincoln, 16 February 1863, Roll 49, Lincoln Papers, LC.

19. Whipple to Usher, 21 April 1863, Box 40, Letterbook 3, Whipple Papers.

20. T. Williamson to Dole, 3 June 1863, Roll 153, M234, LR, Chippewa Agency, OIA, RG75, NA; Williamson to Lincoln, and Day to Lincoln, 27 April 1864, Roll 73, Lincoln Papers, LC, copy in the Lincoln Papers, Minnesota Historical Society.

Williamson went to Washington to see Lincoln about a partial remedy—the release of the prisoners who had never been pronounced guilty. These men had surrendered to Sibley in order to save their families and had been thrown into jail. Commissioner Dole concurred in the need to release them. He calmed Lincoln's fears, "I do not think any injury will accrue to the white people if you should exercise the pardoning power in favor of a portion of their people."[21] On 30 April, Lincoln pardoned twenty-five men. He ordered the release of one more prisoner, Big Eagle, on 26 October. Four weeks later, Lincoln discovered his order had not been carried out, and he ordered again: "Let the Indian Big Eagle be discharged. I ordered this some time ago."[22]

Lincoln never released the rest of the prisoners. In July 1865 (following his death), pleas were still being made to the government on behalf of the prisoners at Davenport.[23]

The Sioux Removal

The prisoners were only part of the Sioux story. There were hundreds more who surrendered to Sibley, mostly women, children, and the elderly. Government officials seemed to ignore the existence of Indian families. Policy was made almost entirely in terms of Indian males. Yet, much of the postwar misery fell on the women and children, and Lincoln knew this. Sibley reported to him on 16 February 1863 that he had in custody sixteen hundred men, women, and children, "mostly the two latter."[24] Their conditions were little better than the prisoners. Bishop Whipple told his wife:

> You have no idea of the very wretched condition of those poor creatures at Fort Snelling. I suppose not less than 300 will die be-

21. Dole to Lincoln, 28 April 1864, Roll 73, Lincoln Papers, LC.
22. Edward Duffield Neill to Minnie Neill, 30 April 1864, Box 2, Edward Duffield Neill Papers; Lincoln's Order for Pardon, 30 April 1864, 7:325–26, Lincoln to the Officer in Command at Davenport, Iowa, 26 October 1864, 8:76, Lincoln to the Commanding Officer, 19 November 1864, 8:116, all Basler, ed., *Collected Works*.
23. H. Price to Edwin M. Stanton, 8 July 1865, Roll 483, M619, LR, AGO, RG109, NA.
24. Sibley to Lincoln, 16 February 1863, Roll 49, Lincoln Papers, LC.

fore Spring. The measles & pneumonia are doing a fearful work of death.[25]

In April 1863, Clark Thompson supervised the removal of the Indians from Minnesota, with the help of the inevitable contractors who profited from removals. Like the Winnebagos, by the time the Sioux arrived in their new homes on the Upper Missouri, they were starving and it was too late to raise crops.[26] S. D. Hinman told Bishop Whipple that the land was "parched with drought" and that the Indians had "neither guns nor horses" to hunt game. Hinman predicted the demise of the Sioux as a people, "These here will diminish by death and intermarriage with the Winnebagoes and Yanktons." The missionary was bitter at what he witnessed: "Bishop, If I were an Ind. I would never lay-down the war-club while I lived. They are right, to be savages is the only hope of the Indian."[27]

Clark Thompson reported in September 1863 that he had one month's provisions left and had been able to find little food or game.[28] Hinman told a different story. The real problem was the corruption of Indian officials. "This is the place chosen where Col. Thompson and parties at Washington may make their last and best effort to repair their fortunes," he informed Bishop Whipple. One hundred tons of freight had been ordered but only fifty arrived. Hinman hinted that some had been stolen en route. He was appalled, "The swindle is an awful one because it is now causing so many innocent and helpless people to suffer."[29]

Whipple wrote Commissioner Dole that the Sioux were "in a starving condition." He flattered the commissioner, saying, "I know you have a kind heart."

25. Whipple to Mrs. Whipple, 13 January 1863, Box 40, Letterbook 4, Whipple Papers.

26. Clark W. Thompson to Barton Able, 14 April 1863, Roll 599, M234, LR, Northern Superintendency, OIA, RG75, NA.

27. S. D. Hinman to Whipple, 8 June 1863, Box 3, Whipple Papers.

28. Thompson to Charles E. Mix, 15 September 1863, Roll 599, M234, LR, Northern Superintendency, OIA, RG75, NA.

29. Hinman to Whipple, 6 January 1864, Box 3, Whipple Papers.

I know no man could have made the plea you did for those who are condemned unless you loved justice. These men are free from crime. They are Christians. They were tried and proved innocent.[30]

Dole told the bishop that he was mistaken, "My information from the Supt. & agents goes to show that while the means at their disposal is very limited, yet they have been able to keep them from suffering."[31] After three years of bitter experience, Dole continued to rely on the testimony of his corrupt subordinates in Minnesota. In June 1864, Congress was still arguing over the funds to be appropriated for subsistence rations for the Santee Sioux.[32]

In Minnesota, however, on 31 March, Dole granted Morton Wilkinson's request that the Sioux reservation be opened for settlement.[33] The white men could move in and the Sioux could be forgotten.

Lincoln and the Minnesota Indians

How can Lincoln's actions in Minnesota be evaluated? In his favor, it is clear that many more men would have been executed without his intervention—probably all 303 condemned prisoners. His humaneness in this must be matched against what he did (or failed to do) following the executions. He made a bargain permitting the removal of tribes from Minnesota, even the innocent Winnebagos. He ordered the permanent incarceration of the pardoned in conditions that led to more deaths than the hangings. His policies left the removed tribes in destitution, partly because of the corruption and mismanagement of officials in the Indian System. Lincoln sanctioned military missions designed to destroy as many Indians as possible in the region, and he acquiesced in sizable land grabs in Minnesota. He installed as secretary of

30. Whipple to Dole, 11 February 1864, Roll 153, M234, LR, Chippewa Agency, OIA, RG75, NA.

31. Dole to Whipple, 3 March 1864, Box 3, Whipple Papers.

32. U.S., Congress, Senate, *Congressional Globe*, 38th Cong., 1st sess., 10 June 1864, pt. 3:2846.

33. Dole to Wilkinson, 31 March 1864, Roll 73, M21, LS, OIA, RG75, NA.

the interior the man who cooperated so closely with the Minnesotans in all these matters.

Lincoln dealt more with the politics of the executions than the welfare of the Indians. This is not to say he did not agonize over the proposed bloodshed. He could have chosen to do nothing. Compared with many actors in the situation, his attitudes appear enlightened. But once the public outcry was over and the political threat was gone, Lincoln seemed to lose interest. It was a "disagreeable subject" he preferred to forget. Like the Kansas refugees, the Minnesota Indians were left to languish by a Lincoln who had other things on his mind.

X. The President and the Reformers "This Indian System Shall Be Reformed!"

1862 WAS A YEAR OF CRISIS for the Lincoln administration. The North was doing badly in the war with the South, and Lincoln was pressured into emancipating slaves and enlisting black troops. It was hardly an ideal time to push for reform of the Indian System.

However, a peculiar juxtaposition of events changed all that. Lincoln was forced to give attention to Indian affairs, because the difficulties with the Indians seemed to be linked to other problems. The Confederate alliances with the southern Indians and the refugee and expedition troubles in Kansas highlighted the bankruptcy of the Indian System. Then came the Minnesota war, fears of a conspiracy in Minnesota by Confederate infiltrators, and the executions. These dovetailed with Lincoln's problems in the South and demanded his personal attention.

Thus, for a brief moment, there was an opening for men who sought reform of the Indian System. When Indian affairs appeared to affect the national welfare and the course of the Civil War, even a president as preoccupied as Lincoln might be ready to listen to some new ideas.

The Commissioner and the Reformers

When the Lincoln era began, most government officials were not interested in reforming Indian affairs. The great cause of the time was abolitionism, and Lincoln's somewhat ambiguous resolution to that question was not reached until the end of his second year in office. The prospects were dim for Indian reform, even though some prominent abolitionists promoted it. William Lloyd Garrison, the arch-symbol of abolitionism, had written an editorial as early as 1829 denouncing the attempt to remove the Indians from the southeastern United States.[1]

John Beeson was another crusader who linked abolitionism and Indian reform. Beeson aided fugitive slaves in Lincoln's home state of Illinois. In the late 1850s, he migrated to Oregon and got involved in Indian causes. He was very nearly the victim of violence as a result of letters and pamphlets he wrote concerning the Rogue River war in 1856. In 1859, the reformer sponsored a meeting in Boston at which abolitionist Wendell Phillips spoke favoring Indian reform. Beeson briefly published a pro-Indian journal, *The Calumet,* but it was a financial failure.[2]

Not long after the Battle at Fort Sumter, Beeson paid a visit to the new commissioner of Indian affairs. Dole took an immediate dislike to the reformer, who attempted to obtain an appointment of special commissioner to the Indians from the commissioner. Dole's response was polite but icy, "Some of your plans are ahead of the age." Dole admitted that the Indian System was often "a legal machine to swindle the ignorant and helpless Indians out of their possessions," but he did not want John Beeson meddling with that mechanism. He told the reformer that the Indian Office already had too many employees and only needed ones that were more honest.[3]

Beeson was an evangelical reformer with scant appreciation for political and social realities. Dole patronized him as one who "fails to appreciate practically, the complicated subject of our relations with the Indian tribes." But the commissioner could not prevent Beeson from pestering everyone in Washington about Indian reform. In December 1861, Beeson petitioned the House Committee

1. Robert Mardock, *The Reformers and the American Indian,* p. 8.
2. Ibid., pp. 10–11.
3. William P. Dole to John Beeson, 3 May 1861, Roll 65, M21, LS, OIA, RG75, NA (for "Abbreviations in Footnotes," see p. vi).

on Indian Affairs for a "suspension of hostilities against the Indians generally."[4]

Dole's problems with reformers went deeper than irritation with fanatical crusaders. The commissioner profited from the very system they sought to transform. As a political appointee, he was distinctly uninterested in undoing the patronage process that had served him so well. There was an empty sound to his complaints during his first year about "liquor sellers" and "unprincipled traders." The commissioner professed to find this corruption overwhelming, "I know not what remedy to propose."[5]

Dole did adopt some reform ideas, including the notion of assigning farms to individual Indians. He noted with pride the "marked success" of severalty experiments in Minnesota, and he agreed with the reformers' argument that land should be allotted to Indians as distinct individuals. It "is the only plan yet devised by which the end we profess to see, viz., the elevation of the Indian as a race in the scale of social existence, can be secured," the commissioner wrote.[6]

Nevertheless, Dole was not a reformer. The policy he espoused most firmly was a policy to concentrate the Indian population in order to accommodate the continued exploitation of Indian lands. Concentration of Indian tribes was the inevitable outgrowth of the increase of white population and subsequent Indian removals. It was an updated removal policy, the logical next step when the continent no longer contained any great uninhabited regions. Reformers were not always comfortable with this policy, although some supported it as a necessary evil. Commissioner Dole had no such qualms. He always coupled the desire "to foster and protect our own settlements" with "the concentration of the Indians upon ample reservations."[7] With a man with this disposition in the commissioner's chair, it would take more than emotional pleas from reformers to move him and the president he served.

4. Dole to Cyrus B. Aldrich, 18 December 1861, Roll 67, M21, LS, OIA, RG75, NA.
5. AR, CIA, 1861, p. 633.
6. Ibid., p. 637.
7. Ibid., pp. 633, 647.

Bishop Whipple Begins His Campaign

The man best equipped to promote the cause coincidentally resided in Minnesota—notorious for its problems with Indians. Henry Benjamin Whipple, the Episcopal bishop of that state, dominated the Indian reform movement in the latter half of the nineteenth century. His appointment in 1859 brought him into direct conflict with the corrupt Indian System in Minnesota and he called at once for reform. In a letter to President Buchanan in 1860, he predicted a Sioux insurrection unless something were done to end the corruption. "A nation which sowed robbery would reap a harvest of blood," the bishop warned the president.[8]

After Lincoln was elected, Whipple determined to make a grand attempt to reform the Indian System. In spite of his Democratic sympathies, Whipple had hopes for the new regime. On 23 February 1861—days before Lincoln took the oath of office—he began his campaign. "I do hope the new administration will give them honest, manly men who have a heart to pity & a hand to help," the bishop wrote Senator Rice. Whipple urged Rice to attempt to influence patronage even though he was a Democrat. The same day he wrote Rice, Whipple corresponded with outgoing secretary of the treasury, John A. Dix. He asked Dix to endorse and pass along a letter to the new secretary of the interior.[9]

Whipple's plea to Caleb Smith was for a change in the method of selecting officials to the Indian service. He wanted "men of unswerving honesty" and urged the secretary to "let men who seek political rewards go somewhere else." It was too late. Lincoln was already busy doing just the opposite by allowing Republican congressmen to select the officials for their region.

Nevertheless, Whipple then turned his rhetoric on two of those appointees, Clark Thompson, the new superintendent of the Northern Superintendency, and Thomas Galbraith, agent to the Santee Sioux. The latter he lectured on "dishonest agents" and

8. Mardock, *The Reformers*, p. 10.
9. Henry Benjamin Whipple to Henry M. Rice, Whipple to John A. Dix, Whipple to the Secretary of the Interior, all 23 February 1861, Box 39, Letterbook 3, Henry Benjamin Whipple Papers.

"corrupt whites" and urged him to watch his step, "May I not believe your agents will be honest & pure men?"[10]

Bishop Whipple failed in his first attempt to influence the Lincoln administration. Lincoln's appointees were as corrupt and bungling as their predecessors, and they helped to bring about the war Whipple had predicted in 1860. It was not easy for the clergyman to continue his crusade. "I have been accused of neglecting my white field & wasting money on Indian missions," he lamented.[11]

Any small hope Whipple had for advancing the reform cause seemed to be destroyed by the outbreak of Civil War. By the time he mailed his letters to Thompson and Galbraith, the fighting at Fort Sumter had already begun. The bishop's attempt to reform the Indian System would have to wait for a more propitious moment.

Bishop Whipple Tries Again—with Lincoln

At the close of Lincoln's first year in office, the reform movement was going nowhere. In spite of Commissioner Dole's views, Lincoln had chosen no clear path in Indian policy. Lincoln tended to discuss Indians only in terms of their impact on the War for the Union.[12] On 6 March 1862, Bishop Henry Whipple set out to change that by writing directly to Abraham Lincoln.[13]

"Where shall a Christian Bishop look for justice if not to you whom God has made the Chief Ruler of the Nation," the bishop asked Lincoln. He told the president that Buchanan had ignored his earlier pleas, and he urged Lincoln to "so instruct the department that something like justice be done to a people whose cry calls for the vengeance of God."

10. Whipple to Clark W. Thompson, 14 April 1861, Whipple to Thomas Galbraith, 15 April 1861, ibid.

11. Whipple to R. M. Larned, 15 April 1861, ibid.

12. LAM, 1861, p. 22.

13. Whipple to Abraham Lincoln, 6 March 1862, Box 39, Letterbook 3, Whipple Papers, also found in Henry B. Whipple, *Lights and Shadows of a Long Episcopate*, pp. 510–14; Henry E. Fritz, *The Movement for Indian Assimilation, 1860–1890*, pp. 40–41.

Whipple went beyond exhortation and provided Lincoln with a cogent analysis of the problem and a clear program for action. Instead of criticizing the government for any malign intent, the bishop blamed the Indian System, with its "dishonest servants, ill conceived plans, and defective instructions." The Indians were degraded because the treaty system destroyed native governments and left Indians without protection. The corrupt patronage system used for selecting agents and the dishonesty of those officials were at the root of the problem.

Whipple believed change was possible. "The first thing needed is *honesty,*" he told Lincoln. Select agents on the basis of merit and character, not politics. Make Indians wards of the government and give them aid so they can build homes, begin farming, and adopt "civilized" life. Provide for the adequate education of every Indian child. Pay Indian annuities in goods, not cash, and thereby undercut dishonest traders. Finally, Whipple urged Lincoln to appoint a three-man commission to investigate Indian affairs and propose further reforms. These commissioners should be "men of inflexible integrity, of large heart, of clear head, of strong will, who fear God and love man." In short, the commission should be "above the reach of political demagogues."

Bishop Whipple proposed a root-and-branch reform of the Indian System that struck at the heart of its political and financial corruption. He wanted a "strong government" because much of the corruption came from an inability of the System to control itself. The centerpiece of the Whipple program was the divorce of this strong system from politics. The present agent, trading, and treaty processes would be wiped away, and price controls would be introduced. The new system would "place the weight of Government on the side of labor." Labor and agriculture were, to the bishop, linked to godliness.

> The Indian must have a home; his wandering tribal relations must be broken up; he must be furnished with seed, implements of husbandry, and taught to live by the sweat of his brow. The Government now gives him beads, paint, blankets and scalping-knives, teaching him to idle away his time, waiting for an annuity of

money which he does not know how to spend. This very autumn the Indian Bureau advertises for hundreds of dollars' worth of goods, and the only implements of labor are one hundred dozen weeding hoes and fifty dozen spades.

This program was overtly assimilationist. The Indian System would be transformed from a political machine that served whites to a mechanism for bringing Indians into the mainstream of American life. It is what Whipple called "a radical reform of the system."[14]

The problem was that Whipple's appeal to depoliticize Indian affairs was made to a man who was a master practitioner of the patronage process. Lincoln responded to Whipple's appeal in a perfunctory manner. He referred the matter to the "special attention of the Secretary of the Interior." Still, the bishop's strategy was not a total failure. Writing the president resulted in a long letter from Caleb Smith on 31 March.[15] At least, this time Whipple was not ignored.

Smith granted that there was truth to much of what Whipple contended, but he claimed that the evils "cannot be remedied without the intervention of Congress." Smith endorsed a partial reform that Congress had thus far refused to consider—concentration, a breakup of the trading system, and payment of annuities in kind, mostly with agricultural implements. Conspicuously missing in Smith's commitment to reform was any mention of Whipple's call for depoliticization.

Nevertheless, Whipple kept the dialogue alive. He responded with approval of the concentration plan but urged that Indians who left the "wild life" have their land secured by inalienable patents. The bishop warned Smith not to break up the trading system without replacing it with a more satisfactory arrangement. "This trade will either be carried on under wise persons, or be done clandestinely by bad men whose cupidity leads them to the Indian country,

14. Whipple, *Lights and Shadows*, pp. 514–19.
15. Lincoln to Whipple, 27 March 1862, Roy P. Basler, ed., *The Collected Works of Abraham Lincoln*, 5:173; Caleb B. Smith to Whipple, 31 March 1862, Box 3, Whipple Papers.

or else the Indian will seek a market amid the temptations of the nearest border town."

Whipple returned to the patronage theme. The crux of the problem, Whipple insisted, was personnel—"competent, faithful and honest men." Supervision was not tight enough: "There is too much left to the discretion of the agent. No system guides him." Even in-kind payment of annuities would not end the corruption if agents and traders were not held accountable. What Whipple wanted was a "definite plan" to govern Indian affairs with justice.[16]

The same day that he responded to Smith, the bishop wrote Lincoln again.[17] He enclosed further recommendations and urged Lincoln to pass them on to the department. Less than a week later, Whipple shared with Lincoln some of his insights on law and government for the Indians, "The Indian must be under law—the good must feel its protection and the bad fear its punishment." The bishop explained to Lincoln that Indians had no protection against theft or murder—no legal framework for protection or self-government.[18] Whipple's contention was that vacuums are inevitably filled, and where no legitimate governmental structure exists, government by thievery and corruption takes its place. On another occasion, Whipple repeated this insight to Alexander Ramsey:

> It is based on a falsehood that these heathen are an independant [sic] nation & not our wards. We leave them really without any government—then after nurturing every mad passion, standing unconcerned to witness Indian wars with each other looking on their deeds of blood, and permitting every evil influence to degrade them we turn them over to be robbed & plundered & at last wonder we have reaped what we sowed.[19]

Bishop Whipple and the Congressmen

Bishop Whipple had managed to engage the president and the secretary of interior in dialogue on reform. He reinforced this small

16. Whipple to Smith, 10 April 1862, Box 39, Letterbook 3, Whipple Papers.
17. Whipple to Lincoln, 10 April 1862, ibid.
18. Whipple to Lincoln, 16 April 1862, ibid.
19. Whipple to Alexander Ramsey, 8 November 1862, Box 40, Letterbook 4, Whipple Papers.

beachhead by obtaining references from Washington friends, including John Dix. Dix praised Whipple to the president, "I know him as a most able, indefatigable man, and am satisfied that any confidence the administration may repose in him will be faithfully responded to."[20]

Whipple next asked for help from his old friend, Senator Rice. Rice told the Bishop, "I will do all in my power to carry out your views." The senator complained that he had little power. He was a Democrat, and the Republicans had taken the places on the Indian Committee, with Morton Wilkinson assuming his seat. Minnesota's Cyrus Aldrich, another Republican, served on the Indian Committee in the House.

Rice's view of Lincoln's Washington was cynical, "All, everything country, Constitution, right—sacrificed upon the Altar of party." The Republican congressmen controlled the Indian patronage in Minnesota and "the Secretary of the Interior and the Comr of Indian Affairs give much *attention* to their suggestions." Rice believed that making Whipple's plan into law would mean nothing "so long as Agents and Superintendents, even Commissioners are appointed as rewards for *political services.*" Rice told Whipple he would try "but I fear the demagogue, the politician & those pecuniarally [*sic*] interested."[21]

Whipple refused to be discouraged. He asked Rice to see Lincoln and urge "the appointment of a commission—simply to devise a plan." Whipple believed Lincoln was "an honest man." "I believe he is not afraid to do his duty. If he could hear the cries which ring in my ears, if he could see what I have seen, if [he] had prayed as I have 'how long, how long O Lord!'—he would act."[22]

Perhaps the bishop thought he saw other signs that the time to act was at hand. Morton Wilkinson introduced a bill in the Senate on 6 March 1862 to protect Indians who had taken their land in severalty. The bill instructed agents to pay "civilized" Indians, as well as whites, for the depredations of "wild Indians."[23] Was it pos-

20. Dix to Lincoln, 21 April 1862, Roll 1, M825, LR, ID, OSI, RG48, NA.
21. Rice to Whipple, 22, 26 April 1862, Box 3, Whipple Papers.
22. Whipple to Rice, 30 April 1862, Box 39, Letterbook 3, Whipple Papers.
23. U.S., Congress, Senate, *Congressional Globe*, 37th Cong., 2d sess., 13 May 1862, pt. 3:2082; Box 2, Clark W. Thompson Papers.

sible that Minnesota's congressmen were ready to listen to the reformers?

On 13 April, Whipple decided to go to work on both Aldrich and Wilkinson. He wrote Aldrich and asked him to deliver another letter to Lincoln. Aldrich had already met the bishop's influence coming from another direction. His House Indian Affairs Committee had been asked by the secretary of the interior to give "very special attention" to Whipple's proposals. Aldrich, however, intended to sidetrack the reform plan. The congressman was not interested in contributing to the destruction of a portion of his own power base.

Aldrich simply denied the need for change. He accused Bishop Whipple of making "general allegations and indefinite charges." The congressman said he knew the Indian agents were honest because he helped select them—a demonstration of the political selection process Bishop Whipple had identified as the wellspring of corruption. But Aldrich said that the real problem was not the System but the Indians. Reform would mean nothing because of "the capacity of the Indian race."[24]

Morton Wilkinson's response to Whipple was so similar to Aldrich's that they must have discussed it. He too accused the bishop of making "general charges." He contended that Lincoln's appointments had eliminated the problem of corrupt agents, thus ignoring the bishop's fundamental point concerning the political premises of the appointment system. Wilkinson also shifted the burden to the Indian. Wilkinson believed Indians were "idle barbarians" and incapable of being civilized. As far as the senator was concerned, "missionary efforts . . . have not produced any adequate or corresponding results." Why reform the System when the real problem lay with the Indians as a race?

> It is easy enough to pull down the present System, to point out defects and to assail the manner of its execution—But it is quite another and more difficult matter to devise and frame in detail a

24. Aldrich to Whipple, 12 June 1862, Box 3, Whipple Papers.

plan which will accomplish all that the good people of our country desire.[25]

Wilkinson and Aldrich either had not read Whipple's program or, more likely, they did not like what they read. The bishop's proposals were not vague. They were especially specific in their attack on political patronage in the Indian System. Neither man was even mildly interested in joining an attempt to undercut his own influence and power.

Thus far, Bishop Whipple's second campaign for reform had elicited words but no action. There had been some encouraging response from Lincoln and Secretary Smith. Commissioner Dole expressed some interest in reform ideas. The commissioner was angry over problems in California and placed reform of that Indian jurisdiction high on his priority list. Dole may have reflected Whipple's influence in his conclusion that

> an honest, upright, true-hearted missionary, I care not what church, who will with his family, settle down with or near some of these people and by example and kindness teach them the arts of husbandry etc., etc., will do more good than all the traveling agents in the Union.

But Minnesota's congressmen, who occupied key seats on congressional committees, had rejected reform. Commissioner Dole, while he complained about the government's Indian policy, still maintained, "I can't see how to change it."[26]

War and a Visit to the President

In July 1862, Bishop Whipple began to lay plans for a trip to Washington. Confident of his ability to sway people, the bishop hoped he could move reluctant officials and President Lincoln. Henry Rice was skeptical and concluded the bishop would have to learn for himself. "When you visit here next fall you will be able

25. Whipple to Morton Wilkinson, 30 April 1862, Wilkinson to Whipple, 8 May 1862, Box 3, Whipple Papers; Fritz, *Indian Assimilation*, pp. 41–42.

26. Dole to Elijah White, 9 June 1862, Roll 59, M574, SF201, OIA, RG75, NA.

to satisfy yourself as to the *intentions* of those in power. . . . From the bottom of my inmost thoughts I wish you success."[27]

Events dramatically changed that gloomy situation. In July, Commissioner Dole traveled to Minnesota to negotiate a treaty with the Chippewas. While there, he found himself in the midst of that "most terrible and exciting Indian war."[28] The Minnesota war appeared to work to Bishop Whipple's advantage. The conflict apparently convinced Lincoln that there was substance in the churchman's arguments. When Whipple reached Washington in September, the war was at its zenith. John Ross was already in the city educating the president about violations of treaty obligations and injustices done to his people. Whipple carried a memorial that identified the new war as a symptom of the need for reform. Whipple said that the real causes of the war lay in the corruption of the Indian System. He skillfully fought opponents of reform with evidence of bloodshed, implying sanction for the suffering in their opposition.

> It is because I would forever prevent such scenes that for three years I have plead [*sic*] with the gover[n]ment to reform a system whose perrenial [*sic*] fruit is blood. Canada has not had an Indian war since the revolution. We have hardly passed a year without one. . . . we shall find that we have reaped exactly what we sowed.[29]

Armed with that argument, Bishop Whipple went to see Lincoln. He took Gen. Henry Halleck, his cousin, along for support. Whipple made the whole case to the president—the corruption of agents and traders, the lack of government protection for the Indians, and examples of how the corruption led directly to bloody war. Whipple believed the president "was deeply moved." Lincoln later told a friend that Bishop Whipple "came here the other day

27. Rice to Whipple, 4 July 1862, Box 3, Whipple Papers.
28. Wilkinson, Dole, John G. Nicolay to Lincoln, 27 August 1862, Roll 40, Lincoln Papers, LC. See Chapter VII.
29. Whipple, "The Duty of Citizens concerning the Indian Massacre," Box 40, Letterbook 3, Whipple Papers.

and talked with me about the rascality of this Indian business until I felt it down to my boots." Lincoln's response was a folksy story:

> Bishop, a man thought that monkeys could pick cotton better than negroes could because they were quicker and their fingers smaller. He turned a lot of them into his cotton field, but he found that it took two overseers to watch one monkey. It needs more than one honest man to watch one Indian agent.

The story was a curious one. Did it imply agreement with Whipple on the need to take Indian affairs out of politics? Or was it a way to say that any reform would be difficult to oversee? After thinking over the bishop's arguments, Lincoln appeared to make a commitment, although it was hedged with two significant "ifs" that betrayed his priorities: "If we get through this war, and I live, *this Indian system shall be reformed.*"[30]

The Executions and Reform

Lincoln pledged reform of the Indian System once the War for the Union was over. However, events intervened once again. The news that Minnesotans wished to execute three hundred and three Sioux prisoners confronted Lincoln with the brutality of the Indian System more directly than ever. Reformers were able to argue to the president that both the war and the execution controversy were the result of corruption. "Our government is *responsible* for this inhuman and horrible neglect and the day of retribution seems now at hand!" one crusader wrote Lincoln.[31]

The controversy over the executions may have been illustrative of Bishop Whipple's arguments. It did not make life simple for the clergyman in war-torn Minnesota. Whipple was attacked in the press. He even became an issue among the congressmen. Senator Rice wrote his wife, "Col Aldrich got knocked down the other night *in a saloon* for abusing Bishop Whipple." Whipple defended

---

30. Whipple, *Lights and Shadows,* pp. 136–37.
31. B. B. Meeker to Edward W. Bates, 2 November 1862, Roll 599, M234, LR, Northern Superintendency, OIA, RG75, NA. See Chapter VIII.

himself, contending that he cared for the suffering whites as much as anyone. They had been hurt because of "a bad system of Indian affairs." If his reform program had been implemented long ago, Whipple maintained, "I believe no blood would have been shed."[32]

Despite his own uneasy position, Whipple understood that the situation was equally uncomfortable for Abraham Lincoln. On 12 November 1862, Whipple sought to exploit the situation by writing Senator Rice and enclosing another letter for Lincoln. This time he linked reform with the war and the executions, "You know it is our culpable mismanagement, robbery & sin which has brought this harvest of blood." The burdens of being a reformer in hate-filled Minnesota were beginning to wear on the usually tireless Whipple. He praised Rice as "the only public man who from the first has recognised the justice of my plea." While maintaining, "We cannot hang men by the hundreds," the bishop worried about executing those actually guilty. He knew anything else would "call down on me a pack of harpies and do no good—but I do earnestly ask a reform, I have the right to demand it and I do so in the fear of God." Rice could only respond, "I shall at the earliest moment place before the President the Memorial and will . . . back it with my entire strength."[33]

Before Rice could reach the president, John Beeson decided to attempt to use the controversy over the executions to convert Lincoln to Indian reform. In a letter to the president, he attacked Commissioner Dole as a man "whose lack of knowledge of Indian nature, and of human rights was shockingly manifested." Beeson's language may have been sufficiently radical to make Bishop Whipple appear more moderate. He called for the recognition of Indian sovereignty and the restoration of land to the Indians, whereas the bishop advocated abandoning the idea of dealing with the Indians as an independent nation. Beeson, however, supported Whipple

32. Whipple to F. Driscoll, 5 December 1862, Box 40, Letterbook 3, Whipple Papers; Rice to his wife, 17 October 1862, Henry Mower Rice Papers; Whipple to Ramsey, 8 November 1862, Box 40, Letterbook 4, Whipple Papers.
33. Whipple to Rice, 12 November 1862, Box 40, Rice to Whipple, 19 November 1862, Box 3, Whipple Papers.

and praised him to the president. "There can be no measure of reform which you can reccomend [sic] that would meet with more general approval than reform of the Indian Department," he told Lincoln.

Beeson regarded the injustice against Indians and the "slave power" as entities in an evil organic whole. It was not going to be enough to end slavery. Injustice to the Indians predated slavery and its source was the same; the nation would achieve salvation only by rooting out the original injustice, "This can be done only by the immediate recognition of the Indians as human beings." Beeson alleged that the "slave power" controlled the Indian Office and connected this with the expulsion of the tribes from the southeastern United States a generation earlier. To reform Indian policy was, in Beeson's mind, "to dry up the principle source from which rebellion has derived its strength." Beeson integrated the Minnesota war into this total picture and closed his letter with a powerful plea not to execute any of the condemned Sioux.[34]

Meanwhile, Senator Rice was finding it difficult to promote Bishop Whipple's proposals. On 25 November, he called on Commissioner Dole to urge more efforts to supply Minnesota Indians with agricultural implements. The commissioner "replied that his hands were tied, that Senator Wilkinson had amended a Bill so as to preclude him from advertising for anything *not estimated by the Superintendent!*" Rice was discouraged and told Whipple, "I can do nothing I fear, without the aid of my colleague, which *I know will not* be given." Rice decried the situation: "I will do my best— Alas! The poor Indian is kept in a savage state by a giant gover[n]ment and his condition renders him, not an object of pity, but of plunder."[35]

Morton Wilkinson's resistance to reforming Indian policy was not passive. He was spearheading a campaign to force Lincoln to execute the three hundred Sioux prisoners. The last week in November was the crucial period for that agitation. Senator Rice, despite

34. Beeson to Lincoln, 18 November 1862, Roll 20, M825, LR, ID, OSI, RG48, NA; Fritz, *Indian Assimilation*, p. 37.
35. Rice to Whipple, 27 November 1862, Box 3, Whipple Papers.

143

his worries, was able to obtain "a long interview with the President" on 26 November, two days before Wilkinson got to see him. Rice carried with him Bishop Whipple's letter and a memorial from several Episcopal bishops.[36]

Lincoln Supports Reform

Events had made Abraham Lincoln extremely sensitive to Indian affairs for weeks. He had been educated on the evils of the Indian System. He had been confronted with Indian warfare in the Indian Territory and Minnesota. By 26 November, he was only days away from a decision on the proposed executions in Minnesota. It is in that context that he met with Senator Rice.

Rice presented Lincoln with Whipple's memorial. Lincoln read it aloud and "said that he would in his [annual] message, call the attention of Congress to the subject." That message was to be delivered on 1 December. Lincoln had apparently changed his mind about waiting until after the Civil War to recommend reform. On 26 November, he led Rice to believe he would seek it immediately. "He is disposed to do all he can," Rice informed Bishop Whipple.

On 1 December 1862, Abraham Lincoln asked Congress to remodel the Indian System. "Many wise and good men have impressed me with the belief that this can be profitably done," he said. Lincoln urged the congressmen to give the matter their "especial consideration."[37] For the moment, it appeared that Bishop Whipple had achieved a great triumph. The president of the United States had endorsed reform of the Indian System.

However, the vagueness of Lincoln's recommendation was troubling. Above all, an endorsement of Whipple's cornerstone proposal—the depoliticization of the System—was conspicuously absent. Instead, the proposal was made in a general way to the men who directly controlled Indian patronage.

That ambiguous posture carried over to subordinate annual reports. Caleb Smith did spell out some details of the reform proposal.

36. Ibid.
37. LAM, 1862, p. 1.

He demanded an end to the treaty process and to the tribes' status as independent nations. "They should be regarded as wards of the government, entitled to its fostering care and protection," said the secretary. His words could have been written by Bishop Whipple:

> The duty of the government to protect the Indians and prevent their suffering for the want of the necessaries of life should be fully recognized. They should be taught to earn their subsistence by labor, and be instructed in the cultivation of the soil.

Among Smith's recommendations were payment of annuities in goods rather than cash and many other aspects of the reformers' program. Smith called it "a radical change in the mode of treatment for the Indians."[38]

Commissioner Dole joined the reform chorus, calling severalty for Indians "the best method yet devised for their reclamation and advancement in civilization." Dole even went so far as to call for "their ultimate admission to all the rights of citizenship." However, Dole was less enthusiastic than Smith. He reserved his greatest attention for his own pet policy, "concentration."[39] But neither official said anything about changing the method of selecting Indian officials, the first step in assuring the successful implementation of the other programs.

Nevertheless, the reformers were ecstatic. A New Yorker, Lewis H. Morgan, wrote Lincoln immediately to support his proposal for reform, "No work is more needed."[40] Bishop Whipple joined in the exultation: "With all my heart I thank you for your reccommendation [sic] to have our whole Indian system reformed. It is a stupendous piece of wickedness and as we fear God ought to be changed." Whipple sent Lincoln more material to read and appeared to believe that his proposed reform commission was a certainty, an implication that Lincoln had promised Whipple that it would be created.

Bishop Whipple knew that his cause had taken only a tentative

38. Ibid., p. 5.
39. AR, CIA, 1862, pp. 169–70, 188, 192.
40. Lewis H. Morgan to Lincoln, 3 December 1862, Roll 20, M825, LR, ID, OSI, RG48, NA.

first step. The significant omission in the government's recommendations had not escaped his scrutiny. "Will you not see that the commission is made up of better stuff than politicians," he addressed the politician in the White House. "It needs the best men in the nation." That same day, Whipple wrote cousin Gen. Henry Halleck. "You have his ear," the bishop wrote, referring to the president. "Do, for the sake of the poor victims of a nations wrong, ask him to put on it something better than politicians."[41] But the reformers had hope where there had been none. Indian affairs had been linked with national concerns and the success of the struggle with the South. As a result, a president of the United States had publicly endorsed reform of the Indian System.

41. Whipple to Lincoln, Whipple to Henry Halleck, 4 December 1862, Box 40, Letterbook 3, Whipple Papers.

XI. The Failure of Reform "The Do Nothing Policy Here Is Complete"

AS DECEMBER PASSED, it became evident to the reformers that it was not going to be easy to translate presidential words into congressional action. Furthermore, Lincoln and his subordinates displayed an unwillingness to take any risks to support the program. Lincoln did not use his executive powers to, in Whipple's words, "instruct the department" or alter the appointment process for the Indian System. On 27 December, Henry Rice wrote Bishop Whipple, "I fear that little or nothing will be done for your Indian project."[1]

Trouble for the Reform Movement

In retrospect, the decline in fervor for reform was predictable. After the executions of 26 December, the dramatic fuel that had fired the enthusiasm had been spent. Also, religious jealousies had surfaced, with Bishop Thomas L. Grace writing officials concerning his fear that because of the new policy, Roman Catholics might be excluded from missionary work with the Sioux.[2] Finally, other Minnesotans were more interested in removal than reform. Bishop Whipple tried manfully to link the two things, "This removal must

1. Henry Benjamin Whipple to Abraham Lincoln, 6 March 1862, Box 39, Henry M. Rice to Whipple, 27 December 1862, Box 3, Henry Benjamin Whipple Papers.
2. Thomas L. Grace to Lincoln, 29 December 1862, Roll 599, M234, LR, Northern Superintendency, OIA, RG75, NA (for "Abbreviations in Footnotes," see p. vi).

not be done without a radical reform of the system."[3] However, the resistance to reform was discouraging to Whipple: "I have plead [*sic*] with all the earnestness of my nature for a reform in this wicked system but I fear I shall be powerless. How sad that a nation should be so deaf. Pray for me—my poor heart aches."[4] On 22 January, Bishop Whipple tried once more to convince Commissioner Dole that if there were no reform, there would be more warfare. "I have so often pressed upon the Department of a need of reform," he wrote. He begged Dole to "examine carefully" the memorial to Lincoln from the Episcopal bishops and "further their prayer."[5]

The crucial roadblock to reform was in Congress, especially the Senate Indian Affairs Committee. The House passed a resolution in January for the appointment of a commission, just as Bishop Whipple had asked, "to investigate the condition of the Indian tribes and remnants of tribes in the United States."[6] The Senate, however, was not interested. Rice gave Whipple the bad news:

> I look for no aid here. In open Senate the other day I called the attention of the Indian Committee to that part of the Presidents message touching Indian affairs. I do not expect any action will be taken. I am powerless and discouraged.[7]

Morton Wilkinson told Whipple directly that he would not help. He agreed that policy should be changed, but his excuse was that there was not time to do it in the current session and no action should be taken in haste. That was Wilkinson's way of killing the program. Rice succinctly summarized the situation, "The do nothing policy here is complete."[8]

3. Whipple, "What Shall We do with the Indians," Box 40, Letterbook 3, Whipple Papers.

4. Whipple to [?], 14 January 1863, Letterbook 4, Whipple Papers.

5. Whipple to William P. Dole, 22 January 1863, Roll 599, M234, LR, Northern Superintendency, OIA, RG75, NA.

6. Cyrus B. Aldrich to John P. Usher, 6 January 1863, Roll 21, M825, LR, ID, OSI, RG48, NA.

7. Rice to Whipple, 7 February 1863, Box 3, Whipple Papers.

8. Morton Wilkinson to Whipple, 1 March 1863, Rice to Whipple, 7 February 1863, ibid.

The Chippewa Treaty

The new Chippewa treaty demonstrated how dead the reform cause was by early 1863. The treaty was negotiated in Washington in March, and Henry Rice claimed he wrote "every word in it (save amendments made by the Senate)." Rice found those amendments "very injurious." The treaty provided for the concentration of the Chippewas and for a board of visitors consisting of two or three churchmen to oversee the payment of annuities, inspect, and report on conditions among the Indians. Rice recommended Bishop Whipple, who was appointed along with Bishop Grace and Thomas Williamson.[9]

The significance of the Chippewa situation is that Bishop Whipple became an instrument of the Indian System in order to implement the very corruption he hated. By June 1863, the Chippewas were intensely unhappy because their "Great Father" in Washington had led them to exchange good land for bad.[10] In November, Bishop Whipple wrote Rice to tell him that the Board of Visitors had been used to sanctify fraudulent dealings. Whipple unsuccessfully tried three times to find out when the annuity payments would be made. Finally, when payments were made, he said, "We were sent blindfolded into the Indian Country, to attend as gentlemanly spectators on a payment without authority to advise or direct." Whipple suspected fraud: "Col Thompson said that he brough[t] 12,000 in gold. You see that only about $5,500 was paid. Some one must make a liberal proffit [*sic*] on the balance." The cleric reported that the annuity goods had been opened and placed in piles so that the board members could not even determine if the promised amount was delivered.[11]

Whipple was angry and humiliated. Officials were talking of another treaty to replace the one that was not working. Whipple

9. Rice to Whipple, 18 March 1863, Box 3, Whipple Papers; Rice to Lincoln, 13 April 1863, Roll 1, M825, LR, ID, OSI, RG48, NA; Dole to Whipple, 4 August 1863, Roll 71, M21, LS, OIA, RG75, NA.

10. Hole-in-the-Day to Lincoln and Dole, 7 June 1863, AR, CIA, 1863, pp. 448–51.

11. Whipple to Rice, 24 November 1863, Box 40, Letterbook 3, Whipple Papers.

called such talk "madness," and he deplored "the farce of another treaty." Treaties were always used by politicians for personal gain. "What we need is not new treaties but honest manly fulfilling of old ones," the bishop complained.[12]

It was not only the Chippewas who made Whipple "sick at heart." It was the conditions of the Sioux prisoners and the removed Sioux and Winnebagos. In spite of all the promises, Whipple witnessed that the Indians of his diocese were worse off than ever before. "I tremble for my country," he told Commissioner Dole, "when I remember that God will compel us to reap what we sow. There is a reason why every advance of civilization is marked with blood."[13]

In a few months, Whipple had gone from exultation to despair.

> The dark mountain of injustice & wickedness has lowered over me so darkly, I have felt such loneliness in trying to do, that often it seemed as if my heart would break if I could not have carried my sorrows and laid them at a Heavenly Fathers feet.

The bishop considered giving up on Indian reform: "I have now decided that it is no use to try and coax." He was unsure of his health, "I feel often my hold on life is very weak." He considered turning his work over to someone else, but the discouraged crusader could not desert his cause. "I beg of you," Whipple wrote Senator Rice, "for the love of God dont be discouraged."[14] In 1864, the bishop escorted Chippewa leaders back to Washington to negotiate a new treaty.[15]

Gen. John Pope and Indian Policy

It was evident that the government was not going to reform the Indian System, despite Lincoln's pledge. Where, then, was

12. Whipple to Dole, 2 November 1863, Letterbook 4, Whipple Papers.
13. Whipple to Dole, 16 November 1863, Letterbook 3, Whipple Papers. See pp. 123–25 in this book on the Sioux prisoners.
14. Whipple to Rice, 24 November 1863, Letterbook 3, Whipple Papers.
15. Whipple to Alexander Ramsey, 12 January 1864, ibid.; Chippewa Treaty, Roll 154, M234, LR, Chippewa Agency, OIA, RG75, NA; James Harlan to Whipple, 24 February 1864, Dole to Whipple, 9 April 1864, Box 3, Whipple Papers; Whipple to Dole, 11 April 1864, Roll 154, M234, LR, Chippewa Agency, OIA, RG75, NA.

policy headed? In the midst of a great war, clues could be found in the thinking of military men. Bishop Whipple wrote Henry Halleck in April 1864, "I hear that the Indian Bureau are down upon General Pope and the entire War Dept. especially Army officers for interfering in their business."[16]

Actually, the military had long been a source of a type of reform agitation, although the soldiers' motivations differed from the more idealistic reformers. Military men felt that they always had to clean up the situations caused by Indian officials, an example of which could be the Minnesota Indian war. The Indian Office had originated in the War Department and there were recurring calls, even among civilian leaders, to transfer it back. Cyrus Aldrich inquired of the Indian Office in 1861 concerning an amendment to accomplish this task. James Doolittle of Wisconsin, chairman of the Senate Indian Committee, told the Senate in 1864 that he had concluded that this solution was best. His grounds were that Indians "respected" military force.[17] This attitude at all levels of government was easily fostered by the war mentality.

Following his experience in Minnesota, Gen. John Pope had some specific ideas along these lines. By October 1862, he was bombarding the War Department with recommendations. Stanton informed him that his proposals had "been submitted to the President, and are now under consideration by him."[18] Pope may have had an impact on Lincoln's recommendation for reform late that year. In 1864, Pope made comprehensive proposals in testimony to the Joint Committee on the Conduct of the War.[19]

Pope corroborated many of the reformers' judgments concern-

16. Henry Halleck to Whipple, 20 April 1864, Box 3, Whipple Papers.
17. Aldrich to A. B. Greenwood, 28 February 1861, Roll 456, M234, LR, Miscellaneous, OIA, RG75, NA; U.S., Congress, Senate, *Congressional Globe*, Debate on the Indian Appropriation Bill, 38th Cong., 1st sess., 11 June 1864, pt. 3:2873; William E. Unrau, "Indian Agent vs. the Army: Some Background Notes on the Kiowa-Comanche Treaty of 1865," p. 135.
18. Edwin M. Stanton to Pope, 14 October 1862, *Minnesota in the Indian and Civil Wars*, 2:276.
19. Pope to Stanton, 6 February 1864, JCCW, 2:192–209, also found in Roll 599, M234, LR, Northern Superintendency, OIA, RG75, NA.

ing the Indian System. He found the same corruption in land speculation, whiskey sales, trade, annuity disbursement, and agent activities. He even accepted the reformers' contention that the root cause
of recent Indian warfare "can be directly traced to the conduct of
the white men who have swindled them out of their money and
their goods." The general pronounced the System an expensive and
"woful [*sic*] failure."

Pope agreed with Bishop Whipple on the need for a strong
government to protect the Indians. He wanted to end treatymaking.
He endorsed the proposal that the Indians receive annuities in payment in kind rather than in cash. Pope encouraged the application
of "the influence of civilization, education, and Christianity." He
suggested a price-control system for traders under his jurisdiction.
Pope, like Whipple, wanted to destroy tribal organization and take
the first steps toward making Indians functioning individuals in
American society.

There were some significant disagreements between the general
and the reformers. One centered on the question of military control.
The cornerstone of Pope's proposals was the transfer of supervision
of the Indians to the War Department. He wanted a military solution "without the interposition of Indian agents." To that end, Pope
proposed the establishment of sizable military posts in Indian country. He would concentrate tribes, isolate them (with or without
their consent), and surround them with soldiers. Behind this shield,
a forcible civilizing process could take place.

Concentration, segregation, military control, and forced civilization were the central features of Pope's program. The old System,
he said, "has worked injustice and wrong to the Indian; has made
his present state worse, morally and physically, than it was in his
native wilderness; and has entailed a heavy and useless expense
upon the government." Surely military control would be better.
Pope sounded a bit unsure of the consequences of this action, partly
because he was less sure than Bishop Whipple about the innate
abilities of the Indian. As far as he was concerned, the safest course
was to treat Indians as a military problem. That was an approach
compatible with a government at war.

Pope's proposals have been praised by some scholars.[20] His analysis of the evils of the Indian System was as cogent as that of any reformer. By implication, military control would have taken the control of Indian affairs away from the politicians. Pope assumed that military men would be more honorable than civilian Indian officials—a proposition that was eventually severely tested in New Mexico and Colorado. The general failed to note the fact that the political ambitions that underlay the Indian System also infected the military, as was demonstrated in Kansas. The Lincoln administration never formally espoused military control, but as the Civil War ground on, the military increasingly assumed responsibility for the Indians.

If anything, Pope's proposals sapped the lifeblood of the reform movement. They were the old policy in new, militaristic dress, with the trappings of reform and not the substance. Pope undercut the reformers at the crucial points of Indian capacity and utility of beneficent policies. Under it, Indians would continue to be removed, concentrated, and generally made to serve the cause of white progress.[21]

The Triumph of Concentration

Lincoln maintained the appearance of keeping his commitment to reform. In his 1863 annual message, he called on Congress to reform the Indian System, proclaiming the "urgent need for immediate legislative action." Lincoln may have thought of Bishop Whipple as he wrote:

> Sound policy and our imperative duty to these wards of the Government demand our anxious and constant attention to their material well-being, to their progress in the arts of civilization, and, above all, to that moral training which, under the blessing of divine Providence, will confer upon them the elevated and sanctifying influences, the hopes and consolations of the Christian faith.

20. Richard N. Ellis, *General Pope and U.S. Indian Policy*, p. 242.
21. See Chapter XII concerning military policy in the last years of the Lincoln administration.

These words were the skeleton at the feast. Congress was not going to remodel the System, and Lincoln surely knew it. More significant, Lincoln's kind words for Indians directly followed sentences expressing pride concerning the removal of many tribes, "sundry treaties," and "extinguishing the possessory rights of the Indians to large and valuable tracts of land."[22]

Lincoln communicated in this general language the fact that his administration had settled on an Indian policy. Commissioner Dole said it more plainly, "The plan of concentrating Indians and confining them to reservations may now be regarded as the fixed policy of the government." Dole still praised the severalty idea as the best way to inculcate "the ideas of self-reliance and individual effort." But his priorities were clear, and they constituted a rejection of any kind of depoliticization of the Indian System. John Usher's report did not even mention reform ideas. Concentration was the policy, and he and Dole both pointed to examples of that policy. One was in New Mexico, where concentration was being carried out by the military. The other they proposed to implement in California by concentrating the tribes there onto two reservations.[23] With or without reform, concentration was being implemented and, with it, politics as usual.

Congress Debates Indian Policy

The executive branch of the government had settled on a tough Indian policy that implicitly rejected depoliticization and placed highest priority on prosecution of the war and development of the West. By 1864, Lincoln and Dole ceased even asking for reform. The last refuge of the reformers was the Congress. It was a feeble reed. Early in 1864, Congress killed a bill "for the benefit and better management of the Indians."[24]

However, the Congress had become more sensitive to Indian

22. LAM, 1863, p. 1.
23. AR, CIA, 1863, pp. 129–30; AR, SI, 1863, p. 22.
24. U.S., Congress, Senate, *Congressional Globe*, 38th Cong., 1st sess., pt. 3:2117, the bill had been introduced by William Windom on 29 January 1864, U.S., Congress, House, *Congressional Globe*, 38th Cong., 1st sess., pt. 1:411.

problems because of a growing public furor over them. The war years had disrupted peaceful Indian-white relations in several regions. The mad scramble for mineral wealth in the West was a source of friction. The war in Minnesota and the refugees in Kansas had upset many white citizens. By the end of 1864, Commissioner Dole admitted that treatymaking policy "has recently attracted a large share of public attention." The secretary of the interior was equally concerned, "Much has been said, and the public mind has late been agitated, against the policy of the Government in making treaties with the Indians."[25]

By June 1864, the accumulated problems were enough to touch off a great debate in the Senate.[26] The senators discovered that it was costing an extraordinary amount of money to implement Indian policies. The removal of the Minnesota Indians had cost $137,000 more than their appropriations. Damage claims in Minnesota exceeded appropriations by $125,000. The pending return of the Kansas refugees to the Indian Territory promised more of the same because they were moved too late to plant crops. Furthermore, there was the question of the government's responsibility for paying the back interest due the Indians on securities issued by seceded states—a matter of $350,000.

The debate on monetary matters evolved into a debate on Indian policy that gave senatorial reformers one last hurrah. John Sherman of Ohio sharply attacked a system that worked so badly and still cost four million dollars a year. "The whole relation between the Indian tribes and the United States is the most ridiculous possible," said the senator, "and I hope some day or other a gentleman familiar with the subject will bring in a bill abolishing the whole system." Sherman maintained that, for all its expenditures, the System did not protect Indians and "our white people constantly encroach on them and do them great wrong."

An agitated Sen. Reverdy Johnson of Maryland joined in the debate, "Of all the injustice that has ever been perpetrated by man

25. AR, CIA, 1864, p. 147.
26. U.S., Congress, Senate, *Congressional Globe,* Debate on the Indian Appropriation Bill, 38th Cong., 1st sess., 10 June 1864, pt. 3:2846–47, 2850, 2871.

upon man the injustice perpetrated upon the Indians is the grossest." The great western states progressed at the expense of the Indians, and the result was that "these poor creatures are houseless and homeless and penniless." The senator shouted: "I protest against it for the credit of the Government. I protest against it in the name of humanity. I protest against it in the name of that higher humanity, Christian civilization."

Unfortunately, the senators on the Indian Committee did not share these sentiments with the reformers. Chairman Doolittle responded that the government had done all it could do. He maintained that the problem was not government policy but the Indians themselves: "We are a different race. God, in His providence has opened this New World to the colonization of a different race from that which inhabited it when our forefathers first landed upon the shores of New England." Indians were inferior, and so they were "a dying, dying race." The government was not wrong, said Doolittle. It was simply a case of "the contact of two races side by side upon the frontiers of Christian civilization." Senator Harlan supported Doolittle's view, contending: "If they refuse to merge into and become part of the superior race, they must necessarily be destroyed. It is a law of humanity."[27]

Morton Wilkinson of Minnesota could not resist such a debate. A longtime opponent of reform, Wilkinson also blamed the problems on Indians and their nature. He called them "a lazy, miserable, thriftless set of beings" and pronounced missionary efforts among them "an utter and entire failure." Besides, to Wilkinson, there was a larger problem—"the character of the American people." Americans just naturally moved into new regions seeking new wealth. No reformed Indian system could stop that great drive.

> The character of the Indian country changes every six months. A gold mine is discovered upon an Indian reservation and you may as well undertake to dam up the Mississippi river and prevent it flowing down toward the Gulf as to stop the tide of emigration in this country. Our people go wherever those developments open an opportunity for wealth and prosperity.

27. Ibid., p. 2874.

Wilkinson's remarks drew fire from an unexpected source, "Bloody Jim" Lane, "I am surprised that any man from the west should be found advocating, or even excusing, or attempting to excuse, our Indian system." Thus joined in debate were two of the great congressional figures in Indian affairs in the Lincoln years. Lane told the senator from Minnesota that a man who knew the frontier, "with common sense and judgement, must have learned that our Indian system was a failure, an utter failure."

Wilkinson was angered at these words, but Lane pressed his attack. He held up the English system, applied in Canada, as much superior and, in the process, Lane endorsed much of the reform program.

> It is not an absurdity that we should pass laws recognizing the Indians as subjects for a time, and then after reaching a certain point of civilization and advancement to recognize them as citizens, and permit them to take the oath of allegiance, if you please or oath of civilization and advancement.[28]

It was remarkable to hear such words from the mouth of a man who had so profited from the Indian System.

Nevertheless, this rhetoric was the only tool of the reformers. They had neither the votes nor the influence in the Indian Committee necessary to pass any kind of reform bill. Doolittle, Harlan, and Wilkinson were opposed to reform, and unless their committee acted, no legislation could ever be enacted. The senatorial debate was a mirror to the reform struggle, ideologically and politically. The reformers had lost in Congress, as elsewhere, because they lacked the political clout to undo a politically and financially profitable system.

Bishop Whipple Gives Up on Lincoln

In February 1864, Bishop Whipple was still pushing for reform. He was writing articles on Indian affairs and still attempting to persuade General Sibley to help the suffering Sioux. In March, he

28. Ibid., pp. 2875–76.

journeyed to Washington to help the Chippewas renegotiate their treaty. While there, he went again to see Lincoln, but this time the meeting brought no dramatic results. Lincoln gave Whipple a perfunctory letter of introduction to the new chairman of the House Indian Committee, William Windom of Minnesota. "Please see & hear Rev. Bishop Whipple about Indians," Lincoln wrote Windom. "He has much information on the subject."[29]

John Beeson was also greeted politely, but his requests were perfunctorily dismissed. Beeson sponsored a meeting at the Hall of the House of Representatives on 9 April 1864. A committee of three was delegated to visit Lincoln and discuss the Indian question. Four months later, the committee had still been unable to secure an audience with Lincoln "on account of the pressure of business." Beeson finally got to see Lincoln and he recalled that the president told him "to rest assured that as soon as the pressing matters of this war is settled the Indians shall have my first care and I will not rest untill Justice is done their and your Sattisfaction [sic]." Lincoln had returned to putting off reform until the Civil War was over.[30]

A disillusioned and ill Bishop Whipple left the country for a restful trip to England. He had given up on Lincoln and his administration. He found hope only in the possibility of a different president and administration. In September, during his voyage, Whipple wrote Lincoln's opponent for the presidency, General McClellan. "I know you too well to appeal to your generous heart to do all you can, if elected Prest to reform this atrocious Indian system," the weary reformer wrote, and he assured McClellan of his support.[31]

Bishop Whipple was disappointed again, because Lincoln won a second term. Whipple wrote his wife from England: "I think

29. Charles Norton to Whipple, 9 February 1864, Henry H. Sibley to Whipple, 17 February 1864, Box 3, Whipple Papers; Lincoln to William Windom, 30 March 1864, Roy P. Basler, ed., *The Collected Works of Abraham Lincoln*, 7:275.
30. Beeson to Lincoln, 12 August 1864, Roll 458, M234, LR, Miscellaneous, OIA, RG75, NA; Robert Mardock, *The Reformers and the American Indian*, p. 13.
31. Whipple to George B. McClellan, 30 September 1864, Box 40, Letterbook 5, McClellan to Whipple, 20 October 1864, Box 4, Whipple Papers.

most of the Americans here felt gloomy. . . . I confess I see no help but in God."[32]

Abraham Lincoln, Reformer?

Was Lincoln's 1862 proposal genuine or mere rhetoric? An evaluation is not easy. Although Lincoln promised a great deal and delivered little, mid-nineteenth century presidents did not generally act as chief legislators in their relations with Congress. Lincoln was Whiggish in his approach on many nonwar issues.[33] However, Lincoln appears to have pushed much harder on other matters, notably the transcontinental railroad and mineral development. More important, Lincoln did not use his executive powers to change what he could without congressional action, especially in the appointment of something besides political supporters to Indian positions. Lincoln never did specifically endorse depoliticization of the Indian System.

To be fair, Lincoln was no worse than the congressmen who profited most directly from the political system the reformers wanted to destroy. Men like Wilkinson and Aldrich were even less willing than Lincoln to talk about giving up a major source of their power. Lincoln at least endorsed the general principles of reform. Given the demands of the War for the Union, he may have believed there was little else he could do.

There is some historic importance to the Lincoln proposal. Historians have long marked the Dawes Allotment Act of 1887 as a watershed in American Indian history. That act enshrined in law the idea that Indians must be assimilated into American civilization to emulate the white agrarian values of individual ownership of property. The Dawes policy proved disastrous in practice, partly due to mismanagement and partly because it ignored cultural patterns thousands of years old. The passage of the legislation required an alliance between the land-hungry and the reformers. It thereby

32. Whipple to Mrs. Whipple, 23 November 1864, Box 40, Letterbook 5, Whipple Papers.
33. David Donald, *Lincoln Reconsidered*, pp. 187–208.

opened Indian lands for settlement so that between 1887 and 1934 the Natives lost 86 million acres of their 138 million acres.[34]

Historians have often described the severalty movement that produced the Dawes Act as an eastern movement. Actually, westerners supported it from the outset, among them Bishop Whipple, Lincoln, Smith, and Dole. This distortion derives, in part, from the scholars' neglect of Indian policy during the Civil War years. The movement began well before 1865 and got its most significant early presidential endorsement from Abraham Lincoln.

The significance of the Lincoln proposal recedes somewhat in the face of the administration's failure to endorse the fundamental political reform sought by Bishop Whipple. Nevertheless, new ideas were raised and significant precedents were set. The corruption of the Indian System received national exposure. Whipple's request for a commission of worthy men paved the way for the Board of Indian Commissioners, begun in 1869 and lasting until 1934. His ideas provided the intellectual foundations for the "peace policy" of the Grant administration under which churchmen administered Indian affairs. All this sprung from that moment when Bishop Henry Whipple confronted Abraham Lincoln and Lincoln responded: *"This Indian system shall be reformed!"*[35]

34. William T. Hagan, *American Indians*, p. 147; Henry E. Fritz, *The Movement for Indian Assimilation, 1860–1890*, pp. 212–13.

35. Hagan, *American Indians*, pp. 110–12, 141–47; Fritz, *Indian Assimilation*, pp. 34, 56–86; Mardock, *The Reformers*, pp. 30–84, 192–228; the idea of individual allotment actually dates back as far as 1633. Treaties featuring allotment were signed in the 1850s. See Howard W. Paulson, "The Allotment of Land in Severalty to the Dakota Indians before the Dawes Act," pp. 132–41; Whipple, *Lights and Shadows*, pp. 136–37.

XII. Concentration and Militarism
"Those Who Resist Should Be Pursued by the Military and Punished"

DURING 1864, ABRAHAM LINCOLN had preoccupations that were bound to distract from Indian affairs. The election, western development, and the transcontinental railroad were all major concerns.

His overwhelming obsession was the War for the Union. This was the year it became evident the North could win. Ulysses S. Grant was appointed leader of that effort on 9 March 1864. Grant began to use his superior numbers to pound the Confederacy into submission. All else was subordinated to winning the war. When Lincoln noticed Indians at all, it tended to be in the context of larger military concerns.

For the most part, the president left Indian matters to the Indian Office. This was a return to normalcy. Lincoln had never really given Indian affairs high priority. The refugees, the Minnesota war, and the executions had forced him out of his normal pattern. Once those matters were past the crisis point, he left them and the difficulties therein largely unsolved. He confined himself mostly to ceremonial duties. In July, Dole wrote Lincoln concerning a visiting Indian delegation: "Will you be kind enough to take these Indians by the hand *this evening*. I wish them to start home by the *early train* in the morning."[1]

---

1. William P. Dole to Abraham Lincoln, 8 July 1864, Roll 77, Abraham Lincoln Papers, LC.

Dole and Concentration Policy

Left to his own devices, Commissioner Dole actively promoted his concentration policy. Dole had long been angry with the state of Indian affairs in California. While never an outstanding advocate of wholesale reform of the Indian System, Dole thought that California could provide a model of modest reform. The California reform, however, retained little of the idealism of Bishop Whipple's reform movement. It was designed to save money, eliminate inefficiency, and end the more outrageous forms of fraud. Where two superintendents existed previously, only one would serve. Other jobs were eliminated. Most important, the tribes of the state were to be consolidated onto no more than four reservations.

Dole obtained the full support of the Senate Indian Committee for his concentration policy in California. Senator Doolittle justified it both because the old system was "altogether too indefinite, too expensive, too loose in its administration" and because it was best for the Indians. The California Indians "have been fading away as the white population has been advancing upon them," said Doolittle. The only way to save them was to remove and concentrate them. The California reform passed the Congress in spring 1864.[2]

Dole's plans for concentration extended beyond California. In his 1864 report, he advocated concentrating all Indian tribes in the nation onto as few as three to five reservations. Dole's arguments showed that he was more in agreement with Wilkinson and Doolittle than he was with the reformers. He said that the loss of Indian country was inevitable because of "the peculiar character of Indians, that they should retire as their country became occupied by whites." To Dole, segregation was the only answer. American history showed "that the white and the red man cannot occupy territory in common, and it follows that a policy which shall be adequate, and adapted to the requirements of the case, must provide for each race a separate abiding-place."[3]

2. U.S., Congress, Senate, *Congressional Globe,* 38th Cong., 1st sess., 18 March 1864, pt. 1:1184, 21 March 1864, pt. 2:1209, 11 April 1864, pt. 2:1523.

3. AR, CIA, 1864, pp. 148–49 (for "Abbreviations in Footnotes," see p. vi).

Militarism and Indians

In the context of a struggle to win the Civil War, this concentration policy took on a harsh character. Interior Secretary John Usher stated it plainly: "This Department will make provision for such Indians as will submit to its authority and locate upon the reservation. Those who resist should be pursued by the military, and punished."[4]

This was the tough policy of a government at war. Usher worried about Indian threats to overland mail routes and the construction of the transcontinental railroad. Insurrection anywhere, whether in the South or by Indian tribes, was not to be tolerated. The massive warfare by Grant, the expeditions across Dakota, and developing military policies toward Indians in New Mexico and Colorado were all cut from the same militaristic cloth.

The real author of this uncompromising policy was Abraham Lincoln. In his 1864 message, his top priority clearly was winning the Civil War.[5] He explicitly rejected "negotiation with the insurgent leader." Said Lincoln of Jefferson Davis: "Between him and us the issue is distinct, simple, and inflexible. It is an issue which can only be tried by war, and decided by victory." The president underlined his resolve, "The public purpose to reestablish and maintain the national authority is unchanged and, as we believe, unchangeable."

This attitude cannot be directly linked to Indian policy but the priorities therein dictated much of what happened in 1864–1865. Lincoln's determination to develop the West was tied to a commitment to win the war. He perceived that the exploitation of the minerals and the railroads located in Indian territory as necessary resources to accomplish that end. He was therefore exultant that "the steady expansion of population, improvement, and governmental institutions over the new and unoccupied portions of our country has scarcely been checked, much less impeded or destroyed,

4. AR, SI, 1864, pp. 21–22.
5. LAM, 1864, pp. 2–4.

by our great civil war." Lincoln noted "indian hostilities" that hampered organizing governments in Idaho and Montana, but he believed those governments would soon go "into speedy and full operation." He praised "the great enterprise of connecting the Atlantic with the Pacific States by railroads and telegraph lines." Gold and precious metals were being discovered all over the West. A nation at war was becoming richer and more powerful.

It was in this context that Lincoln spoke of Indians. The very order of his topics demonstrated Lincoln's priorities—new territories, railroads, minerals, and finally Indians. While he spoke of "the welfare of the Indians," his first concern for the West was "to render it secure for the advancing settler." Then and only then could Lincoln view the war effort with this perspective, "The national resources . . . are unexhausted, and, as we believe, inexhaustible." Come what may, this president was not going to let Indians get in the way of obtaining those resources.

Thus, Indians were treated increasingly as a military problem. Many troop contingents, like the Iowa Seventh Cavalry, never saw action in the South. Instead, they spent the years 1863-1865 in Dakota, Colorado, Wyoming, Kansas, and Nebraska.[6] Lincoln himself revived the once-stymied Confederate prisoner-of-war project in September 1864. Secretary of War Stanton opposed using them to fight Indians, and Lincoln personally went to the War Department to order Stanton to comply.[7] By 1865, the government had twenty thousand troops on the frontier, a large army considering the needs of the war in the South.[8] Lincoln's government never officially adopted John Pope's proposals for military control of the Indians. It did, however, adopt a de facto policy of militarism toward Indians. This policy was to provide a test of Pope's belief that military men would treat Indians better than civilians, with the laboratories in New Mexico and Colorado.

6. Eugene F. Ware, *The Indian War of 1864*, pp. xi, 176.

7. Roy P. Basler, ed., *The Collected Works of Abraham Lincoln*, 5:531; Carl Sandburg, *Abraham Lincoln: The War Years*, 3:501–5.

8. Robert M. Utley, *Frontiersmen in Blue: The U.S. Army and the Indian, 1848–1865*, p. 216.

Military Concentration in New Mexico

The great Civil War gave military men everywhere a special stature. Gen. James Carleton was given a relatively free hand when he went to New Mexico in the spring of 1862 to deal with the Indian situation. He found a situation where white and Indian relations were very bad.[9] To further complicate the situation, gold had been discovered on Indian land.

Commissioner Dole had advocated a concentration policy in New Mexico as early as 1861. He called then for the use of "military force" to punish the tribes for "the barbarous atrocities they are continually committing." Battles were also fought with Confederate soldiers in New Mexico during 1861 and that brought General Carleton into the territory.[10]

Carleton acted decisively. Under his auspices, Kit Carson launched expeditions against the Apaches. Carson's orders resembled those given by General Pope in the Minnesota war: "The Indians are to be soundly whipped." Women and children were to be taken prisoners and "all Indian men of that tribe are to be killed whenever and wherever you can find them." Carson was to "lay waste the prairies by fire."[11]

Carleton drew up plans to concentrate the Navajos on the Bosque Redondo, a reservation on the Pecos River. He set 20 July 1863 as the deadline for the Indians to surrender. Carson was then sent on a similar scorched-earth campaign against the Navajos.[12]

Carleton was not just being a good soldier. He had a passion for gold. He begged for funds to build a road to gold fields in Navajo country. Carleton plagued his superiors with stories of

9. Edmund Danziger, *Indians and Bureaucrats: Administering the Reservation Policy during the Civil War*, pp. 73–75.

10. E. R. S. Canby to The Adjutant General, 1 December 1861, OR, 1:4, pp. 77–78; AR, CIA, 1861, p. 636; Dee Brown, *Bury My Heart at Wounded Knee*, p. 20; these conflicts may have nourished Lincoln administration illusions about Confederate activity in the Minnesota war.

11. James Carleton to Kit Carson, 12 October 1862, *Report of the Joint Committee on the Condition of the Indian Tribes in the United States*, Senate Report 156.

12. Brown, *Bury My Heart*, pp. 22–25.

"extraordinary discoveries of gold and silver in Arizona territory." The general sent gold nuggets to cabinet members and even asked Salmon P. Chase to "give the largest piece of gold to Mr. Lincoln."[13]

Under Carleton, New Mexico became a major theater of conflict between Indian officials and the military. Michael Steck, the superintendent, objected to Carleton's methods, his waste of money, and his selection of the Bosque Redondo as a reservation for the Navajos.[14] Carleton, however, refused to back down. By early 1864, he proclaimed a victory over the Indians. The general congratulated himself on subduing "this formidable band of robbers and murderers." The Navajos, he proudly announced, "will have abandoned an area of country larger than the State of Ohio, to the pastoral and mining purposes of our citizens."[15]

Carleton completely misled Washington officials. He told them there was plenty of good land for the Navajos to sustain themselves at the Bosque Redondo. Commissioner Dole was led to believe that the Indians there "will soon become self-sustaining." In fact, just the opposite was true. The Indians began to suffer intensely and Carleton's fight with the Indian Office officials only made the situation worse.[16] The Carleton operation cost nearly a million dollars the first year, and it became a focus of national controversy. It merged into the debate over control of the Indians between the War and Interior departments.[17] Congress argued that question in May

13. Carleton to Henry Halleck, 10 May 1863, p. 110, Carleton to Halleck, 14 June 1863, pp. 113–14, Carleton to Lorenzo Thomas, 2 August 1863, p. 122, Carleton to Salmon P. Chase, 20 September 1863, p. 140, all *Report on the Condition of the Tribes*.

14. Michael Steck to Dole, 19 September 1863, AR, CIA, 1863, pp. 228–29; Edmund Danziger, "The Steck-Carleton Controversy in Civil War New Mexico."

15. Henry Connelly to Edwin M. Stanton, 12 March 1864, Roll 553, M234, LR, New Mexico Superintendency, OIA, RG75, NA.

16. Carleton to Thomas, 6 September 1863, *Report on the Condition of the Tribes*, p. 134; Dole to John P. Usher, 4 April 1864, *Senate Miscellaneous Document 97*, 1:2; Carleton to Thomas, 12 December 1863, Roll 551, M234, LR, New Mexico Superintendency, OIA, RG75, NA; H. D. Wallen to Ben F. Cutler, 12 February 1864, Roll 283, M619, LR, AGO, RG109, NA; Danziger, "The Steck-Carleton Controversy," p. 104.

17. Steck to Dole, 10 October 1864, AR, CIA, 1864, pp. 327–31; Carleton to Thomas, 19 March 1864, *Report on the Condition of the Tribes*, pp. 168–69; William B. Baker to Dole, 27 March 1864, Roll 552, M234, LR, New Mexico Superintendency, OIA, RG75, NA.

1864 when the Indian Office requested $100,000 to settle the Indians on the Bosque Redondo. Senators were shocked to learn that the military had four thousand prisoners. Nevertheless, the appropriation passed the Senate.[18]

Carleton's policies produced a disastrous situation. Secretary of War Stanton ordered an investigation of the large contracts Carleton had made. By July, Carleton had more than six thousand captives. In August, the number had grown to seventy-five hundred, including twelve hundred children. Carleton called them "the happiest people I have ever seen." That was not quite accurate. In September 1864, Carleton admitted having eight thousand prisoners, including "hundreds of naked women and children . . . likely to perish." Winter was approaching. Carleton became desperate, "Now the cold weather is setting in, and I have thousands of women and children who need the protection of a blanket."[19]

It wasn't until three investigations had been conducted that Carleton was relieved of his command. In September 1866, the War Department reversed his concentration policy, and the Navajos were returned to their own country.[20] Carleton continued to advocate General Pope's proposal to isolate and concentrate Indians behind military posts as a shield behind which Indians would be taught to farm and acquire the arts of civilization.[21] However, no one man did more to discredit these ideas.

The New Mexico situation confirmed Commissioner Dole's conviction that military control was a bad idea. In his 1864 report, he lashed out against the militarists and used New Mexico as an example. He compared it to the Indian Territory, which was man-

18. U.S., Congress, Senate, *Congressional Globe,* 38th Cong., 1st sess., 9 May 1864, pt. 3:2172–74.

19. Stanton to E. A. Hitchcock, 20 July 1864, Letterbook 43, Edwin M. Stanton Papers; Carleton to Thomas, 6 March 1864, p. 163, Carleton to Thomas, 8 July 1864, p. 187, *Report on the Condition of the Tribes;* Carleton to Usher, 24 August 1864, Roll 21, M825, LR, ID, OSI, RG48, NA; Carleton to Dole, 16 September 1864, p. 197, Carleton to Thomas, 30 October 1864, p. 207, *Report on the Condition of the Tribes.*

20. Danziger, "The Steck-Carleton Controversy," p. 111; Brown, *Bury My Heart,* p. 33.

21. Carleton testimony, 25 July 1865, *Report on the Condition of the Tribes,* p. 437.

aged by civil authorities. This comparison presented "a fair practical test of each line of policy." In New Mexico, there had been
continuous war. In the Indian Territory, only the Confederacy had
disrupted the peace. To Dole, New Mexico proved the bankruptcy
of the military control plan.[22]

Militarism in Colorado

Colorado provided the second major arena of military confrontation with the Indians in 1864. The impetus for the crisis was similar to elsewhere. Discoveries of gold brought large numbers of
white immigrants into the territory. The Indian System in Colorado
was typically corrupt. Agent Samuel Colley was a gold prospector
and politician before being appointed agent by Lincoln—on the
recommendation of his cousin, Commissioner William P. Dole.
Colley became one of a number of agents notorious for corrupt involvement with the Indian trade in Colorado.[23]

Like Minnesota and New Mexico, the Colorado situation was
shaped partly by the Civil War. Washington officials were concerned about protecting mail routes, railroads, and telegraph lines
as actual and symbolic links to northern unity. In April 1862, Lincoln authorized Brigham Young to raise a hundred men for ninety
days to protect these routes against Indians. Also, there were rumors
that the Confederates were plotting with the plains Indians. These
worries grew because of the Minnesota war and because General
Sully's expeditions in Dakota drove some of the Sioux into the
region, resulting in violence and destructive raids. The Cheyennes
and Arapahos were blamed for most of these incidents.

These matters came to a head in 1864 because the Colorado
government, under Gov. John Evans, embarked on a concentration
policy. In mid-1863, Evans had held unsuccessful council meetings
with tribal leaders.[24] In December 1863, Evans claimed there was a

22. AR, CIA, 1864, p. 150.
23. Harry Kelsey, "The Background to Sand Creek," p. 298.
24. G. Wright to J. W. Nye, 22 November 1861, AR, CIA, 1861, p. 360; Frank
Fuller (et al.) to Stanton, 11 April 1863, Brigham Young to John N. Bernhisel,
14 April 1862, AR, CIA, 1862, pp. 356–57; Lincoln to Stanton, 26 April 1862, Basler,
ed., *Collected Works*, 5:200; Danziger, *Indians and Bureaucrats*, p. 32.

conspiracy to form "an alliance of several thousand warriors" among the Sioux, Cheyenne, Kiowa, Comanche, Apache, and Arapaho tribes. He sought troops and arms from the War Department. In June 1864, Evans warned that "the Indians of the Plains are combining together for the purpose of waging war against the whites."[25]

During the summer of 1864, Colorado was in an uproar. Ranches were burned, livestock were stolen, and prisoners were captured by the Indians. Agent Colley concluded about the hungry Indians, "I now think a little powder and lead is the best food for them." The Indians were equally fearful. The Cheyennes heard that "the Big War Chief in Denver, [Col. John M. Chivington] had told his soldiers to kill all their squaws and papooses," and their fears were not groundless. Chivington was reported to have made a speech in Denver advocating the scalping of Indian infants.[26]

The crisis reached its peak in August. Evans sounded desperate: "We are left almost defenseless when the most powerful combination of Indian tribes for hostile purposes ever known on the Continent is in open hostilities against us." The War Department received reports of attacks on the overland mail route.[27] However, Washington officials had read similar reports from Minnesota two years earlier only to find out later that they were exaggerated. Evans did not wait for reluctant officials in Washington. He issued a proclamation on 11 August, calling on whites to "kill and destroy as enemies of the country wherever they may be found, all such hostile Indians." Evans implied that friendly Indians should not be killed, but citizens found it safer to kill Indians first without waiting to ask who was friendly. That inclination was encouraged by Evans's offer to let them retain any property retained as a result of killing the Natives. A war of defense merged into a war of plunder and extermination. When the War Department authorized the

25. John Evans to Stanton, 14 December 1863, Roll 64, Lincoln Papers, LC: Evans to Dole, 15 April 1864, Uriah Curtis to Evans, 28 June 1864, Roll 197, M234, LR, Colorado Superintendency, OIA, RG75, NA.

26. Kelsey, "Sand Creek," p. 284; H. T. Ketcham to Evans, 1 July 1864, Roll 197, M234, LR, Colorado Superintendency, OIA, RG75, NA; Brown, *Bury My Heart*, p. 89.

27. Evans to Dole, 9 August 1864, Roll 197, M234, LR, Colorado Superintendency, OIA, RG75, NA; S. E. Curtis to Halleck, 10 August 1864, JCCW, p. 63.

creation of a militia force for one hundred days, to be employed exclusively in killing Indians, the stage was set for a bloodbath.[28]

Officials in Washington, including Lincoln, paid little attention to all this. They were more concerned with Grant's battles with Lee in Virginia and Sherman's march into Georgia. The momentum of the Civil War was shifting toward the North. Unlike 1862 and the Minnesota war, Lincoln and his subordinates did not intend to let an Indian war in Colorado distract them from winning the War for the Union.

That left the initiative in Indian conflicts with military men in the field. On 28 September 1864, Gen. Samuel Curtis gave a fateful order to Colonel Chivington and the Colorado militia, "I want no peace until the Indians suffer more." Governor Evans confirmed the harsh policy thay had adopted, "A peace before conquest, in this case would be the most *cruel* kindness and the most *barbarous* humanity." The Indians were to be sought out and punished. Militarism had triumphed in Colorado.[29]

A Distracting Election Campaign

The Lincoln administration paid little attention to what was happening in Colorado. There was an election campaign going on and it was one more reason not to notice the situation in Colorado. There was a growing peace movement in the country in 1864 and Lincoln had significant opposition, even in his own party. The Democratic party had nominated Gen. George McClellan as its candidate, and with the growing peace sentiment, it appeared possible until September that McClellan might unseat the president. Then, Sherman's dramatic triumphs in Georgia began to reverse the trend of public opinion.

Commissioner Dole paid little attention to Colorado because he was too busy with the election campaign. As a political ap-

28. Danziger, *Indians and Bureaucrats*, p. 38; Evans testimony, August 1865, *Report on the Condition of the Tribes*, p. 85.
29. Curtis to John M. Chivington, 28 September 1864, AR, CIA, 1864, p. 365; Robert Mardock, *The Reformers and the American Indian*, p. 19; Evans to Dole, 15 October 1864, AR, CIA, 1864, p. 366.

pointee, Dole had work to do. He was very busy with his "political file" and corresponded almost more often with John Usher and Lincoln on political matters than on Indian affairs. Dole paid special attention to New York and Kansas, where agents kept him informed as to "the *true* friends of the President."[30]

The busy Indian commissioner did not write his annual report until the week after the 1864 election was over. In it, he praised "the energetic action of Governor Evans" in Colorado. Dole took note of the hundred-day volunteers and the military actions taking place. He also expressed some doubts, "I am unable to find any immediate cause for the uprising of the Indian tribes of the plains, except the active efforts upon their savage natures by the emissaries from the hostile northern tribes." Dole feared that the chance for peace had been lost, "It is a great deal cheaper to feed them . . . than to fight them."[31]

Chivington and Evans had no intention of pursuing a policy of peace. "What shall I do with the Third Colorado Regiment if I make peace?" asked Evans. "They have been raised to kill Indians, and they must kill Indians."[32]

Sand Creek and the Discrediting of Military Control

On 9 January 1865, a shaken Sen. James Doolittle rose in the Senate to introduce a bill to investigate "the condition of the Indian tribes and their treatment by the civil and military authorities." Doolittle informed the Senate he had received news to "make one's blood chill and freeze with horror." Doolittle said that Colonel Chivington and his soldiers had attacked five hundred unsuspecting

30. Dole to Usher, 20 February 1864, Roll 68, Lincoln Papers, LC; Simeon Draper to Dole, 3 March 1864, Roll 69, Lincoln Papers, LC; Thomas Ewing to Dole, 26 August 1864, Roll 80, Lincoln Papers, LC; Ewing to Dole, 21 September 1864, Roll 97, Lincoln Papers, LC; J. S. Emery to James H. Lane, 23 November 1864, James H. Lane Papers; Dole to Lincoln, 18 June 1864, Roll 76, Lincoln Papers, LC; Draper to Dole, 7 September 1864, Roll 81, Lincoln Papers, LC; William Frank Zornow, "The Kansas Senators and the Re-election of Lincoln."

31. AR, CIA, 1864, pp. 167–68.

32. Brown, *Bury My Heart,* p. 79.

Indians at Sand Creek, Colorado, in November of the previous year. They had killed one hundred and fifty Natives, mostly women and children.[33]

News of Sand Creek brought a sharp public reaction. Three different investigations were launched, and all agreed that Sand Creek was a "massacre," an unusual label to be attached to the actions of white soldiers. Black Kettle, leader of the Cheyennes, had raised a white flag and an American flag—to no avail. Chivington had told his men, "I want no prisoners." Eyewitnesses reported the slaughter of children, the scalping of women, the butchering of pregnant women, and castrations. The atrocities were, in Agent Colley's words, "as bad as an Indian ever did to a white man."[34]

Chivington and Evans defended their actions. Chivington called his performance "an act of duty to ourselves and civilization."[35] The public did not accept this. Besides the investigations, there was talk of court-martialing Chivington. The Congress passed Doolittle's bill with a fifteen-thousand-dollar appropriation and provision for three senators and four representatives on a joint committee to investigate Indian affairs.[36]

The scandal over Sand Creek produced debate in the Senate. On 13 January 1865, the senators argued a resolution to suspend pay of the officers and soldiers involved with Sand Creek until the investigations were completed.[37] The promoters of the action included Indian Committee members who had been normally unsympathetic to Indians and opposed to reform.

33. U.S., Congress, Senate, *Congressional Globe*, 38th Cong., 1st sess., 9 January 1865, pt. 1:158; Marvin A. Garfield, "Defense of the Kansas Frontier, 1864–65," p. 144.

34. Kelsey, "Sand Creek," pp. 279–80; Samuel G. Colley testimony, 7 March 1865, pp. 29, 34, Cramer testimony, 27 July 1865, p. 74, Robert Bent testimony, 22 [?] June 1865, p. 96, all *Report on the Condition of the Tribes*.

35. Evans testimony, 8 March 1865, *Report on the Condition of the Tribes*, p. 49; Chivington testimony, 26 April 1865, JCCW, p. 104.

36. Garfield, "The Kansas Frontier," p. 145; U.S., Congress, Senate, *Congressional Globe*, 38th Cong., 2d sess., 19 January 1865, pt. 1:326; the House passed it 24 February 1865 (pt. 2:1057) and the conference report was adopted 3 March 1865 (p. 1380).

37. U.S., Congress, Senate, *Congressional Globe*, 38th Cong., 2d sess., 13 January 1865, pt. 1:250–56.

Sen. James Harlan attacked the militarism exhibited at Sand Creek. He labeled it a departure from previous benevolent policies. "That policy is being reversed without any authority from the Federal Government by the agents of the Government remote, away from the capital." Harlan called it a plan for the "extermination of the Indians," a war to end all wars. The Iowa senator directly linked Sand Creek with the actions of General Carleton in New Mexico.

Senator Nesmith opposed suspending pay for the soldiers and condemned such "misguided sympathy for the Indians." He called Indians "a degraded, thieving, murdering, plundering race" incapable of civilization. White men had long endured atrocities by Indians. "Most of my sympathy is on the side of the white man," declared the senator, "because I believe he has generally been in the right and has only resorted to this sort of retaliation as a matter of self-defense."

The debate grew more heated. Sen. John Conness of California raged at the unjust treatment of the Indians:

> And I say these wars have been fomented by the miserable kind of human fungi that now hang upon the vitals of the nation making money and crying for money when no man could tell whether the nation should live or die; and they were instituted for plunder, carried on with the hand of murder, maintained by the basest cowardice that the human mind can conceive, because the blows were directed at those who could not and had not the power to strike back.

Even Charles Sumner, lion of the Radicals, jumped into the debate. Sumner normally held his peace on Indian issues, but the heated exchange drew him in. The man who had made "the crime against Kansas" household words pronounced Sand Creek "an exceptional crime; one of the most atrocious in the history of the country."

Senator Doolittle demonstrated how thoroughly militarism in Indian affairs was discredited by Sand Creek. Doolittle denied "any overweening sympathy in behalf of the Indian race." Indians were a dying race. That was inevitable given the advance of civilization.

Nevertheless, Doolittle concluded: "I am unwilling that the flag and the Government of the United States shall be stained by any outrages such as it is alleged have been perpetrated by Colonel Chivington and the men under his command in this expedition."

Doolittle had once been an advocate of military control of Indians. The chairman of the Senate Indian Affairs Committee changed his mind when confronted with events in New Mexico and Colorado. He condemned the military in both places. "It is time," he said, "the country should wake up to these military expeditions inaugurated, in my judgement, without the direct authority of the War Department here at Washington, against these Indian tribes."

The pay suspension measure passed the Senate but was defeated in the House of Representatives. Chivington was already out of uniform and beyond the reach of military law. Congress salved its conscience by providing $39,050 in the next session in gifts to the Cheyenne and Arapaho bands attacked at Sand Creek.[38]

The blunders and brutality of the military did what the reformers, with Lincoln's help, had been unable to do. They moved the power structure in the Congress to launch serious investigations that promised change in Indian policy. While the controversy over civilian and military control continued for another decade, the actions in New Mexico and at Sand Creek did much to discredit John Usher's idea that all Indians "should be pursued by the military, and punished."

38. Garfield, "The Kansas Frontier," p. 145.

XIII. Lincolnian Attitudes Toward Indians: "A Dying Race . . . Giving Place to Another Race with a Higher Civilization"

IT WAS NOT JUST POLITICS that undid the movement for reform of the Indian System. Americans of the Lincoln era accepted a fabric of ideas and attitudes that supported their political and military actions toward Indians. The reformers failed to break up the "political machine" that exploited the tribes partly because they were unable to break the chain of ideas whites held that bound Native Americans. Those ideas reinforced the great European-American cultural migration of hundreds of thousands of persons that led almost inevitably to tragedy. Given the premises on which that migration and European-American civilization were based, it is difficult to imagine another outcome.

The Indian as Savage

What is an Indian? White leaders in the 1860s agreed that he was a *savage*. The word had great meaning for both reformers and nonreformers. A savage was not like a white man. He was clearly inferior. Savagery presumed an opposite—*civilization*. Civilized men were therefore the ones who decided who and what was labeled savage.

The idea of the savage had more specific meanings. It denoted violence, especially in the aftermath of wars like the one in Minnesota in 1862. Agent Thomas Galbraith identified this savage characteristic, contending the Sioux prized "theft, arson, rape and murder" and that Indian children were raised "to regard killing as the highest of virtues." Galbraith also identified a second savage characteristic, "idleness," and argued that Indian men hated labor and left it only for their women. Galbraith found the Indians' heathen religion at the root of savage behavior, "They are bigoted, barbarous and exceedingly superstitious." Superstition, in white man's jargon, meant that Indians were non-Christian. Galbraith specifically blamed the medicine men for creating a situation where "ignorance, indolence, filth, lust, vice, bigotry, superstition, and crime, make up the ancient customs of the Sioux Indians." These religious leaders taught the Indians to be "ignorant, deluded, super-stitious, and wicked creatures, degraded and brutal in all their habits and instincts, and always prepared to do any bad thing." To Galbraith, "This is the Sioux Indian as he is."[1]

This image of the violent, indolent, superstitious savage was buttressed by a fear of Indian male sexual aggression. The "savage" was a masculine concept, enunciated by white males about Indian males. The Minnesota war brought these emotions to the surface. The atrocity tales of that war were filled with accounts of rape. Morton Wilkinson described a scene of rape to his Senate colleagues and railed against "these violators of our women." Gen. John Pope matched Wilkinson with his tales of "women violated and then disemboweled." The military trials of the Sioux resulted in the condemnation of nearly all the male prisoners. Lincoln, when he reviewed the trial transcripts, looked first for evidence of rape, thereby ranking that crime ahead of murder. Yet, Lincoln's report indicated he could find proof of only two rapes among the three hundred and three condemned.[2] If this were the case, the insecurity of the white males rendered them almost irrational. The image of the savage was psychologically linked to fears of Indian male sexual violence.

Most white leaders concluded that the savage was unchange-

1. Thomas Galbraith to William P. Dole, 27 January 1863, AR, CIA, 1863, pp. 395-97 (for "Abbreviations in Footnotes," see p. vi). A major study of the idea of savagism up to 1851 is Roy Harvey Pearce, *Savagism and Civilization*.

2. See pp. 88, 98, 110 of this book; U.S., Congress, Senate, *Congressional Globe*, 37th Cong., 3d sess., 1862, p. 13; John Pope to Henry Halleck, 23 September 1862, OR, 1:13, p. 667; Abraham Lincoln to the Senate, 11 December 1862, Roy P. Basler, ed., *The Collected Works of Abraham Lincoln*, 5:550-51.

able. Cyrus Aldrich held that view, "It is very questionable to my mind whether under the most favorable circumstances the native Aborigine 'to the manor born' is capable of attaining a high or even mediocre state of civilization."[3] Morton Wilkinson agreed:

> The efforts to improve & civilize the Indians are misdirected. . . . So long as an Indian feels that his mode of savage life is preferable to the civilization of his neighbor, just so long your efforts to educate him will prove abortive, because education in no wise aids him in the gratification of savage ambitions.[4]

Senator Nesmith called Indians "a degraded, thieving, murdering, plundering race" and concluded this was "the instinct of their nature." Thomas Galbraith believed the Minnesota war was evidence of "the fixed hostility of the savage barbarian to reform, change, and civilization." Nesmith summarized the unchangeable savage, "Sir, you cannot civilize the Indian."[5]

Thus, Indians were seen as idle, heathen, violent, sexually aggressive, and unchangeable. The Indian wars seemed to confirm whites' fears as to the consequences of these savage traits among Indians. Furthermore, they believed savages were always conspiring together against the whites. These conspiracy fears surfaced in the Lincoln administration's acceptance of the explanation of the cause of the Minnesota war as a Confederate conspiracy.[6] Commissioner Dole called conspiracy part of "the well known character of Indians having a common enemy." Whites feared that, as the result of a "deep-laid plan," Indians would fall upon them at any moment. This syndrome helps to explain the exaggerated reports of the numbers, power, and brutality of the Indians. It bears a similarity to the fears of revolt so common among white slaveowners. Whites had a deep-rooted fear that they simply could not be safe in proximity to Indians, no matter how peaceful.

All these fears are similar to the ideas that whites, North and

3. Cyrus B. Aldrich to Henry Benjamin Whipple, 12 June 1862, Box 3, Henry Benjamin Whipple Papers.

4. Morton Wilkinson to Whipple, 8 May 1862, ibid.

5. U.S., Congress, Senate, *Congressional Globe*, 38th Cong., 2d sess., 13 January 1865, pt. 1:251; Galbraith to Dole, 27 January 1863, AR, CIA, p. 397.

6. See pp. 78–79.

South, articulated concerning Afro-Americans. The fear of rape and the complex of ideas surrounding male sexual aggressiveness and primitive unchangeability were often applied to blacks. Scholars like Winthrop Jordan have identified these fears of safety as fundamental to the attitudes underlying slavery, although with subtle shades of difference in attitudes toward Indians.[7]

Although reformers assumed a more humanitarian view, they did agree that the Indian was a savage. Bishop Whipple said, "The North American Indian is a savage and like all other heathen men fierce, vindictive[,] cruel and his animal passions are unrestrained by civilization & Christianity."[8]

This label did have different connotations for the reformers than it did for other whites. Bishop Whipple, for example, concentrated on the "Noble Savage" characteristics of the Indian. The Indian had "natural virtues," according to the bishop. Whipple maintained, "The Indian is the only heathen who is not an idolater, he is naturally a brave man & has manhood."[9] Whipple made the noble savage a fundamental factor in his contention that a reform program could succeed.

> The North American Indians are the best of the heathen uncivilized races. They are not idolators. They believe in a Great Spirit. They have home affections. They have strong national pride and love of country. They are generally chaste, truthful, honest, generous and hospitable.[10]

Why Indians Are Degraded

Reformers and nonreformers agreed that the Indians lived in terrible conditions. The majority believed the tribes were responsi-

7. AR, CIA, 1862, p. 188; see p. 78 of this book; John H. Baker to Edwin M. Stanton, 21 August 1862, OR, 1:13, p. 591.
8. Whipple, "The Duty of Citizens concerning the Indian Massacre," Box 40, Letterbook 3, Whipple Papers.
9. Whipple to Galbraith, 15 April 1861, ibid.
10. Whipple to the Secretary of the Interior, 23 February 1861, ibid. A significant study of Jeffersonian origins of the "noble savage" stereotype is Bernard Sheehan, *Seeds of Extinction*, pp. 89–116.

ble for their destitution and the wretched conditions of the Indians reinforced their image of the unchangeable savage. The reformers, however, came to a significantly different conclusion: the noble savage was not naturally that way but had been degraded from a higher level of life. "If all this has been changed until degradation & poverty are stamped upon a race," Whipple charged, "it is a curse given to them by a Christian people."[11]

Reformers argued that Indians were degraded because an evil system exposed them to the worst in white society. Whipple made the point: "Dishonest agents or careless servants have made way with his money. Corrupt whites have polluted his home wife & daughters & blasted his home by the accursed fire water."[12] In short, reformers argued that the Indian was in the wrong environment; if the environment were changed, the Indian could change.

Many policymakers rejected this approach with the view that the problem was the Indian, not the environment. Caleb Smith held this view, "It is apparent to all acquainted with Indians that they are incompetent to manage their own business or to protect their rights in their intercourse with the white race." In Smith's view, something about the Indian made him acquire the worst white traits and reject the best. Commissioner Dole admitted reformers were right that "the worst classes of our own people collect around his reservation." Nevertheless, Dole contended that the vices of the whites, "gambling, the whiskey traffic, and every species of vice and immorality" were things "to all of which the Indian seems to be unusually prone." The Indian, argued Senator Nesmith, "has contracted all the vices of the white man, but none of his virtues."[13]

Reformers found this explanation unacceptable. Bishop Whipple differed on the basis of his religion, "As a Christian I take issue with anyone who claims that God has created any human being who is incapable of civilization or who cannot receive the gospel of

11. Whipple to the Secretary of the Interior, 23 February 1861, Box 40, Letterbook 3, Whipple Papers.

12. Whipple to Galbraith, 15 April 1861, ibid.

13. AR, SI, 1861, p. 12; AR, CIA, 1863, p. 130; U.S., Congress, Senate, *Congressional Globe,* Debate on the Indian Appropriation Bill, 37th Cong., 2d sess., 13 May 1862, pt. 3:2095.

Jesus Christ." Occasionally, William Dole appears to have been attracted by this reform argument, "Innumerable instances have demonstrated that he possesses capacities which, properly developed, would enable him to live creditably amongst the most enlightened nations."[14]

Make Him Like a White Man

If the Indian could be changed, it remained for the reformers to define the kind of change that was desirable. The reformers furnished a paternalistic answer—make the Indian like a white man. Clark Thompson was no reformer but he expressed this attitude with clarity: "His whole nature must be changed. He must have a white man's ambition, to be like him. He must have the objects and aims of a white man." Thompson identified the characteristics of Indian life—the chase, medicine dances, irregular work patterns for males, dress, and nonmaterialistic values. But he perceived these values as inferior rather than as a different culture. The solution was to introduce white man's work and "change the disposition of the Indian to one more mercenary and ambitious to obtain riches, and teach him to value the position consequent upon the possession of riches."[15]

Reformers and nonreformers agreed on one thing: In order to change the Indian it was first necessary to put him to work. They were offended by what they perceived to be Indian idleness. Morton Wilkinson said it:

> Labor is the great civilizer up in our country; and as the white men are pretty well civilized, because they all labor, so we think if we can induce the Indians to labor and earn their own living by cultivating farms, that will be one of the highest evidences of civilization.[16]

14. Whipple, "The Duty of Citizens," Box 40, Letterbook 3, Whipple Papers; AR, CIA, 1861, p. 647.

15. Clark W. Thompson to Dole, 30 October 1861, AR, CIA, 1861, p. 683.

16. U.S., Congress, Senate, *Congressional Globe,* 37th Cong., 2d sess., 13 May 1862, pt. 3:2082.

Indians, however, seemed not to like such work. Galbraith found idleness "idolized among the Sioux braves, and labor is regarded as a debasing institution, fit only for squaws."[17] If the Indian was to be transformed, the leaders of the Lincoln era agreed that he had to labor like a white man.

This Northerners' idealization of labor may have been reinforced by the struggle over slavery. The idea of "free labor" had become sharply etched in their minds. It stood in sharp contrast to the idleness of the slavocracy and the debasement of labor represented by slavery. As Lincoln articulated this attitude: "Labor is prior to, and independent of, capital. Capital is only the fruit of labor, and could never have existed if labor had not first existed. Labor is the superior of capital, and deserves much higher consideration." Lincoln extolled "the free hired laborer" and "the prudent penniless beginner in the world" who "labors for wages awhile" and moves up the ladder. "No men living are more worthy to be trusted than those who toil up from poverty," proclaimed the president in this mid-nineteenth century version of the Protestant ethic.[18]

The bloodshed of the Civil War raised the deification of labor to a new level. And because whites, including Lincoln, perceived that Indians did not live by this philosophy, their response to Indians could only be negative. Morton Wilkinson summarized the attitude: "Labor is a great civilizer. I do not believe that the efforts to civilize or convert to Christianity an idle race of Barbarians will ever succeed unless you first induce them to become industrious, prudent and thrifty."[19]

Wilkinson belittled the impact of Christianity on Indians, but Christian dogma provided further support for the deification of labor. Bishop Whipple called for placing "the weight of government on the side of labor. Man must live by the sweat of his brow."

17. Galbraith to Dole, 27 January 1863, AR, CIA, 1863, p. 397.
18. LAM, 1861, p. 2. For a more complete explanation of Republican ideology on labor, see Eric Foner, *Free Soil, Free Labor, Free Men: The Ideology of the Republican Party Before the Civil War*, pp. 9–39.
19. Wilkinson to Whipple, 8 May 1862, Box 3, Whipple Papers.

That famous phrase from the book of Genesis was commonly used in reference to Indians. Senator Rice quoted it to Whipple just before going to see President Lincoln and concluded that those "words of Holy Writ are as unchangeable as the Heavens."[20]

White men were so obsessed with the stereotype of Indians' laziness that they often failed to perceive Indian labor when it took place. Clark Thompson challenged this assumption about the Indian, "I believe, in fact, that he is naturally just as fond of labor as a white man; that labor is as essential to his civilization as it is to the civilization of the black or white man." That was an extraordinary statement to come from an Indian official in the 1860s. Thompson charged that whites themselves had created the myth of the Indian who would not work. His evidence was irrefutable:

> Armies are raised, attacks are made, long night marches are undertaken and endured, large amounts of plunder are taken and carried away; they can kill; they can destroy; they can bear up under almost any amount of hardships and fatigue.

Thompson pointed to robberies of wagon trains, the loading of grain, and the driving of teams. Indians built canoes and hunted wild animals as large as deer and buffalo. "Now, is it to be proved that they cannot labor?" argued Thompson. "Indeed, can they do all these things without immense labor?"[21]

Thompson's view was in the minority. The majority view was presented in a letter from C. Wood Davis to Sen. Jim Lane concerning the opening of Indian lands for settlement, "It is certainly for the interest of all citizens to have these lands settled by enterprising white settlers rather than have them remain in the hands of the indolent, improvident Red Man."[22] The logic of such rhetoric was inescapable. The only hope for the Indian was to learn to labor like a white man.

20. Whipple, "What Shall We Do with the Indians," Box 40, Letterbook 3, Whipple Papers; Henry M. Rice to Whipple, 19 November 1862, Box 3, Whipple Papers.

21. Thompson to Dole, 1 October 1864, AR, CIA, 1864, p. 543.

22. C. Wood Davis to James H. Lane, 28 November 1864, James H. Lane Papers.

The Cornerstone of Civilization

Whites not only agreed that Indians needed to engage in labor according to their own definition, but there was also an overwhelming consensus that the kind of labor that would be best was farming. This was the natural bias of a nation where the largest proportion of labor was agricultural. Agriculture, however, meant more than that to Americans in the Lincoln era. It was, especially when linked with private property, the cornerstone of civilization. To the men of the 1860s, no clearer criterion existed for measuring the degree to which Indians were "savage" and white men were "civilized."

The agrarian bias was rooted in Christianity. Thomas Galbraith called Christianity "the true basis of civilization." He linked it to the myth of the Garden of Eden and the "sweat of the brow" doctrine found in Genesis. Although not all arguments were based so directly on Christianity, most whites reached similar conclusions. Augustus Wattles contended that to go "from barbarism to civilization it is of the first importance that the Agency be supplied with a farmer & a carpenter to work with and for the Indians, and teach them in these necessary occupations."[23]

This idealization of agricultural labor was a dominant feature of American ideology during the era. The Homestead Act was the embodiment of it, and attitudes toward the plantation South reinforced it. The reform movement made individualized farming central to proposals for change and underlined the reformers' distaste for collectivistic tribal organizations. Lincoln's own legend as the rail-splitting frontiersman participated in the mythology of agriculture.

Thus, policymakers strongly advocated that Indians farm. Caleb Smith praised individual allotment, "A continuance of this policy, by familiarizing them with the habits of agricultural life,

23. Galbraith to Dole, 27 January 1863, AR, CIA, 1863, p. 397; Augustus Wattles to Dole, 1 June 1861, Roll 59, M574, SF201, OIA, RG75, NA. For more on the agrarian myth, see Henry Nash Smith, *The Virgin Land: The American West as Symbol and Myth,* and Leo Marx, *The Machine in the Garden: Technology and the Pastoral Ideal in America.*

will gradually lead them to depend upon the cultivation of the soil for subsistence." Commissioner Dole advocated pushing Indians "to adopt the customs of civilization" and "the ideas of self-reliance and individual effort, and as an encouragement of those ideas, the acquisition and ownership of property in severalty." The "first efforts for the attainment of civilization," wrote Dole, "should be directed toward the acquisition of a knowledge and practice of the simple arts of husbandry and pastoral life." Land allotment would, in Dole's judgment, lead the Indian "to abandon the ancient customs of his tribe, and engage in the more rational pursuits of civilization."[24]

This policy led to the creation of two classes of Indians. Dole labeled them "farmer" and "blanket" Indians. During the war in Minnesota, the trouble was blamed on the "blanket" Indians. This confirmed to Dole that individual ownership of "the soil was the step that was the most important in their progress toward civilization."[25]

The most complete statement of agrarian ideology came from Lincoln's new Department of Agriculture in 1862. The commissioner, Isaac Newton, said very little about Indians, but the implications of his vision were profound for the Natives of America.[26]

Agriculture, claimed Newton, was the "great civilizer in the world's progress." He identified four stages in the development of civilization—a period of wild growth, a pastoral period when men were herdsmen, a third age when men settled on the fertile plains, and a final era when there was a "migration of races" to plant new empires in the wilderness and practice agriculture as "the great and essential art of life." In this perspective of evolution, Indians were perceived as near the bottom of the ladder of civilization, and whites were on top.

To Newton, the process of civilization offered dangers as well as potential progress; if civilization could rise, it could also fall.

24. AR, SI, 1861, p. 12; AR, CIA, 1863, p. 130.
25. AR, CIA, 1862, pp. 170, 179.
26. AR, Commissioner of Agriculture, 1862, Roll 46, Abraham Lincoln Papers, LC.

Rome was his example. Rome fell because "labor became disrespectable; the soil a monopoly, and the masses of the people reckless, unpatriotic and degraded." Rome's decline had a great lesson for America: "Any nation that desires permanent prosperity and power, should learn it well, wisely protecting labor and capital and encouraging the division and cultivation of the soil." This reasoning implied that deviation from the acceptable occupation of agriculture was not merely an irritant—it was dangerous. That logic could lead to the conclusion that Indian ways constituted a threat to the foundations of civilization itself.

Newton extolled the progress of civilization in America. In so doing, he made his only direct reference to the Indians, "The first settlers had many and great difficulties to encounter in clearing the land, in bringing it under cultivation and in defending themselves against the Indians." The commissioner saw these settlers as a vanguard of civilization. Newton took no note of the contribution of Indian agricultural products like corn or tobacco, although the statistical portion of his report did refer to "Indian corn." He was caught up in "the spirit of enterprise which urges our young men and adopted citizens to become free-holders." The symbol of American progress was "the noble homestead law." Newton quoted a political economist, "Every acre of our fertile soil . . . is a mine which only waits the contact of labor to yield its treasures; and every acre is opened to that fruitful contact by the Homestead Act." No Indian land was secure when "every acre" was so coveted.

The glories of yeomanry were linked, in Newton's perspective, to nationalism. The nation most needed "increased respect for labor" of the type practiced by the freeholder. "He has no master," wrote the commissioner. "He has a sturdy independence of character." Agriculture tamed the ambitions of men and healed divisions. "Whatever improves the condition and character of the farmer feeds the life springs of National Character, wealth, and power," Newton proclaimed. He distrusted cities and thought they encouraged selfishness and corruption. The commissioner had no doubt about the proper course, "The United States are and must always remain an agricultural nation."

Newton was an eloquent articulator of the American conviction that agriculture was fundamental to civilization. "It is the cause and the evidence of true civilization," he wrote, "for when tillage begins, barbarism ends." Americans of Newton's time saw the Indians as the most accurate representation of barbarism. They were a clear and present symbol of what had ruined Rome. They were a tragic remnant of the savage past, before men learned to till the soil in severalty. The logic of such thinking led to a harsh conclusion—Indians must change or die.

Lincoln and the Agrarian Myth

Abraham Lincoln accepted these ideas concerning labor, agriculture, and civilization. He and those around him also recognized their implications for Indians. John G. Nicolay, his secretary, often went on missions for the Indian Office. Nicolay thought Indians were savages and accepted the notion that they were unchangeable. He doubted the Indian could be taught to farm because of "his ineradicable habits of indolence and carelessness." Nicolay even saw problems with them being herdsmen because of their "improvidence and wastefulness." To Nicolay, war was "the normal condition of savage life."[27]

Lincoln's personal views were similar. He accepted the stereotype of the Indian as a heathen savage, in need of civilization and religious instruction. In 1863, he spoke of "their progress in the arts of civilization, and, above all to that moral training which, under the blessing of divine Providence, will confer upon them the elevated and sanctifying influences, the hopes and consolations of the Christian faith."[28]

Lincoln appears to have entertained little doubt as to the first step toward helping Indians obtain "the arts of civilization." They would have to become farmers. In March 1863, Lincoln and Indian leaders from several tribes met in the East Room of the White House. The Indians spoke of the great numbers of people and large

27. John G. Nicolay to Dole, 10 November 1863, AR, CIA, 1863, pp. 267–68.
28. LAM, 1863, p. 3.

buildings they had seen. Lincoln responded in paternalistic tones, "We pale-faced people think that this world is a great, round ball." He told them how his people had come from far away, and he had a professor lecture the tribal leaders, using a world globe for illustration.

Then Lincoln commented on the "great difference between this pale-faced people and their red brethern both as to numbers and the way in which they live."

> The pale-faced people are numerous and prosperous because they cultivate the earth, produce bread, and depend upon the products of the earth rather than wild game for a subsistence. This is the chief reason of the difference; but there is another. Although we are now engaged in a great war between one another, we are not, as a race, so much disposed to fight and kill one another as our red brethern.[29]

There is no record of what went through the chiefs' minds at this incredible recitation by the president of the United States. In three sentences, Lincoln managed to tie together the stereotype of the savage, nonfarming hunter with the inherently violent barbarian who was inferior to whites. Considering the bloodiness of the Civil War in 1863, it was a remarkable statement.

Removal Ideology

Lincoln's advice to Indians to take up farming clashed with the harsh realities. His own troops had destroyed Indian farms in Minnesota only months earlier. Efforts by the Indian Office to promote agriculture had failed again and again through bad management and outright fraud. Furthermore, such rhetoric ran into the reality of Indian removal.

When Indians were removed, it was nearly always to agriculturally inferior land. Lincoln told the Indians, "I can only say that I can see no way in which your race is to become as numerous

29. Meeting with Indian Leaders, 27 March 1863, Washington *Daily Morning Chronicle*, 28 March 1863, reprinted in Basler, ed., *Collected Works*, 6:151–52.

and prosperous as the white race except by living as they do, by the cultivation of the earth." At that very moment, Lincoln's subordinates were preparing to move Minnesota's Sioux and Winnebagos onto land that was practically unarable. The Minnesota Indians, in fact, were forced to leave good land for soil where they would be forced to subsist on hunting or government handouts. Government leaders preached something that their own policies made impossible. It was impossible because the Homestead Act implied that all Indian lands were open to settlement. Farming could not be begun when troops were chasing Indians all over Dakota or moving them from good land in New Mexico. The evidence was overwhelming that ambitious white men were not inclined to permit Indians to have farmland that would permit them "to become as numerous and prosperous as the white race."[30]

In order to get that land, Indians had to be removed. That practical concern underlay removal policy. Nevertheless, a number of justifications arose for removing the Indians. Sometimes these were self-serving rationales to justify land grabs. Often, however, they coincided with arguments advanced by reformers justifying removal as a benefit to the Indians.

A major justification for removal was that it was protecting the Indians. Reformers contended that Indians were degraded by contact with whites. The solution was isolation. Bishop Whipple sanctioned such removal after the Minnesota war, in order to separate the tribes from evil white influences. Commissioner Dole worried about "the pernicious efforts arising from the intercourse of vicious whites with the Indians. . . . I have long believed," he said, "that the civilization of the Indian and the perpetuation of his race depend upon his isolation from the whites." Dole thought concentration offered the best solution. General Pope agreed with the isolation plan because "no sufficient protection is afforded to the Indians."[31]

30. Basler, ed., *Collected Works*, 6:152.
31. Whipple, "The Duty of Citizens," Box 40, Letterbook 3, Whipple Papers; AR, CIA, 1862, p. 179; Dole to Caleb B. Smith, 22 November 1862, AR, CIA, 1862, p. 493; AR, CIA, 1863, p. 130; JCCW, 2:195. See pp. 151–53 of this book for Pope's plan. Pope's report to the committee contains many of the other ideas common to the prevailing attitudes outlined above.

Opportunists found the argument useful. Jim Lane, calling for the removal of the Kansas Indians from his state, said, "They are surrounded by the whites pressing upon them on all sides, destroying them." Lane said that the removal was "not for the benefit of the whites"; it would help the Indians. "Then you can protect the Indians from controversies and wars with each other; and there they can live and develop the highest civilization of which the Indian race is capable."[32]

Lane's use of the phrase, *Indian race,* points to an obvious perspective on removal that links it to European-American attitudes toward other nonwhite groups. Removal was fundamentally racial segregation. In the minds of whites, it did not differ essentially from the already well documented separatist attitudes whites expressed toward blacks in American life. Race, rather than behavior, was the foundation for categorization and removal just as in segregation. Nowhere was this racism more evident than in Lincoln's description of Indians "as a race."[33]

Some men protested the racial double standard. Sen. William Pitt Fessenden of Maine was an eloquent opponent of racism. Fessenden criticized Jim Lane for his arguments for removal, complaining that "all the rights, and all the justice . . . are to be reserved exclusively for the whites and that the Indians do not seem to have any rights in relation to the matter." Fessenden questioned the logic of racial removal. He forecast that moving the Kansas Indians to Indian Territory would be only a temporary remedy; then the cycle of white domination over Indian lands would begin all over again. The senator scoffed at the statement that the Territory would belong to the tribes forever. "Forever," he said, really meant "until the white people want it."[34]

Fessenden's role as the senatorial conscience on anti-Indian racism was a lonely one. In 1862, Senator Nesmith advocated remov-

32. U.S., Congress, Senate, *Congressional Globe,* 37th Cong., 3d sess., 26 January 1863, pt. 1:505–6.

33. Basler, ed., *Collected Works,* 6:152.

34. U.S., Congress, Senate, *Congressional Globe,* 37th Cong., 3d sess., 26 January 1863, pt. 1:506.

ing some Oregon Indians to protect them. There were ten thousand whites on the Nez Perce reservation, and Nesmith said "no power can remove them." Fessenden asked why the law-breaking whites were not driven away and suggested employing bayonets. The senators were horrified at the idea of using weapons against whites on behalf of Indians. Fessenden pressed his argument:

> There is no difficulty, I take it, in Kansas or Oregon in keeping men off the lands that are owned by white men. . . . The sympathy is with the possessor and the owner; public opinion is with the possessor and the owner, and he can be kept in possession of his land, notwithstanding his neighbor wants to get it away from him. But when the possessor happens to be an Indian, the question is changed altogether; the law of God, the higher law . . . requires that the white man should steal from the Indian; and if he cannot do it in any other way, he is to cut his throat; and if he is not strong enough to do this, the Government of the United States is to help him![35]

Fessenden exposed the racism in removal ideology. By implication, he exposed a weakness in the reform argument that Indians should sometimes be removed for their own protection. The reformers assumed that, once done, the same rules would be applied to white men as to Indians. The racial double standard prohibited that.

Removal also functioned psychologically as a means of getting rid of a bothersome problem without actually solving it. After the 1862 Indian war, Lincoln demonstrated this in his forgetfulness concerning the Sioux and Winnebagos.[36]

In this respect, removal performed a similar function as the movement to colonize blacks. Lincoln was a colonizationist. He openly advocated it, obtained appropriations for it, and authorized two abortive experiments in Latin America.[37] The subtle link between the colonization movement and removal appears more sub-

35. U.S., Congress, Senate, *Congressional Globe*, 37th Cong., 2d sess., 13 May 1862, pt. 3:2095–97.
36. See Chapter IX.
37. LAM, 1861, p. 3; LAM, 1862, p. 4; Jacob R. S. Van Fleet to Lincoln, 4 October 1862, Van Fleet to Lincoln, 4 October 1862, Roll 42, Lincoln Papers, LC; James M. McPherson, *The Negro's Civil War*, pp. 95–97.

stantial when it is noted that the two approaches to racial problems coincided with each other in 1862. It was September 1862, in the midst of the Minnesota war, that colonization activity was most feverish. On 10 September, Lincoln appointed an advocate of Indian removal, Sen. Samuel Pomeroy of Kansas, to supervise the Chiriqui colonization project in Panama. This was two days before Lincoln met with John Ross. Pomeroy's project was abandoned in October, almost simultaneous with the end of the Minnesota Indian war. Pomeroy made a natural shift in thinking from colonization to removal. On 15 November 1862, he called on the Indian Office to enact a program for "the *removal* and *consolidation* of the small tribes into one distinctive Indian country."[38]

The arguments in favor of both colonization and removal were to serve whites, to protect the minority group, to be rid of the problem, and to prevent racial friction. Lincoln especially worried about racial friction. In August 1862, he met with black leaders and advised them to accept colonization. Why? Because "you and we are different races."[39] He did not think they could live together. How similar were those sentiments to the ideas expressed to the Indian leaders in March 1863. He did not advise the Indians to colonize, but he spoke at a time of massive Indian removals in Minnesota. His advice to them to take up farming was, in a sense, a similar ultimatum. "I can see no way in which your race is to become as numerous and prosperous as the white race except by living as they do."[40] Common to all this advice, to blacks or Indians, was Lincoln's great pessimism about white attitudes on race. Lincoln was a perceptive politician and knew white public opinion. He had seen the hatred in Minnesota and the bigotry that fueled the fighting of a

38. Lincoln to Samuel Pomeroy, 10 September 1862, Roll 41, Lincoln Papers, LC; see p. 86 of this book; Smith to Lincoln, 20 September 1862, Roll 41, Lincoln Papers, LC; John P. Usher to Pomeroy, 13 October 1862, John P. Usher Papers; McPherson, *The Negro's Civil War*, p. 97; Pomeroy to Dole, 15 November 1862, AR, CIA, 1862, pp. 491–92.

39. Meeting with a committee of black leaders, 14 August 1862, New York *Tribune*, 15 August 1862, reprinted in Basler, ed., *Collected Works*, 5:370–72.

40. Basler, ed., *Collected Works*, 6:152. Winthrop Jordan explores the psychological function of colonization ideology for whites in *White Over Blacks: American Attitudes toward the Negro, 1550–1812*, p. 567.

Civil War. He could "see no way" that either group could ever live peacefully with whites. To fight the dominant white attitude was to invite destruction.

Americans justified removal as a means to protect the Indians. It was racial segregation. It helped ease racial frictions. These all merged, however, into an even more sweeping justification that directly addressed the categorization of the Indian as a "savage." This great justification was that the Indian had to be removed to make way for the advance of civilization.

The Advance of Civilization

During the 1860s, *civilization* was a magic word. It symbolized a dynamic force, moving upward and onward, conquering new lands, making new machines, and launching bold ventures. Civilization was on the march, advancing up the evolutionary scale and across the landscape of the United States. This sense of "manifest destiny" justified the greatest drives of American society and provided an overpowering rationale for sweeping aside the Indians.

Every major figure gave voice to a belief in progress. Isaac Newton called the fourth and highest stage in civilization the "migration of races" to plant new empires in the wilderness. Commissioner Dole spoke of a "scale of social existence," along which civilization moved. The idea of a civilization in progress had an inevitability about it. Caleb Smith stated the case forcefully, "The rapid progress of civilization upon this continent will not permit the lands which are required for cultivation to be surrendered to savage tribes for hunting grounds." These words were doubly significant, coming in the same 1862 report that advocated reform of the Indian System. Smith continued, "Indeed, whatever may be the theory, the Government has always demanded the removal of the Indians when their lands were required for agricultural purposes by advancing settlements." This was, in Smith's opinion, "a necessity which they could not resist."[41]

41. See p. 184 of this book; AR, Commissioner of Agriculture, 1862, Roll 46, Lincoln Papers, LC; AR, CIA, 1861, p. 647; AR, SI, 1862, p. 7.

Commissioner Dole held the same assumptions. He spoke of "our rapidly extending settlements, and the consequent organization of new Territories and admission of new States." Dole wanted a special domain for the Indians. Nevertheless, despite promises to the Natives, "it is found that, as our settlements advance, the Indians, through the instrumentality of treaty negotiations, by military force or by stress of circumstances which they are powerless to resist, are compelled to retire before them." For Dole, this showed the nature of things in human society. It was almost inevitable that there would be Indian dispossession by "civilization with its attendant blessings."[42]

Lincoln's Program for the West

Lincoln's program for the West must be seen not only in the context of economic reward but also as linked to the national destiny in the progress of civilization. In particular, three specific policies came to symbolize the upward and outward thrust of white civilization.

The first symbol of progress was the Homestead Act. The homestead policy is normally discussed in terms of its operation and it exploitation by speculators. An Indian perspective on the subject is illuminating. The legislation's purpose was clearly to promote settlement in the West. It constituted a national commitment to growth and progress that irrepressibly led to conflict over Indian lands.[43]

The second symbolic policy related to mineral development. William Rector was right when he said, "Gold is the lever that moves the age." Gold fever reflected perfectly the chasm between the cultures. Indians did not value gold in the way white men did, another indication that Indians were uncivilized. Senator Nesmith's description of ten thousand settlers crowding onto an Oregon reser-

42. AR, CIA, 1864, p. 147; Pearce, *Savigism and Civilization*, pp. 239–42, finds this idea in an earlier period.

43. Dole to John and Lewis Ross, Lewis Downing, 24 May 1864, Roll 74, M21, LS, OIA, RG75, NA; LAM, 1864, p. 3; Foner, *The Republican Party*, pp. 27–29.

vation in search of gold demonstrates the strength of the white drive for mineral wealth. The senator's solution was also typically American—remove the Indians and let the whites have the gold.[44]

Commissioner Dole described what happened to the California Indians when gold was found there, "Resorting to precisely the same means as those employed towards the wild beasts of the country, a tide of emigration sets in upon them and begins to despoil them of their homes, the graves of their ancestors, and the means of supplying their rude and simple wants."[45]

Leaders knew the relationship of the Indian System to the development of mining. In 1863, Morton Wilkinson made a plea for increased appropriations for the Indian service precisely on these grounds:

> There is a very good reason why the appropriations for the Indian service should increase. We have been opening and settling a large tract of country, rich in mineral wealth. In the territory occupied by the Indians the American people are now digging out millions and hundreds of millions in gold every year. The enterprise of the American people drives them into such places. They go into the fastnesses of the mountains and find gold there, and they enrich this nation by it.[46]

The third Lincolnian symbol of western development and the progress of civilization was the transcontinental railroad. Economic gain and regional interests certainly were central in the conception of this great project. But it was also sanctified with the air of destiny that surrounded the whole western development program. No other mechanism in the new industrialism so perfectly embodied the "manifest destiny" spirit. The railroad and its ribbons of iron were solid symbols of progress across the continent. Congressmen argued over where to build the railroad but not whether to build it.

44. William H. Rector to Dole, 1 November 1861, Roll 613, M234, LR, Oregon Superintendency, OIA, RG75, NA; U.S., Congress, Senate, *Congressional Globe,* 37th Cong., 2d sess., 13 May 1862, pt. 3:2095.

45. AR, CIA, 1863, p. 135.

46. U.S., Congress, Senate, *Congressional Globe,* Debate on the Indian Appropriation Bill, 37th Cong., 3d sess., 25 February 1863, pt. 2:1281.

One senator said: "Nearly all of us are committed to a Pacific railroad. . . . The people are for a Pacific railroad."

Sen. Henry Wilson of Massachusetts called the transcontinental line "a great national undertaking" and essential to the Union. "I believe," he said, "it to be of vital importance to this nation that we should commence this work, and unite the people of the Atlantic and Pacific coasts in interest." Another senator called the railroad "a great national measure to cement the Union, to bind with a belt of iron the Atlantic and Pacific, and, as had been said, to transfer the commerce of the world upon these iron rails."[47]

These men made selfish arguments for the railroad but their belief that they were part of a great undertaking shines in their rhetoric. The vision of uniting the continent with "a belt of iron" was cut from the same fabric as the homestead policy and the plans for mineral development. Selfish arguments were, in that era, considered good arguments. Lincolnians generally believed that their materialism was ordained by God and nature. Conversely the Indian's lack of materialism designated him a savage. The Indians held land needed for the building of civilization, no greater symbol of which was the railroad. The railroad was, to Lincolnians, like civilization itself, destined to exist, to dominate, to push aside anything in its path.

Homesteading, mining, and railroading all furnished proof to Americans of the progress of their civilization. It was an exhilarating time when a man could get rich quickly and simultaneously feel he was doing the will of the ages. The advance of civilization made a powerful justification for doing things to Indians that could not have otherwise been justified.

A Dying Race

Lincoln's program for the West carried with it the implicit doom of the Indians. Viewed as savages, there was no way they could logically survive. Thus, many leaders concluded that Indians

47. U.S., Congress, Senate, *Congressional Globe,* Debate on the Transcontinental Railroad, 37th Cong., 2d sess., 17 June 1862, pt. 3:2753, 2805.

were headed for extinction. Commissioner Dole worried that the tribes, in conflict with a "superior race," might "finally fade from the face of the earth." Dole saw Indians "in the pathway of a race they are wholly unable to stay" and "in active competition with their superiors in intelligence and those acquirements which we consider so essential to success."[48] Senator Doolittle called Indians "a dying race."[49]

> It is dying through natural causes growing out of its contact with a superior race inhabiting the same country. . . . And the warfare when once begun between civilized and savage life becomes an eternal and irrepressible conflict which, in the very nature of things, will only cease when the savage life ceases.[50]

This was the "irrepressible conflict" in the Indian Civil War. The linking of racism with the progress of civilization made a barrier of thought over which Indians could never triumph. Doolittle said that Indians were "giving place to another race with a higher civilization." This was sanctioned by God, who "in his providence is giving this continent to a hundred millions of human beings of higher civilization, of greater energies, capable of developing themselves, and doing good to themselves and the world, and leading the advance guard of human and Christian civilization."[51]

Divided Minds over Indians

Here lay the roots of the ideological failure of the reform movement. The combination of a civilization on the march, sanctioned by God, buttressed by white supremacy, and personified in homesteads, goldmines, and railroads was too powerful for the Indian. In the white man's mind he was the opposite—a static, uncivilized impediment to the progress of civilization. This chain of ideas was

48. Dole to Smith, 22 November 1862, AR, CIA, 1862, pp. 169, 493.
49. U.S., Congress, Senate, *Congressional Globe,* Debate on the Indian Appropriation Bill, 38th Cong., 2d sess., 13 January 1865, pt. 1:254.
50. U.S., Congress, Senate, *Congressional Globe,* 38th Cong., 2d sess., 13 January 1865, pt. 1:254.
51. U.S., Congress, Senate, *Congressional Globe,* Debate on the Indian Appropriation Bill, 38th Cong., 1st sess., 10 June 1864, pt. 3:2873.

strong, and reformers shared too many of its premises. Leaders occasionally expressed sympathy for Indians, but their priority lay with the advancing civilization. Even this concern was undercut by a fatalism that labeled Indians a dying race.

Therefore, the reformers' major proposals contained unresolvable contradictions. They sought to isolate the Indian while trying to assimilate him. They sought to find him a place in the face of an advancing civilization that envisioned only continuous removal and eventual extinction. They wanted to advance the Indian to civilization while presuming a civilization that was in dynamic progress, symbolized by an accelerating locomotive that Indians could never catch.

Commissioner Dole reflected these contradictions. He attempted to promote settlement of the West while still protecting the Indians. He seems never to have understood the conflict. In New Mexico, Dole's purpose was "to foster and protect our own settlements, to secure the ultimate perpetuity of the Territory, and a speedy development of its resources, and to reclaim and civilize the Indians."[52] The result was removal, concentration, and great suffering for the Indians.

John G. Nicolay, Lincoln's secretary, demonstrated the same priorities, though even less sympathetically than Dole. He described to Dole "the sudden growth" taking place in Colorado Territory. What had once been a lawless wilderness, "is already a civilized country, with courts, schools, churches, and telegraphs—a land of active enterprise, where all classes of people are prosperous." Nicolay was also excited about the "great iron highway" intersecting Colorado. He believed the railroad would bring new prosperity and new settlements that would provide protection "against the Indians."

Nicolay saw the purpose of his trip to the West in 1863 as to act as the emissary of advancing civilization. He was to help negotiate a treaty with the Utah Indians in 1863, opening "one of the largest tracts of land ever ceded to the United States in a single treaty."

52. AR, CIA, 1861, p. 637.

Nicolay saw little hope for the Utes. White settlement would inevitably inundate them. The treaty commissioners were "looking forward to the possible future discovery of rich mines in the land retained by these Indians." Therefore, they had made sure that the treaty allowed prospecting. This would furnish "a sufficient excuse" to negotiate for more land in the future.

Nicolay wasted little sympathy on the Indians. His priorities were clear: "The safety of the white settlements on the frontier should be an object of special care and solicitude on the part of the government." In order to do that, military force was needed. As for the Indians, "they are poor ignorant and weak, while the government is rich, wise and powerful."[53] The president's secretary could not know, of course, that the implementation of this ideology of advancing civilization in Colorado was, a little over a year later, to lead to tragedy at Sand Creek.

Abraham Lincoln's priorities were no different, although he stated them in less harsh rhetoric. Lincoln enthusiastically promoted western development. He actively supported the three symbols of the advance of civilization in that region. The Homestead Act was designed, Lincoln told Congress, to offer "inducement to settlers." He wanted settlement even if it cost the government revenue. Homesteads and land grants to railroads both implemented this objective. Lincoln spoke of "gratifying evidence of increasing settlement upon the public lands." Almost in the same breath, he linked this settlement to Indian removal, mentioning "sundry treaties" and "extinguishing the possessory rights of the Indians to large and valuable tracts of land." All this came two sentences before a statement on reform of Indian policy.[54] The priorities were evident in that recital.

The same was true of mineral development. "The immense mineral resources of some of those Territories ought to be developed as rapidly as possible," Lincoln told the legislators. He was pleased that "the mineral resources of Colorado, Nevada, Idaho, New Mexico, and Arizona are proving far richer than has been heretofore understood." The president hardly noticed that those regions were

53. Nicolay to Dole, 10 November 1863, AR, CIA, pp. 261–69.
54. LAM, 1862, p. 2; LAM, 1863, p. 3.

inhabited by large numbers of Indians. He called instead for the importation of cheap foreign labor to develop the resources. "It is easy," said Lincoln, "to see that, under the sharp discipline of the civil war, the nation is beginning a new life." Lincoln saw this as part of a great national destiny. "This noble effort demands the aid, and ought to receive the attention and support, of the Government."[55]

Lincoln reserved some of his greatest enthusiasm for the transcontinental railroad. His description of the Minnesota Indian war to Congress in 1862 was followed by a statement on "the progress that has been made in the enterprise of constructing the Pacific railroad." In 1864, the president spoke with fervor he never expressed concerning Indian reform, "The great enterprise of connecting the Atlantic with the Pacific States by railways and telegraph lines has been entered upon with a vigor that gives assurance of success."[56]

Lincoln may have talked less ideologically about the advance of civilization than others but his program was their program, with all its apocalyptic implications for Indians. His sympathies for Indians, however genuine, never altered his priorities for the development he deemed essential to the prosecution of the Civil War and the nation's destiny. To be fair, it is difficult to see how Lincoln could have chosen any alternative path acceptable to his European-American constituency and the extraordinary circumstances of Civil War. Thus, he ordered the continued removal and concentration of Indian tribes while espousing reform of the Indian System. Lincoln never really faced the contradiction inherent in his desire for the West, "to render it secure for the advancing settler, and to provide for the welfare of the Indian."[57]

Reformers Fail to Break the Chain

The reformers never broke the chain of ideas that bound the Indian and doomed him. They failed to alter the fundamental con-

55. LAM, 1862, p. 1; LAM, 1863, pp. 1–2.

56. LAM, 1863, p. 2; LAM, 1864, p. 3.

57. LAM, 1864, p. 3; Don E. Fehrenbacher tells of the impact of railroads on Lincoln's Illinois in the 1850s and Lincoln's active representation of railroads in his law practice, *Prelude to Greatness: Lincoln in the 1850s*, pp. 7–9.

ceptions of men like Lincoln or reorient their priorities. Partly, this was because of their own confusion. They agreed that the Indian was a savage, faced by a superior, advancing civilization. Despite their humanitarian attitudes, they accepted too many of the opposition's fundamental premises to challenge effectively their pattern of thought about Indians.

What could have broken the chain? This is where the historian must view the situation as a historic tragedy rather than circumstances in which personal blame can be assigned. The only solution would have been the acceptance of ideals of racial and cultural equality for which nineteenth-century white Americans were not prepared. Neither reformers nor nonreformers respected Indian culture. Indeed, they did not even perceive the existence of a Native culture. Their recitals of Indian characteristics (imagined or real) occasionally approximated descriptions of cultural patterns but were not conceptualized as such. To them, those traits and behavior patterns were, if anything, an anticulture. *Civilization,* not *culture,* was their key word-concept. "Savage" characteristics were anticivilization, something heathen and evil to be stamped out rather than praised. There was only one civilization in the world and it was theirs—white, Christian, materialistic, agrarian, and on the march.

John Beeson alone denounced to Lincoln "the Atheistic idea that they the Indians must necessarily perish before the march of Civilization," but he was ignored by the president and Dole. Beeson rejected white supremacy as well. "The truth is," he told the president, "the Indians as a Race have the common characteristics of humanity varied only by circumstances and surroundings. They have as few vices and as many virtues, and as much capacity and as great desire for improvement as is possessed by the average of mankind."[58]

The men of the 1860s were not ready for such radical thinking. Neither was Lincoln. Four months after Beeson made his startling declaration, Lincoln demonstrated his rejection of Beeson's ideas in his meeting with Indian leaders. Indians, he said, were not like

58. John Beeson to Lincoln, 18 November 1862, Roll 20, M825, LR, ID, OSI, RG48, NA.

white men and did not till the soil. There were racial differences. "Although we are now engaged in a great war between one another," Lincoln continued, "we are not, as a race, so much disposed to fight and kill one another as our red brethren." The racism of the frontiersman and his fellow European-Americans had won out over the egalitarianism of the reformer.[59]

Why were policymakers so incapable of accepting such logical arguments? The answer lay somewhere in their inner selves, as they faithfully reflected the biases of their culture. Their precise and impassioned definitions of savagery and civilization served important psychological functions. These ideas provided reassurance for European-Americans concerning their identity and the meaning of their existence. Their conception of Indians as savage was linked to their self-images. What frightened them about Indians was pinpointed by Senator Nesmith when he said that the Indian "has contracted all of the vices of the white man, but none of his virtues."[60] The vices of white men were uncomfortably real. The characteristics these white men labeled "savage"—violence, idleness, sexual aggressiveness, inclination to roam, thievery, drunkeness—were all too often found to exist among white men in the American West. These were the appetites they feared in themselves. The Indians became, for them, the embodiment of the dark side of their own natures. It was the "savage within" they feared most of all and projected on the Natives.[61]

Given that fearful perception, only one conclusion was possible for the leaders of the restless American culture in the Lincoln era. The savage had to be leashed, removed, and perhaps even exterminated. This was the "irrepressible conflict" of the Indian Civil War. The insecurity of white Americans about themselves and their civilization made tragedy inevitable for the "savages" of Lincoln's America.

59. Basler, ed., *Collected Works,* p. 152.
60. U.S., Congress, Senate, *Congressional Globe,* Debate on the Indian Appropriation Bill, 37th Cong., 2d sess., 13 May 1862, pt. 3:2095.
61. This projection theory in respect to colonial America is discussed in Wilbur R. Jacobs, *Dispossessing the American Indian,* p. 4. It is applied to early American attitudes up to 1851 in Pearce, *Savagism and Civilization.* The most significant use of it is found in Jordan's study of American attitudes toward blacks in *White Over Black,* p. 572.

XIV. Lincoln and the Indians
"A Great Revolution in the Conduct of Our Indian Affairs"

ABRAHAM LINCOLN CAME to the presidency knowing the Indian System only as a rich source of political patronage. Harsh experience educated him to the fact that it was also a system of institutionalized corruption that served as a vehicle for white economic and political gain, not service to Indians. Lincoln learned the truth of Bishop Henry Whipple's assertion that the Indian System "commences in discontent and ends in blood."[1]

Lincoln's perception of the System did not change until blood was shed. He ignored the warnings of reformers and investigators early in his first term. The Indians first demanded his attention because of the War for the Union. Confederate alliances with the southern tribes and "Bloody Jim" Lane's persistence pushed the president into accepting the Kansas senator's scheme for a great southern expedition. As a result Indian troops were eventually enlisted into the Union army, the expedition was aborted, and the Indian refugees suffered greatly.

A corrupt Indian System exploded into war in Minnesota in 1862. That bloody affair demanded men and supplies needed in the war with the South. It nourished the Northern administration's fears that the conflict had been inspired by a Confederate conspiracy. The Indian war confronted Lincoln with an agonizing decision concerning the fate of more than three hundred Sioux men that had been condemned to death by the military because of atroci-

1. Henry Benjamin Whipple to William P. Dole, n.d., Box 40, Letterbook 4, Henry Benjamin Whipple Papers.

ties they had allegedly committed. Lincoln risked political retaliation when he reduced the number of executions. However, his decision to trade lives for land and money left the Minnesota Indians in worse condition than before the war.

In all these matters, Lincoln tended to respond to the political consequences of Indian affairs rather than to the substance of the difficulties that demanded his attention. He addressed the fundamental problem only when confronted dramatically and personally, as in the executions. Even then, he put it out of mind as quickly as he could.

Lincoln was personally confronted by the events in the Indian Territory and Minnesota, the proposed executions, and the incessant arguments of reformers like Bishop Whipple. The convergence of these in late 1862 apparently convinced Lincoln of the need for reform in the Indian System. He proposed its modification to the Congress that December, although he never made the crucial commitment to depoliticize that System nor did he use his executive powers to modify its operation. In any event, Congress refused to undercut a major source of influence for its members. The reform movement floundered and Lincoln concentrated his attention on the War for the Union.

When the reform movement failed, the Lincoln administration adopted the expedient policy of concentration. Given war priorities, this plan to consolidate Indian tribes merged with militarism. Military concentration in New Mexico was a fiasco and, in Colorado, military brutality produced the tragedy at Sand Creek and consequently discredited schemes for military control of the Indians.

The failure to reform the Indian System was tragic for the Indians. That failure came, in part, because reformers could find no way to transform the political and economic machinery of the System. They failed because they could not break the chain of ideas that bound Native Americans. This was not so much a personal failure as the consequence of thousands of years of prejudice that had become fundamental to European-American culture. This culture produced men like Lincoln who believed in a white, Christian, materialistic, and rapidly advancing civilization that was personified in homesteads, gold mines, and the transcontinental railroad. They believed that the pursuit of political and financial gain at the expense of the Indians was both proper and inevitable. The "savage" was the antithesis of their civilization as far as they were concerned. Therefore, the demise of the savage was probably inevitable. Indians had to become like white men or perish. Most leaders believed that they were a dying race.

A Revolution?

This larger cultural perspective must be kept in mind when asking what the impact of the Lincoln era was on Indian affairs. In 1863, Morton Wilkinson argued: "I believe there has been a great revolution in the conduct of our Indian affairs since this Administration came into power."[2] That was not true and Wilkinson knew it. In fact, abundant evidence existed that very little of importance had changed.

In 1865, the first negative evidence was the condition of the tribes. In Dakota, the remnants of the Santee Sioux and Winnebagos continued to suffer. In New Mexico, the Navajos and Apaches still lived under the disastrous care of General Carleton. Colorado had been the scene of a war of near extermination. In other localities, the killing and looting of Indians through the corrupt Indian System continued unarrested.

Conditions were best symbolized by the situation in the Indian Territory. In early 1865, the formerly proud tribes of that region were destitute. In March, Congress debated a $750,000 appropriation to alleviate their misery. Senator Doolittle told the Senate that Cherokee women and children were near starvation. One senator suggested putting the Cherokees under military control, but Doolittle responded that, based on the experience in New Mexico, that would cost three times as much. The need was immediate. Jim Lane told the senators: "They will starve to death."[3]

More negative evidence of the accomplishments of the Lincoln

2. U.S., Congress, Senate, *Congressional Globe,* 38th Cong., 3d sess., 25 February 1863, pt. 2:1281.

3. U.S., Congress, Senate, *Congressional Globe,* 38th Cong., 2d sess., 2 March 1865, pt. 2:1299–1301.

years can be found in the actions of the Congress. Congress had always held the key to reform of the Indian System because its actions provided the fuel for the corruption that made it operate. Congressmen talked nobly of the plight of the Cherokees, but there was a hollow sound to the rhetoric. Some of the legislators were preparing a new indignity for the residents of the Indian Territory.

On 2 March 1865 (the same day as the debate over relief for the starving Indians), the Senate took up a bill "to provide for the consolidation of the Indian tribes, and to establish civil government in the Indian Territory."[4] Jim Lane was set to assault that last refuge of the Natives. Organizing a territory of the United States there would begin the chain of events that nourished the corrupt Indian System. American civilization was set to advance again, and it seemed nothing could stop it.

The bill set off the last debate on Indian policy during the Lincoln years. Opponents of the legislation pointed out that the bill was introduced prior to obtaining consent from the tribes. Sen. Lafayette Foster of Connecticut called the bill farcical and "fraught with danger and dishonor to the country." Foster demanded:

> What is the purpose of the bill? Is it honest? I ask again, do we mean to send these officers there to organize this government, and are these officers, after they get there with commissions in their pockets, to negotiate with the Indians first whether they may stay and organize the government?

Foster understood what was going on. He prophesied that "the organization of this territorial government would bring in the whites and surround Indians there with what are called the 'blessings of civilization' which are the curse and bane of the Indians." Once the government was organized, "our people will go upon the Territory, and there will be no power to stop them."

The members of the Indian Committee calmly argued away these objections. They invoked the old justification that "The design of the bill is to protect these Indians from annihilation—not to

---

4. U.S., Congress, Senate, *Congressional Globe*, Debate on Territorial Government for Oklahoma, 38th Cong., 2d sess., 2 March 1865, pt. 2:1304–10. Despite this legislation, Oklahoma did not become a territory until 1890.

establish a government there for white men." The debate disclosed that John Ross opposed the legislation, but that did not deter the senators. Jim Lane supported the bill with the quiet reasoning that it differed little from other legislation of the type. Lane had long sought to penetrate the Indian Territory. Now he had the vehicle and he had no need to engage in powerful debate. He had the votes. The Senate passed the legislation 17 to 9.

That senatorial action embodied the fundamental corruption of the Indian System and in a larger context, the basic acquisitive drives of Western civilization. Congressmen pursued their regional political and economic interests. They did so at a time when starving Indians could not resist. It was a continuation of the great contradictions inherent in white policies ever since the ordinances of 1785 and 1787 provided the means to bring new states into the Union. Those early laws had promised to observe "the utmost good faith" toward the Indians. At the same moment, they proclaimed the objective of organizing an American empire out of lands occupied by Natives.[5] For European-Americans, it was the familiar and inevitable story of the march of their superior civilization through primitive lands at the expense of primitive peoples.

Business as Usual in the Indian System

As the Lincoln era closed, it was business as usual in the Indian System. Secretary Usher was negotiating with Jim Lane in a scheme to deprive some Indians of land and circumvent treaty stipulations to make way for the Union Pacific Railway. Once they figured out the details, Usher told Lane, "the Executive is to approve the contract." Lincoln had apparently learned little from his troubles with Jim Lane. On 11 February 1865, Lincoln gave Stanton orders on a matter concerning military patronage: "Please have . . . Senator Lane's request complied with."[6]

As he began his second term, Lincoln continued to do his political patronage duty in the Indian System, just as he had done

5. Henry Steel Commager, ed., *Documents of American History*, p. 131.
6. John P. Usher to James H. Lane, 25 February 1865, Roll 5, M606, LS, ID, OSI, RG48, NA; Abraham Lincoln to the Secretary of War, 11 February 1865, James H. Lane Papers (for "Abbreviations in Footnotes," see p. vi).

years earlier. He accepted recommendations from congressmen for appointments to Indian agent positions and passed them on to the secretary of the interior with the endorsement, "Appoint according to herein."[7]

Despite the incident at Sand Creek, the fate of the Indians was still approached primarily as a military problem. Gen. John Pope worried about protecting overland routes and "defense against the Indians." Gen. Alfred Sully was still conducting missions against the Indians in the Dakotas. Gen. G. M. Dodge spoke to superiors of "offensive operations against the Indians, who, I am satisfied, are determined to make aggressive war upon all our overland routes this spring and summer." Lincoln's last proclamation concerning Indians was militaristic. He said he had "reliable information" that the Indians were being smuggled arms "and are thereby enabled to prosecute their savage warfare upon the sparse settlements of the frontier." Lincoln ordered that any soldier found to be participating in this "nefarious traffic" be court-martialed and possibly executed.[8]

Because of this preoccupation with the War for the Union, Lincoln knowingly allowed the Indian System to function normally until he died. On 13 April 1865, Commissioner Dole sent out advertisements for Indian lands in Kansas: "Notice—Valuable Lands for Sale." On 14 April, payments were arranged for contractor R. S. Stevens, who had long ago been accused of massive fraud in Kansas. Dole accepted payments for Winnebago lands in Minnesota that same day. On 14 April, the day Lincoln died, Commissioner Dole wrote Vital Jarrot: "You have been appointed by the President . . . to be Agent of the Upper Platte Agency." Another political appointment was made and the Indian System lived.[9]

7. Lincoln to the Secretary of the Interior, 16 March 1865, Roy P. Basler, ed., *The Collected Works of Abraham Lincoln*, 8:358.

8. John Pope to Henry Halleck, 8 February 1865, OR, 1:48, p. 778; Alfred Sully to the Assistant Adjutant General, 17 March 1865, OR, 1:48, pp. 1204-5; G. M. Dodge to Joseph McC. Bell, 5 March 1865, OR, 2:8, pp. 358-59; Proclamation of 18 March 1865, OR, 1:48, p. 1205.

9. Dole to the Leavenworth, Kansas, *Times*, 13 April 1865, Roll 77, M21, LS, OIA, RG75, NA; Usher to Dole, 14 April 1865, Roll 5, M606, LS, ID, OSI, RG48, NA; Dole to E. H. Smith & Company, Dole to Vital Jarrot, 14 April 1865, Roll 77, M21, LS, OIA, RG75, NA.

The Reaction to Sand Creek

The condition of the Indians, congressional actions, and continued corruption all support the conclusion that the Lincoln administration implemented little significant change in the Indian System. That evaluation, while reasonable, is overly simple.

The American drives for wealth, property, social mobility, and power were still there. However, there had been some change in thinking that is historically significant. The slaughter at Sand Creek produced a public scandal. It discredited men like Chivington and even led to calls for the resignation of Commissioner Dole. The mass death of Indians had occurred before but why, in 1865, was there a public outcry?

Several theories are plausible. One is that the rising peace movement in 1865 made the public more open to peaceful relations with the Indians. Another is that people throughout the United States were sensitized by the growing disruption in the West, partly in retaliation for Sand Creek, and the consequent threats to the transcontinental railroad, communication lines, and settlers.[10] Perhaps the public arguments of reformers had provided a new perspective on these events.

A provocative explanation for the scandal can be based on Lincolnian ideas about Indians. In earlier Indian warfare, the public normally heard only about "savages," male Indian warriors. Leaders like Sen. James Doolittle were shocked at the action at Sand Creek because they learned that women and children had been killed and mutilated. The news from Sand Creek, seemingly irrefutable, shattered their monolithic image of savagery.

The report of the Joint Committee on the Conduct of the War expressed this terrible realization. The atrocities were committed by "men claiming to be civilized." They had done, as Agent Colley put it, things "as bad as any Indian ever did to a white man." The writer of the committee's report found it "difficult to believe" that American soldiers would commit deeds of "savage cruelty." Terms

10. Robert Mardock, *The Reformers and the American Indian*, p. 19.

normally reserved for Indians were now applied to whites. The committee called Sand Creek a "massacre." Colonel Chivington, it said, "deliberately planned and executed a foul and dastardly massacre which would have disgraced the veriest savage among those who were the victims of his cruelty."[11]

Cherished notions of the contrasts between white "civilized" men and Indian "savages" lay in shreds. If both acted similarly, what was the difference? Much of the whites' confidence in the destiny of their civilization had been based on a constant comparison with the natives they perceived to be savage. For them, the Indians were a projection of the fearful side of their own natures. The "savage within" had broken loose at Sand Creek. White men there sought, in the words of the committee report, "to gratify the worst passions that ever cursed the heart of man." The resulting dissonance was the life-blood of the scandal. Something had to be done so that whites would not be reminded that they, too, could be savage. Sand Creek and the scandal surrounding it can thus be viewed as a significant crack in the public consensus on the inevitable superiority of Western civilization and the so-called civilized men it produced.

Beyond Lincoln

The Sand Creek massacre initiated the actions that reformers had earlier pursued. It moved the Congress to action. Investigations were launched. In July 1865, Congressman William Windom asked Bishop Henry Whipple for help in uncovering fraud "and in discussing some better plan for the management of the Indians." A joint congressional committee studied the condition of the Indian tribes under the mandate that resulted from the Sand Creek scandal. The committee produced its report in January 1867. Its findings were the basis for the "peace policy" of the Grant years, with its attendant objectives of preserving the tribes and depoliticizing the

11. Colley testimony, 7 March 1865, *Report of the Joint Committee on the Condition of the Tribes in the United States*, Senate Report 156, p. 129; JCCW, pp. iii–vi.

Indian System by turning its administration over to churchmen.[12]

The joint committee reached several significant conclusions. First, the Indians were diminishing in number, and the root cause was the migration of the white population onto their lands. Second, most Indian wars could "be traced to the aggressions of lawless white men." Third, the Indians were fast losing their food sources and hunting grounds, especially due to railroad construction and gold mining in the West. Fourth, the committee confirmed the consensus that had emerged in the aftermath of the disasters in New Mexico and Colorado—that the Indians should remain under civil rather than military control. Finally, the committee recommended boards of inspection be established to supervise Indian affairs and reduce fraud and violence. This recommendation led eventually to the formation of the Board of Indian Commissioners in 1869, a body that functioned until 1934.[13]

Lincoln did not live to read the committee's report. He probably would have supported the reform recommendations. At the time he called for reform in 1862–1863, there was no public outcry and no action in the Congress. It is true that Lincoln's priorities for winning the war and developing the West conflicted with his commitment to reform, as did his conception of Indians as hunter-savages who could be saved only by becoming like white men and his view of the Indian System as a political patronage machine. However, Lincoln and the reformers must be given some credit for preparing the public mind and the Congress for a change of direction. Lincoln could do relatively little until there was a change in public opinion mediated through Congress. That did not happen until Sand Creek and the investigations generated by it. By then, Lincoln was gone.

The change during the Lincoln era was intellectual rather than practical. There had been no "revolution," as Wilkinson claimed. Only the seeds of reform had been sown. A president of the United

12. William Windom to Whipple, 25 July 1865, Box 4, Whipple Papers; Mardock, *The Reformers*, p. 21.

13. *The Condition of the Tribes*, pp. 1–10; Donald Chaput, "Generals, Indian Agents, Politicians: The Doolittle Survey of 1865."

States had endorsed reform but had been unable to effect it and unwilling to risk higher political, economic, and military priorities to promote it. That he spoke for reform at all forecast a change in American racial attitudes that would require another century to mature. How long that transformation has taken is a measure of the task that Lincoln and the reformers confronted. Thus the reform that followed his death fell far short of the need. Lincoln's call to "bind up the nation's wounds" was never applied to Native Americans.[14] They continued to be deprived of life, land, and their just roles in the histories of Lincoln's presidency.

14. Basler, ed., *Collected Works*, 8:333.

Bibliography of Materials Cited

This bibliography reveals only a portion of the materials consulted in research on the subject. In the interests of a concise and usable bibliography, a listing of the consulted works has been omitted. With only a few exceptions, the sources noted below were consulted for the years 1861–1865.

I. Primary Sources

A. Unpublished Papers

Orville Hickman Browning Papers. Illinois State Historical Society, Springfield.

Cable-Cody Collection. Kansas University, Lawrence.

Correspondence of the Kansas Governors, 1861–1865. Kansas State Historical Society, Topeka.

Mark W. Delahay Papers. Kansas State Historical Society, Topeka.

William Jayne Papers. Illinois State Historical Society, Springfield.

James H. Lane Papers. Kansas University, Lawrence.

Abraham Lincoln Collection. Blue Earth County Historical Society, Mankato, Minnesota.

Abraham Lincoln Papers. Library of Congress, Washington, D.C.

Abraham Lincoln Papers. Minnesota Historical Society, St. Paul.

Edward Duffield Neill Papers. Minnesota Historical Society, St. Paul.

Samuel C. Pomeroy Papers. Edmund Gibson Ross Collection. Kansas University, Lawrence.

Alexander Ramsey Papers. Minnesota Historical Society, St. Paul.

Henry Mower Rice Papers. Minnesota Historical Society, St. Paul.

Charles Robinson Papers. Kansas University, Lawrence.

Henry Hastings Sibley Papers. Minnesota Historical Society, St. Paul.

Edwin M. Stanton Papers. Library of Congress, Washington, D.C.

Clark W. Thompson Papers. Minnesota Historical Society, St. Paul.

John P. Usher Papers. Kansas State Historical Society, Topeka.

Thomas S. Williamson Papers. Minnesota Historical Society, St. Paul.

Henry Benjamin Whipple Papers. Minnesota Historical Society, St. Paul.

B. Published Papers

Browning, Orville Hickman. *The Diary of Orville Hickman Browning.* Edited by James G. Randall and Theodore C. Pease. 2 vols. Springfield, Illinois: Illinois State Historical Library, 1925–1933.

Chase, Salmon P. *Inside Lincoln's Cabinet: The Civil War Diaries of Salmon P. Chase.* Edited by David Donald. New York: Longmans, Green and Company, 1954.

Hay, John. *Lincoln and the Civil War in the Diaries and Letters of John Hay.* Edited by Tyler Dernett. New York: Dodd, Mead, & Company, 1939.

Lincoln, Abraham. *The Collected Works of Abraham Lincoln.* Edited by Roy P. Basler et al. 9 vols. New Brunswick, N.J.: Rutgers University Press, 1953.

Ware, Eugene F. *The Indian War of 1864.* Lincoln: University of Nebraska Press, 1960.

Welles, Gideon. *The Diary of Gideon Welles.* Edited by Howard K. Beale. New York: W. W. Norton, Inc., 1960.

Whipple, Henry B. *Lights and Shadows of a Long Episcopate.* New York: The Macmillan Company, 1899.

C. Unpublished Federal Documents, National Archives

Records of the Office of Indian Affairs
    Letters Received from: Central Superintendency, Cherokee Agency, Chippewa Agency, Colorado Superintendency, Delaware Agency, New Mexico Superintendency, Northern Superintendency, Oregon Superintendency, St. Peter Agency, Southern Superintendency, Winnebago Agency, Yankton Agency
    Letters Sent
    Report Books
    Special Files 85, 201
Records of the Office of the Secretary of the Interior
    Indian Division: Letters Received, Letters Sent
Records of the War Department
    The Adjutant General's Office: Letters Received
    Office of the Secretary of War: Letter Received, Letters Sent
Sioux Trial Transcripts. Military Commission, U.S. Army. Senate Executive Documents, 1862. Also found at Minnesota Historical Society, St. Paul.

D. Published Federal and State Documents

Congressional Globe, 37th and 38th Congresses.

Supplemental Report of the Committee on the Conduct of the War. 2 vols. Washington, D.C.: Government Printing Office, 1866.

Lincoln's Annual Messages, 1861–1865. Appendixes to *Congressional Globe,* 37th and 38th Congresses.

Annual Reports of the Secretary of the Interior, 1861–1864. Appendixes to *Congressional Globe,* 37th and 38th Congresses.

U.S., Congress, House of Representatives. *Annual Report of the Commissioner of Indian Affairs, 1862.* Executive Document 1, 37th Congress, 2d session (Serial 1157).

———. *Annual Report of the Commissioner of Indian Affairs, 1863.* Executive Document 1, 38th Congress, 2d session (Serial 1182).

———. *Annual Report of the Commissioner of Indian Affairs, 1864.* Executive Document 1, 38th Congress, 2d session (Serial 1120).

———. *Executive Document 58,* 39th Congress, 1st session, pt. 9 (Serial 1189).

U.S., Congress, Senate. *Annual Report of the Commissioner of Indian Affairs, 1861.* Executive Document 1, 37th Congress, 2d session (Serial 1117).

———. *Executive Document 7,* 37th Congress, 3d session, pt. 1 (Serial 1117).

———. *Miscellaneous Document 97.* 38th Congress, 1st session, pt. 1 (Serial 1177).

———. *Report of the Joint Committee on the Conduct of the War,* "Massacre of the Cheyenne Indians," Report 142, 38th Congress, 2d session, pt. 3 (Serial 1214).

———. *Report of the Joint Committee on the Condition of the Indian Tribes in the United States.* Report 156, 39th Congress, 2d session (Serial 1279).

E. Miscellaneous Documents

The American Annual Cyclopedia and Register of Important Events of the Year. vol. 2 (1862). New York: P. Appleton and Company, 1867.

Documents of American History. Edited by Henry Steel Commager, 7th ed. New York: Appleton-Century-Crofts, 1963.

II. Secondary Sources

A. Books

Abel, Annie H. *The Slaveholding Indians.* 3 vols. Cleveland: Arthur H. Clark, 1915–1925.

Brown, Dee. *Bury My Heart at Wounded Knee.* New York: Holt, Rinehart & Winston, 1971.

Buice, Sammy David. "The Civil War and the Five Civilized Tribes." Ph.D. dissertation, University of Oklahoma, 1970.

Carley, Kenneth. *The Sioux Uprising of 1862.* St. Paul: Minnesota Historical Society, 1961.

Carman, Harry J. and Luthin, Reinhard H. *Lincoln and Patronage.* Gloucester, Mass.: Peter Smith, 1964.

Castel, Albert. *A Frontier State at War: Kansas, 1861–1865.* Ithica, New York: Cornell University Press, 1958.

Cornish, Dudley. *The Sable Arm.* New York: W. W. Norton and Company, 1956.

Danziger, Edmund. *Indians and Bureaucrats: Administering the Reservation Policy during the Civil War.* Urbana: University of Illinois Press, 1974.

Donald, David. *Lincoln Reconsidered.* New York: Vintage Books, 1961.

Ellis, Richard N. *General Pope and U.S. Indian Policy.* Albuquerque: University of New Mexico Press, 1970.

Fehrenbacher, Don E. *Prelude to Greatness: Lincoln in the 1850s.* Stanford: Stanford University Press, 1962.

Foner, Eric. *Free Soil, Free Labor, Free Men: The Ideology of the Republican Party before the Civil War.* New York: Oxford University Press, 1970.

Foreman, Grant. *Indian Removal: The Emigration of the Five Civilized Tribes of Indians.* Norman: University of Oklahoma Press, 1953.

Fritz, Henry E. *The Movement for Indian Assimilation, 1860–1890.* Philadelphia: University of Pennsylvania Press, 1963.

Hagan, William T. *American Indians.* Chicago: University of Chicago Press, 1961.

Jacobs, Wilbur R. *Dispossessing the American Indian.* New York: Charles Scribner's Sons, 1972.

Johnson, Ludwell H. *The Red River Campaign.* Baltimore: The Johns Hopkins Press, 1958.

Jones, Robert Huhn. *The Civil War in the Northwest.* Norman: University of Oklahoma Press, 1960.

Jordan, Winthrop P. *White Over Black: American Attitudes Toward the Negro, 1550–1812.* Chapel Hill: University of North Carolina Press, 1968.

McPherson, James M. *The Negro's Civil War.* New York: Pantheon, 1965.

Mardock, Robert. *The Reformers and the American Indian.* Columbia: University of Missouri Press, 1971.

Marx, Leo. *The Machine in the Garden: Technology and the Pastoral Ideal in America.* New York: Oxford University Press, 1964.

Minnesota in the Indian and Civil Wars. 2 vols. St. Paul: Pioneer Press Company, 1890–1893.

Monaghan, Jay. *Civil War on the Western Border.* Boston: Little, Brown, and Company, 1955.

Pearce, Roy Harvey. *Savagism and Civilization.* Baltimore: The Johns Hopkins Press, 1953.

Quarles, Benjamin. *Lincoln and the Negro.* New York: Oxford University Press, 1962.

Randall, James G. *Lincoln the President.* 3 vols. New York: Dodd, Mead, & Company, 1952.

Sandburg, Carl. *Abraham Lincoln: The Prairie Years.* New York: Blue Ribbon Books, 1926.

———. *Abraham Lincoln: The War Years.* 3 vols. New York: Harcourt, Brace and Company, 1936–1939.

Sheeham, Bernard. *Seeds of Extinction.* Chapel Hill: University of North Carolina Press, 1973.

Smith, Henry Nash. *The Virgin Land: The American West as Symbol and Myth.* Cambridge: Oxford University Press, 1950.

Utley, Robert M. *Frontiersmen in Blue: The U.S. Army and the Indian.* New York: The Macmillan Company, 1967.

Whitney, Ellen M., ed. *The Black Hawk War, 1831–32.* Illinois Historical Collection, 35, 1970.

Williams, T. Harry. *Lincoln and the Radicals.* New York: Alfred A. Knopf, 1952.

B. Articles

Caldwell, Martha B. "Pomeroy's 'Ross Letter': Genuine or Forgery." *Kansas Historical Quarterly* 13 (August 1945):463–72.

Chaput, Donald. "Generals, Indian Agents, Politicians: The Doolittle Survey of 1865," *Western Historical Quarterly* 2 (July 1972):269–82.

Danziger, Edmund. "The Office of Indian Affairs and the Problem of Civil War Refugees." *Kansas Historical Quarterly* 35 (Autumn 1969):257–75.

———. "The Steck-Carleton Controversy in Civil War New Mexico." *Southwestern Historical Quarterly* 74 (October 1970):104–24.

Franks, Kenny A. "The Confederate States and the Five Civilized Tribes: A Breakdown of Relations." *Journal of the West* 12 (July 1973):439–54.

Garfield, Marvin H. "Defense of the Kansas Frontier, 1864–65." *Kansas Historical Quarterly* 1 (February 1932):140–52.

Kelsey, Harry. "The Background to Sand Creek." *The Colorado Magazine* 45 (Fall 1968):279–300.

———. "William P. Dole and Mr. Lincoln's Indian Policy." *Journal of the West* 10 (July 1971):484–92.

Langsdorf, Edgar. "Jim Lane and the Frontier Guard." *Kansas Historical Quarterly* 9 (February 1940):13–25.

Lewis, Lloyd. "The Man the Historians Forgot." *Kansas Historical Quarterly* 8 (February 1939):85–103.

Moulton, Gary E. "Chief John Ross During the Civil War." *Civil War History* 19 (December 1973):314–33.

———. "John Ross and W. P. Dole: A Case Study of Lincoln's Indian Policy." *Journal of the West* 12 (July 1973):414–23.

Neet, J. Frederick. "Stand Watie, Confederate General in the Cherokee Nation." *Great Plains Journal* 6 (Fall 1966):36–51.

Paulson, Howard W. "The Allotment of Land in Severalty to the Dakota Indians before the Dawes Act." *South Dakota History* 1 (Spring 1971):132–41.

Phillips, George H. "The Indian Ring in Dakota Territory, 1870–1890." *South Dakota History* 2 (Fall 1972):345–76.

Unrau, William E. "Indian Agent vs. the Army: Some Background Notes on the Kiowa-Comanche Treaty of 1865." *Kansas Historical Quarterly* 30 (Summer 1964):129–52.

Zornow, William Frank. "The Kansas Senators and the Re-election of Lincoln." *Kansas Historical Quarterly* 19 (May 1951):133–44.

Index